THIS IS
EAR HUSTLE

THIS IS
EAR HUSTLE

UNFLINCHING STORIES OF EVERYDAY PRISON LIFE

**NIGEL POOR AND
EARLONNE WOODS**

CROWN
NEW YORK

Published in the United States by Crown, an imprint of Random House, a division of Penguin Random House LLC, New York.

Crown and the Crown colophon are registered trademarks of Penguin Random House LLC.

Edited excerpts from the following *Ear Hustle* podcast episodes included with permission of *Ear Hustle* and PRX/Radiotopia: Chapter Five: Objects, "The Christmas Boxes" (Season 6, 9/23/20, Episode 46); Chapter Six: Alliances, "Cellies" (Season 1, 6/14/17, Episode 1); "Looking Out" (Season 1, 7/12/17, Episode 3, Rauch); "Unwritten" (Season 1, 9/13/17, Episode 7, AR & Drew); "Us and Them" (Season 5, 4/1/20, Episode 39, Carlos). Chapter Seven: Memory, "This Place" (Season 3, 10/10/18, Episode 22); Chapter Eight: Family "Crew No. 7" (Season 6, 11/25/20, Episode 50, Michelle); Chapter Nine: Three Strikes, "Left Behind" (Season 1, 9/27/17, Episode 8); Chapter Ten: Commutation, "Bittersweet" (Season 3, 12/12/18, Episode 26); Chapter Eleven: With and Without, "Kissing the Concrete" (Season 4, 7/3/19, Episode 29, Ronnie); "Locked Down Again" (Season 5, 3/18/20, Episode 38), which was an updated/re-aired version of "Birdbaths and a Lockbox" (Season 3, 9/12/18, Episode 20); "The Trail" (Season 6, 12/9/20, Episode 51, Pat).

Library of Congress Cataloging-in-Publication Data
Names: Poor, Nigel, author. | Woods, Earlonne, author.
Title: This is ear hustle / Nigel Poor and Earlonne Woods.
Description: First edition. | New York: Crown, [2021] | Includes index.
Identifiers: LCCN 2021012924 (print) | LCCN 2021012925 (ebook) | ISBN 9780593238868 (hardcover) | ISBN 9780593238875 (ebook)
Subjects: LCSH: Prisons—United States. | Prisoners—United States. | Criminal justice, Administration of—United States. | California State Prison at San Quentin
Classification: LCC HV9471 .P67 2021 (print) | LCC HV9471 (ebook) | DDC 365/.973—dc23
LC record available at https://lccn.loc.gov/2021012924
LC ebook record available at https://lccn.loc.gov/2021012925

Printed in the United States of America on acid-free paper

crownpublishing.com

987654321

First edition

Book design by Lizzie Allen

Ear Hustle logo on jacket by Cal Tabuena-Frolli

TO ALL THOSE WHO ASK QUESTIONS,
OBSERVE, AND LISTEN

CONTENTS

THIS IS
EAR HUSTLE

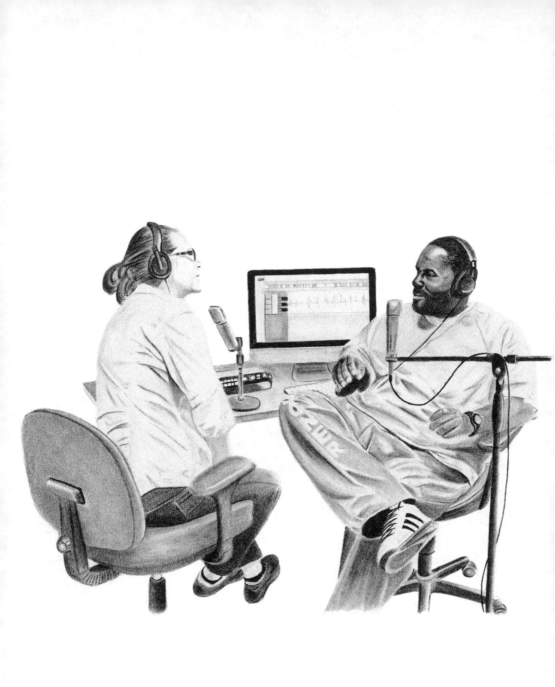

PROLOGUE

MEDIA LAB, SAN QUENTIN PRISON, NORTHERN CALIFORNIA
Summer 2017

EARLONNE All right! We need quiet now; we're about to record.

NIGEL It's so freakin' hard to make it quiet.

EARLONNE It's prison.

NIGEL Can we turn that fan off?

EARLONNE It's gonna get hot . . .

NIGEL It's never quiet enough in here.

EARLONNE That's prison for you . . . All right, everybody, we're gonna need some quiet! Hey, can we get a minute?

NIGEL We're recording.

EARLONNE Ay, ay, can we get about ten minutes so we can get this line out?!

NIGEL Do you hear that?

EARLONNE Hear what?

NIGEL It's . . . It's finally quiet.

EARLONNE Well, okay then. Let's do this.

PART I

LET'S

DO

THIS

EARLONNE

I grew up in the late 1970s in South Central Los Angeles in a two-parent home with my older brother, Trevor. My mother, Alyce Faye Woods, worked for the post office. My father, Walter Earl Woods, was an alcoholic who hustled in the streets and never really had a job. We only interacted when I was in trouble. He never played with me, never watched me play sports, never talked to me, never helped me with my homework—but he'd fasho whoop my ass . . . like I wasn't learning what he was teaching.

Trevor and I fought a lot—as brothers do—but he was also my protector. He was four years older, so my parents always left him in charge. To him, that meant he owned me and had the right to beat me up as he pleased. I'd always be the one crying after a round of fisticuffs. One time he beat me up badly enough that I was hungry for revenge, so I conceived of a plot to get back at him. I paid close attention and observed his routine when he was watching football. He'd lounge on the couch until the commercials came on, at which point he'd always get up to do something. Every time he ran back to the couch—without fail—he'd do a swan dive right into his pillow, headfirst . . . *Hmm*. At the next opportunity, I was prepared. As soon as he got up, I quickly removed the pillow from the case and shoved a typewriter in its place, fluffed it, then ran outside. I watched through a crack in the door as the game came back on and, true to form, he did his swan dive head-first into the couch. POW!

"AHHHHOOOW!!! Um'ma kick yo ass!"

Chalk up a victory for the little guy.

When I think about some of the earliest contributing factors in my introduction to crime, I go to 1978 and '79, when my brother would sneak into my parents' room when they were sleeping, and quietly bring our dad's pants out of the room. He'd rifle through, take a dollar or two, and give me fifty cents, which I earned by being the one to creep back in and put the pants back. I'd use my fifty cents to buy as many boxes of Lemonheads, Now & Laters, or sunflower seeds as I could afford. I'd sell a ten-cent pack of Now & Laters for a quarter at school, and be *the man* that day—I was a hustler before I even knew what that meant.

Parmelee Avenue Elementary School, where I went from second through sixth grade, was located in the heart of my neighborhood, on the east side of South Central Los Angeles. School interested me—not the education aspect so much as the getting-in-trouble part. I was embarrassed throughout my time in elementary school, because my classmates could read but I couldn't. Due to lack of practice or desire, I didn't really learn how to read until closer to junior high. Maybe it was a defense mechanism, but the class clown mask fit me perfectly. Plus, I was a magnet for trouble.

I took note of the fact that one class got out of school at 12:30 p.m., while the rest of us got out at 2:15. I investigated how I could get into that class and, after a few weeks of plotting, I too was getting out at 12:30. I had played myself into the special education class, and I was damn proud of it. The schoolwork was easy and no one else could read either. Unfortunately, my mother caught wind eventually and voiced her concerns. As a result, I was shipped to an after-school learning center called Kedren, where they sit you down with private tutors. *Awww man . . . I fucked up.*

During lunchtime, you'd get a tray and slide it down the conveyor, telling the cafeteria worker what you wanted. I guess there was a sign somewhere declaring "YOU MUST EAT EVERYTHING ON YOUR PLATE," but I sure couldn't read it. One day, I left some untouched spinach on my plate, and the staff told me that if I didn't eat it I'd have to go to "the box": a room with nothing in it but a mirror. So there I was, standing in this tiny room that was about the size of a school bathroom stall, looking at myself in the mirror. Bored, I took out my house keys and carved my name in the wall. My mother had to come get me and, when they told her that I had carved my name in the wall, I insisted that they were lying—*I did no such thing!* They gave me every opportunity to tell the truth, but I stuck to my story.

That was the first time I learned about mirrors you could see through. They literally led me to the other side. Wow. They had watched me do it. They showed my mother where I had written "KAOS" (my nickname for a while). There was drywall dust on the floor from the carving—shit, it was probably still on my keys too—but I held my ground, stubbornly. My only response was to keep it real, claiming, "I didn't write on no wall."

When I wasn't making trouble in school, I was playing park ball. Our sponsors were the local county sheriff's department. It was all about community. There were Black detectives from the Firestone Park Station who spent their off-time coaching and mentoring the youth in the neighborhood. As a youngster I really looked up to police officers—those guys were involved in my life. I came to know them well. Myself and other local kids used to go up to their offices and hang out with them. If they were ever driving through the neighborhood and saw us, they would often pull over, jump out, and just have a conversation with us. I respected them.

That all changed when I was nine years old. I was at Roosevelt Park leaving the swimming pool. Across the street, on the railroad tracks, a long train of "K" Line containers followed by hot dog–shaped chemical tanks went rolling by. The caboose passed and I watched the train go down the track for about a mile, but the railroad crossing gates never lifted. Cars started driving around the guard gates, so I did what I'd done before: I lifted one of the train-crossing arms to let cars go by. Motorists seemed to appreciate my gesture, though not trusting a nine-year-old's judgment, the drivers all looked both ways to make sure a train wasn't coming.

About four or five minutes later, a couple of sheriffs I didn't know pulled up and yelled at me to put my hands on the hood of their car. I let go of the gates and followed their instructions. They rifled through my shorts pockets, put me in handcuffs, and placed me in the back of the police car. None of the drivers stopped to see why they were messing with me. And initially, I truly thought they were just playing. But then both of the officers got in the car, closed the doors, and told me I was going to jail. I started crying immediately, but they just ignored me. On the way to jail, they got a call about a local disturbance, so they took me on tour to some grocery market. While they were in the store, I sat in the back of the police car as people walked by, looking at me as I bawled my eyes out, hoping someone would just open the door and let me go.

When we finally made it to the sheriff's department, they put me in a cell with nothing in it. I was terrified. I had to pee, so I started knocking on

the door as officers passed by, asking if I could please use the bathroom. They all ignored me, like I wasn't their business (as if I were not nine years old). I had to go *bad,* but I didn't want to get in trouble for peeing on the floor. Left without any other choice, I took off my checkerboard Vans shoes and urinated in them. That was the only thing that made sense to me.

I stayed in that holding cell all day. They couldn't reach my parents; my mother was at work and my father was in the streets. I gave them the only phone number I knew by heart, for my Auntie Donzell, my mother's older sister. The sheriffs eventually dropped me off at her house, about three miles away. I don't remember what she had to say about it. I only remember my father's words the next day, when he came to get me: "You know um'ma beat your ass when we get home." He had nothing to say to me except those words. Tears started falling. He never once asked me what had happened. All he needed to know was that I'd been arrested.

I had to show up with my family in juvenile court, because—as I would learn—lifting those guardrails is a federal crime. I genuinely thought I was being a Good Samaritan. To make it far worse, I discovered in court that those sheriffs had lied about me, claiming I was charging each car a dollar to go by. I didn't have a penny on me when they took me into custody.

Weekends as a kid were times for tuning into Kung Fu Theater. I remember a specific Monday, when my friend Julian "JuJu" Arnold and I were sparring, doing our rendition of karate and pretending to be Bruce Leroy. I must have karate-chopped JuJu too hard, because suddenly we started American fighting. He had a gang called the JuJu Gang, so after I fought him I had to fight the rest of them, one at a time. I performed righteously—mainly because of all the experience I had fighting off my older brother. JuJu and I both got suspended from school, but our fight didn't stop us from being friends.

The following weekend, JuJu, our friend Juan "Zoot" Carlos, and I created our own gang, and called ourselves the Crip Boys. We took the name from the older guys' gang, Shack Boy Crip. The "Shack" was because one of those older kids, who were anywhere from sixteen to twenty-five, had a shack behind his house. We walked around calling ourselves CBS—

I didn't know what the "Crip" part really meant (I still don't know what the S stood for), nor did I have any idea that the Crips extended beyond my neighborhood. It was just kid stuff, just something to belong to. If anyone wanted to be down with the Crip Boys, we would walk him to the local supermarket and he'd have to steal candy or grab a bike, to show us that he was loyal.

We'd strike up (graffiti) on the walls around the neighborhood, with a mission to make it known who we were. The older gang wasn't concerned with us kids. As the years passed, we started jumping guys into our gang through fights. One time, we were jumping our friend Tuffy in the alley behind JuJu's house, on Parmelee and 76th. I fought Tuffy; JuJu fought someone else. One of the homies from the older gang was there, a guy named Mac, and noticed I was getting the best of Tuffy. Out of nowhere, Mac, who was a little bigger than I was—though not by too much—socked me a couple of times. Surprised, I quickly redirected my focus and started unloading a volley of knuckles in his direction. He hadn't been expecting that at all, and dropped on his ass. His first words were "This nigga should be from the hood," meaning I should be in the big kids' real gang.

I didn't want to be from the big gang. I was more interested in climbing roofs, hitting people's fruit trees without permission, breaking into birdcages (people would raise fancy tumbler pigeons, which we'd steal . . . a skill that came in handy later in life), knocking on doors and then running, smashing the occasional car window, and playing sports. We called ourselves a gang, but it's not like we had any enemies or were looking to hurt anybody. And we definitely didn't realize that—based on the Crip part of our name—we were inherently enemies of all Bloods.

I was in seventh grade when the Crip Boys disseminated and were dissolved by the bigger gang. They weren't called the Shack Boy Crips any longer; they were 76 Street East Coast Crips—a big gang on the east side of Los Angeles. I didn't immediately join, but as time passed, I became a walk-on member. That meant I was never jumped into the gang; I just started representing the hood. My homies called me E-Mac (for Earl Mac), but there was an older homie with that name, so I became LiL E-Mac or E-Mac II.

The gangs were like a family, a fraternity, a brotherhood. We grew up together, hung out, spent nights at each other's houses—most of all, we protected one another. As Crips, blue was the color. But I've always loved two colors: royal blue and lipstick/fire engine red. I was that dude in the hood who used to wear the shit out of red, the Bloods' color—before, during, and after being affiliated with the Crips. My dress code wasn't going to be regulated, nor was it going to define me or my loyalties.

I was fourteen when I started selling joints for a dollar. It seemed cool, but it was time-consuming. I didn't need much money; I just needed enough to buy food, clothes, and more weed. That kept me going until my homie Black—my roll dog—showed me a small baggie with little yellowish-white rocks. He said they were worth five hundred dollars! On a good day I was making twenty dollars slang'n joints and my boy was clearing five hundred–plus a day? So, without much thought and with dollar signs in my eyes, I started selling rock cocaine. I'd give Black twenty-five and he'd give me a fifty-dollar gram. It was circular-shaped, flat on the bottom, and raised on the top. Black would place a razor blade halfway through and apply just enough pressure to break it. Then he'd cut those halves in half. Suddenly, there I was on the block selling cocaine—or rather just holding it, because in those days that shit was selling itself.

It was the end of 1985, and for the first time in my life I witnessed Blacks becoming instantaneously, dangerously wealthy, in real time. The crack boom for the Black community was probably like the tech boom for the white community. It was like a bank vault left open in a poverty-stricken neighborhood where there were no available jobs. I witnessed all kinds of shit: grandmothers selling crack, women selling their bodies for a hit, strong people turning weak. No one knew the long-term effects of it, and if we did, we certainly didn't care. People who looked like me were becoming filthy rich.

I never used, but its influence still grabbed ahold of me. I became materialistic. I wanted the clothes that celebrities and my drug-dealing friends were wearing—the clothes that the girls noticed. Those kinds of labels—Fila Bjorn Borg bomber jackets, Diadoras, Ellesse, Guess, Gucci— were not in my mother's budget. Through dealing, I could afford them. And the ladies noticed. Talk about sex . . . I was only fifteen years old, fucking all the girls my age and those who had *kids* my age. My parents never gave me the birds-and-the-bees talk, so I was careless; and there were consequences to my recklessness. But I was hooked. Sex was the drug that made me happy. It was the life for me.

Around the same time, my brother, Trevor, was working for some big-time drug dealers, so I was just getting my stuff from him. In my eyes, he was living the life. He was getting paid a thousand dollars a week, working for a guy who sold drugs wholesale. He bought an El Camino and hooked it up custom-style: candy gold with a pair of rims that were known as killer Daytons (so called because people got killed for them). Within a year though, my bro was blackballed by the dealers, because he knew some dudes—his girlfriend's cousins—who kidnapped and robbed drug dealers as a profession. Those dudes kidnapped the guy my bro worked for. Legend was they caught this kingpin in front of his father's house and threw him in the trunk of their car at gunpoint. While they were on the freeway, the kingpin worked the trunk open and somehow jumped out and escaped.

Bro had gotten accustomed to living the good life, and suddenly none of the drug dealers he knew would mess with him. So, he resorted to the very thing he was blackballed for—he hooked up with the jackers and started robbing dealers. That's when the real money and power started coming in. I was fifteen when he took me on my first lick (robbery).

We got a Sterling rent-a-car—either Trevor's girlfriend or her mom must have rented it—and I drove them to Hawthorne, a nice, middle-class neighborhood. I'd been driving for years, or at least since my brother started stealing our mom and dad's cars. The sun was setting and the sky had a dusty orange color to it. Residents were watering their grass or putting out their trash cans. We knew this dude was in the house, but his girlfriend's car wasn't in the driveway yet. The plan was for my brother and his homie Twon to get in the bushes, and when the girlfriend got back they'd follow her into the house. All I had to do was drive. I dropped them off on the corner and watched them creep up to the sides of the front door. The neighbors didn't seem to notice. I drove down the street, turned around, and parked, then sat in the car daydreaming about what I'd do with the money I didn't have yet.

After maybe ten minutes of picturing myself at the Gucci store on Rodeo Drive, I saw the girlfriend's car round the corner and pull into the driveway. She grabbed a grocery bag and walked to her front door. My heart started racing as I turned the ignition, knowing it was all about to go down. As soon as she opened the door they were right behind her, pushing her in and closing the door quickly. I looked around at the other houses on the block—no one was the wiser. I anxiously waited a few seconds, then slowly drove down the street, keeping my eye out for any movement as I busted another U-turn to pull up in front of the house. The neighbors remained oblivious. Within minutes (which felt like an hour), I saw the front door opening, so I leaned over and opened both passenger doors. They came rushing out with all kinds of bags of cash. I remember Twon had a Gucci purse with so much money stuffed in it that cash was flying out of it and he was turning back to grab every bill. They jumped in and my dumb ass burnt rubber like we were in the movies.

"Damn, nigga, tell everyone!" my bro shouted; I should have just casually driven off the same way we came in. Lesson learned. We drove to a Comfort Inn and dumped all the loot out of the bags and onto the bed. We counted a little over sixty thousand dollars. In that moment my whole life changed. We started dancing, giving high fives, hollering. It was that surprise-come-from-behind-win feeling. They gave me the big bag with all the small bills, which by that point were like pennies for them ballers. My cut amounted to about five thousand. I was rich!

I guess my brother felt bad about my tiny cut, because two days later he bought me a 1976 Buick Regal Custom from a street hustler named Juice. It was painted candy gold with a Black Phantom top, laces, and Vogue tires. The stereo system blared. I rode into the tenth grade in a car that adult hustlers drove. Every day became Friday. I was the shit, partying all the time, and I loved every second of it. There were consequences, of course. I ended up in a probation school for two years, but it was easier than real school and my priority at the time wasn't learning, anyway.

Within a few months, my brother and I were broke again, waiting on the next come-up. In the meantime, my little crew and I had been going around jacking street dealers, running up in crack or weed spots, or—if it came to it—just robbing regular people. One time my friends and I needed some gas money, so we went out and started snatching pockets. I'll never forget being on Slauson Avenue, in the Crenshaw district of Los Angeles, robbing a Black couple in their forties. The guy stepped in front of his wife, pulled out his wallet, and hit me with some real shit: "Why are you in the hood, robbing people?" It was more of a statement than a question. "We ain't got shit—you should be in Beverly Hills," he continued. I had them at gunpoint, and took a pause to contemplate what he had just said. I lowered my weapon, embarrassed.

"You're right," I said. I mumbled an apology and walked away. It had never occurred to me. In that moment, that couple's faces became my parents', or my homies' parents, and that really stuck with me. What the fuck *was* I doing? How did I fall into this? I wasn't in my own neighborhood, but I might as well have been.

There's a saying that's been important, and rung true, in my life: If you know better, you'll do better. This was something that I had heard in my community, though I'm not sure who originally said it. Point is, I didn't know better. The gun was a bluff tactic, but that wasn't the issue. This lifestyle was the only way I had been taught to make money. It was the only one I was accustomed to. In a weird way, by being questioned about what I was doing—being made to step away from myself for a second—I received more guidance from a total stranger I was holding at gunpoint than from anything my own father had ever shared. In retrospect, it was twisted guidance, as he was telling me to go rob someone else. And of course he could have added, "Get a job, son." But if he had, I would have fasho robbed him.

I kept doing what I was doing. Taking homies on these little licks instantly boosted my hood rep. I was the Stickup Kid. For fun, me and the homies would team up and lurk, looking for people in pimped-out cars to carjack. I could never fathom taking a life, especially over bullshit. I'd hear of drug dealers getting robbed and killed, and it always struck me as tragic. Especially because, nine times out of ten, the deceased knew the killer. *Fuck*, I'd sometimes think, slowly becoming aware that I was dependent on a lifestyle filled with betrayal.

Growing up, I had never contemplated going to jail for a significant amount of time. I used to go to juvenile hall for up to thirty days, for minor violations like getting in a fight at the probation school, but even that was like a little vacation; I'd see homies I knew from all over LA County. I'd watch the older homies going to prison, then I'd see them a year or two later getting out looking like bodybuilder Lee Haney, with muscles everywhere. Going to prison and getting out with muscles wasn't a deterrent. Those guys never talked about their experiences, so I assumed they were just happy to be out. They came back to their hoods as the OGs, but in their absence young homies were now the OGs on the block, and they had money. All the older homies (those eighteen and up) were locked up or smoking crack cocaine—and they couldn't begin to tell us shit. They were compromised! We had all the drugs, all the guns, all the power.

During the rise of the crack era, a shitload of guns started flooding into the hood. I would protect myself if pushed upon, but I never woke up like, "Today is a good day to snatch someone's birthday away." I ain't never been that dude. I was too cool and too mellow for that. That didn't make me special. Most people from the hood ain't killers; just like most people in prison for murder are not murderers. They may have participated, but they didn't pull the trigger. Each hood or ghetto in the world only has a chosen few who truly possess that "I don't give a fuck" attitude. Those are the killers of the hood. I would never take one of those homies on a lick with me, because I knew they had no control. I'd seen those cats go on what were supposed to be simple robberies and then get trigger-happy . . . Suddenly I would know three homies facing murder. No one else would have known that guy was going to shoot and kill—he himself may not have even planned on it. But none of that matters.

The closest I ever came to being a killer was one night in the hood when I had a 12-gauge shotgun on me. We were about a dozen deep and we all had guns. The idea came up to go bust on some Madd Swan Bloods in the neighboring hood. We were separated by a main street, Central Avenue. We crept across Central and down some alleys, and when we got to the end we were all bent down looking at some guys wearing red. Our plan was just to run down the alley, yell out the hood, and squeeze our triggers. It's crazy, but that's all it would take for us to unload murderous gunfire and end some other African Americans' existence—guys living with the same struggles as we were. Just as we were all crouched down, my roll dog Jap—who had a .357—paused, stood back, then was like, "Nah, I'm outta here," and started sprinting back down the alley. He was my boy so, without hesitation, I followed him. Everyone else followed suit.

Later, I asked Jap what was up, and he was like, "Out of twelve dudes, six are going to brag about it and four of those six are going to tell the police who was there." I had never even thought that far ahead. Damn, was each one of these cats loyal enough for me to put my life in their hands? I started contemplating what happens when two or more cats are on the same case: someone always tells. Who knows what would have happened across Central? It could have been a few bodies taped off. A friend once told me, "Once it leaves your lips, you no longer own it." Jap was right: somebody would have told. Twenty-five years to life to the death penalty . . . It was another incident that put my lifestyle into perspective. I learned to keep shit I didn't want others to know to myself.

———— ▮▮▮▮▯▯ ▬ ▫▫▫▫ ————

At 12:50 a.m. on December 28, 1997, when I was twenty-six years old, two things happened simultaneously. My best friend, Furman "F-Dog" Little, stopped breathing; and I was captured.

Fifty-five minutes earlier, at the end of a brief police chase, we had exited my Jeep Cherokee. I had assaulted a man. I never hit him with a gun—the gun was in my waistband. I ran up on him and tackled him like a football hit. He fell, I fell, and when I jumped up to pull my gun out of my waistband to demand his car keys, all the bullets fell out the bottom of the clip.

Furman, who was with me, came up and sprayed him with some

Mace. Boom. When he did that, we started picking up these bullets. He was of course scared and screaming, and then his wife came out of the house and started screaming at us too. We finished gathering up the bullets, and then we just left—we didn't demand anything from him.

We were subsequently pulled over by the Manhattan Beach police. In our minds, when it came to criminality, nothing serious had happened; I'd only tackled the guy. But when the cops were approaching our vehicle, our main objective was to get rid of the gun. So we took off—my friend Chapple Sims was driving and was doing like eighty. We were in a Jeep but he turned a corner like it was a Porsche. It was too much too quick and we crashed into the curb and some bushes. We all jumped out and started running, still with the objective of getting rid of the gun. Without further provocation, the police just opened fire.

The gun in my waistband couldn't have been seen, so it wasn't the reason forty-one shots were fired in the direction of our torsos. Mid-stride, I was shot in the side of my chest, just under my armpit. The bullet hugged my rib cage and exited the middle of my chest. Later, after injections of dye and CT scans, the doctor told me if I had been running a hair faster the bullet could have splintered one of my ribs and pierced my heart. But I didn't even need surgery. The bullet just went through tissue and muscle. All I needed was a tetanus shot and bandages. I was the lucky one: I survived.

Furman did not. Though he was unarmed, the police officers shot him five times in the back. They used the same phrase most police officers say when they kill an unarmed Black or brown man: "He was reaching in his waistband. Out of fear for my safety and the safety of other officers, I fired my weapon." Actually, what those bold-ass officers said was, "While he was running he turned his body facing the officers and was going into his waistband running backwards and that's when I fired." What? He was shot in the back. When did they invent boomerang bullets? From that night forward, I went through a lot of introspection. The one question I could never get past was: *What was it all for?*

That night was the culmination of my destructive life. I was a part-time criminal—part-time because, when I hit a good lick, I would go on vacation for six months. My targets of choice were always drug dealers—

people who would rarely report the crime (except when I was seventeen, but we'll get back to that). I had been robbing drug dealers since that first time when I drove my bro. A little over a decade later, I was handcuffed to a gurney, tears welling up in my eyes, and thinking about my friend lying spiritless on some other gurney in the same hospital. What was it all for, if this was the end result?

I was transferred to LA County General Hospital and escorted to the thirteenth floor, where the prisoners are transferred after they're triaged in the emergency department. A white female officer sat at the check-in desk. She asked the officer what had happened to me. He told her it was an officer-involved shooting in Manhattan Beach. Her response stunned me. She saw I was conscious and listening, and then had the audacity to fix her lips and say, "Manhattan Beach needs to get new bullets." Wow. She knew nothing about the circumstances. All she knew was that I was Black. In her mind, I should have been dead.

When I got into the medical cell—a big room with about ten hospital beds and two phones on the wall—I prepared for perhaps the most difficult conversation of my life. I had to call Furman's wife and tell her what had happened. How in the fuck do I call Kelley (a mother of a one-year-old, and five months pregnant with their child), and shatter her life with the worst possible news?

While I was in county jail I made up my mind that I was done with destroying whatever remained of my life. I was done being a gang member. I was done with crime. Though nothing made sense anymore, immediately following Furman's murder I decided—like flipping a light switch—that I needed to stop subscribing to the shit I'd been involved with for the past fifteen years. It was like I had just snapped out of a trance and had finally woken up. I stayed in county for seventeen months.

After that, I was sent to prison, sentenced to 31 years to life for attempted second-degree robbery, and 26 years to life for assault with a deadly weapon.

Walking into prison and seeing the environment was the most depressing sight ever. It was the architecture that stressed me the fuck out. All of the newer prisons, like Corcoran, Donavan, and Ironwood had the same 270-degree design. It's U-shaped, built that way so the police can see everything. I had already served time in this chaotic environment, when I got caught for kidnapping and robbery at seventeen years old. To see this shit and acknowledge I was about to be trapped within it again was more than a little devastating, especially since, prior to paroling, I had vowed to the homies on Level IV—a maximum security prison, with cell blocks and guards at every corner—that I'd never return to prison alive.

Incarcerated people and prison levels are classified according to a point system: placement "scores" are ascribed based on age, the crime, whether violence was used, prior convictions, and other factors, like if there's gang involvement. Those with scores of 0 through 18 are placed in Level I facilities, where inmates are usually housed in open dorms with a low-security perimeter. Placement scores of 19 through 35 get you sent to Level II prisons, which have a secure perimeter that may be patrolled by armed guards. Scores of 36 through 59 qualify for Level III locations, which have armed guards and units of cells abutting the prison's exterior walls. Incarcerated people with scores of 60 and higher are housed in Level IV prisons, which have internal and external armed coverage and blocks of cells separated from the exterior walls. Incarcerated people can reduce their scores through good behavior and participation in programs (when offered). Scores can also be increased for disciplinary actions incurred during incarceration.

I had 52 points against me, which had landed me there in the first place. The first time I had gone to prison I chalked up two convictions: kidnapping and robbery. And here I was right back there. With this charge for second-degree robbery, I had, in the eyes of California's archaic Three Strikes Law, struck out. I was looking down the barrel of two life sentences.

Once a year, all prisoners have to go to an "annual," which means going before the Classification Committee, who will review your incarceration program from the previous year. It's the one time all year when you can request to be transferred to another prison. My yard in Centinela—a California state prison located about an hour and a half from San Diego—was a Level III prison. I was interested in transferring to the San Francisco Bay Area's San Quentin State Prison, a low-custody Level II prison, which means incarcerated people are housed in cell living, not a dorm setting. There were only two Level II prisons in California that were cell living: San Quentin and Soledad State Prison, an hour or so from Monterey. For some reason, if you were sentenced under the California Three Strikes Law—as I was—you were on Closed Custody, meaning your movements around the prison were limited, and you were treated as if you were a mass murderer. At my annual, 8 points were taken off of my total points due to my good behavior, meaning I was now classified as Level II and eligible to put in for a transfer to San Quentin. My alternate choice was Soledad. About a month later I received a response that San Quentin was closed to intake, and instead of sending me to Soledad they hit me with CPP, which means Continue Present Program. I wasn't going nowhere. FUCK!

Year after year for the next four years, I'd put in for a transfer to San Quentin but a month later would receive the same decision: CPP. It was depressing. I tried to keep my program clean, but in between my annuals I'd stand the chance of getting written up, because some officers are petty as fuck and are out to punish. I eventually decided to appeal the decision, and was denied under a section in the California Code of Regulations, which essentially stated that my current institution could house me until my custody dropped to Level I. I was devastated. As a Three Striker, I knew my custody would never drop below Level II. Because we're repeat offenders? The logic behind that decision remains unclear.

In my twelve years at Centinela, I had completed training for two trades—graphic arts and print press—and I had taken a college course on business. But I was continuously being denied appropriate placement, so I just resigned myself to never leaving. The last straw was when I appeared before the Classification Committee in 2011. My cellie, Kobi, had been caught making pruno—basically the equivalent of prison malt liquor, made from fermented apples and a sugar source (if not the real thing, then something like jelly)—in the confines of our cell, and we had both been written up for it and found guilty. The thinking was that I should have known he was making it, based on the pungent smell. Even if I did know, it's not my job to tell a grown man what he can or can't do. The committee told me that I couldn't go anywhere. "We'll see you next year," they said.

"I'm depressed," I said calmly.

They laughed and joked, "Do you want us to refer you to Mental Health?" I walked out of the program office, strolled to Medical, and retrieved a request to see the psychologist. The nuclear-option countdown was on.

There's a stigma about going to the psychologist in prison, because it's assumed you're crazy and mentally ill if you see one. Plus, prisoners thought that the Board of Prison Hearings would never let you out if you'd seen a psychologist. I didn't care about all that stigma shit anymore—after all, it's not like there's no stigma about going to prison.

Prior to asking to see the psychologist, I'd been paying close attention to the Zoloft commercials on TV. That bouncing ball had become my teacher. I had observed all of the symptoms associated with depression: severe despondency and dejection, feelings of inadequacy and guilt, lack of energy, no appetite, loss of sleep . . . Game on or not, I needed to talk to a psychologist. (Even though seeking psychological help has been taboo in prison for decades, I now believe it should be mandatory for *every* prisoner to talk to someone other than other prisoners or correctional officers.)

I told the psychologist that I was depressed. He asked how long I had been depressed. I thought about it for a while before speaking my truth. I had been depressed ever since the judge had sentenced me to 31 years to life for attempted second-degree robbery, and 26 years to life for assault with a deadly weapon. Who wouldn't be depressed after receiving a life sentence for a non-homicidal violation? I mentioned I wasn't sleeping well, so he put me on medication that I willfully took for about two weeks. It did make me sleep a lot, but boy were my side effects weird. If someone dropped something, the shutter speed of my eyelids would take at least five hundred pictures per second before it hit the ground. Don't ask me why; I assume that's why they call it a side effect, and that was one of mine.

Within two weeks of hitting that nuclear button I was back in front of the same committee that had denied me a transfer. They had to transfer me now, because Centinela State Prison doesn't have a psychiatric program— they only have a few psychologists. I was up outta that biiiitch! It took about ninety days to complete the transfer. I trans-packed (packed my property) and took it to Receiving and Release (R&R) on September 9, 2011, twelve years to the day from arriving there. My destination was Soledad. I was pissed about that, because I had been watching the Discovery Channel and seen this dude named Troy Williams, who I knew from Centinela State Prison. He and other prisoners were on a show called *San Quentin Film School.* Observing him learn about a skill set that had always intrigued me immediately made me want to do anything possible to get to San Quentin—it had to be a progressive prison to think outside the box like that. But not this time.

The day I left Centinela State Prison was sooo beautiful. It was the first time in a dozen years that I had been in a vehicle as we left the grounds of that institution. That thought alone was profound. How can anyone be contained in one location for so long? Especially me, a free spirit? There I was, naked other than see-through paper boxers and a see-through paper jumpsuit, with a waist chain and handcuff on each side and a tiny Master Lock affixed to it, plus ankle chains. Would it sound far-fetched to say I felt like I was on a modern-day slave ship? For an African American, it's not hard to make the comparison—we always think of this shit as today's slavery. But mentally, I felt as free as the people in the cars next to our bus as we drove away. I observed and took in every rock, mound, car, house, and person, registering them with a whole new appreciation.

It took us forever to get to Highway 60, and the landscape was nothing but barren land consisting of dirt, dust, and an occasional tumbleweed rolling by. I thought about everyone who had taken that trek to Centinela to visit me for the last twelve years, and felt such gratitude. I will always be indebted to them. I had known the trips were long, but sheesh.

Our first destination was Chino State Prison, about forty minutes inland from Los Angeles—our layover for the night. They didn't assign us cells; they just left about thirty of us packed into three three-feet by fifteen-feet cages in a hallway. Each held eight to ten men, seated on a long metal bench, enclosed by a skinny cage. It has to be one of the most unethical confinement practices in California.

Ten hours on those cold benches and we were back on the road again. I returned to my sightseeing, back to dreaming that my circumstances were different, back to being visually free, back to fantasizing about being in the cars I saw speed by us. On these transfer trips, you either blocked out the sight of everyday routines of freedom or you used the time to confront what you were missing out on in life.

When we arrived at Soledad State Prison, I didn't know when I'd next be out on a "field trip," so when I got off the bus to enter R&R, I felt as dejected as a kid leaving Disneyland (which is about forty-five minutes from where I grew up, so I actually knew the feeling). If I hadn't been depressed before, I was now. Soledad was a Level II prison, but they didn't allow Closed Custody prisoners like me to be out of our cells at night. How could this be? I had just left a Level III higher-security prison that allowed us to go out at night. Plus, they had me in an administrative segregation overflow building, which was a lockdown program . . . meaning it was "the hole," so nearly all the guys were always in handcuffs. The space wasn't set up for any kind of indoor program whatsoever for those of us who weren't in cuffs.

It took two weeks to see my counselor, and when I finally did we only talked for a minute. I let him know that my first choice had been San Quentin. "Oh, yeah, well you know that we have a volunteer list for people to be shipped to San Quentin. They just opened up West Block; it's no longer a reception center," he said. Converting the West Block would make room for a thousand additional beds.

"Where do I sign?"

I stayed at Soledad a whopping sixty-seven days before I got on that bus of volunteers headed for San Quentin—the destination that I had tried to get to for what seemed like *forever*. Back to Disneyland! The bus ride wasn't as long as the one to Soledad; it was about three hours. But it was where I wanted to be going, so I felt great about the whole trip. *Hopefully this is the last prison that I'll be sent to,* I thought. All I could do was hope that my next transfer would be from the parking lot at San Quentin, bound for home.

CHAPTER TWO

NIGEL

I make a lot of phone calls from the San Quentin State Prison parking lot. In fact, I spend most of my time there—in the parking lot and in the prison itself. I'm at San Quentin more hours than at home or my university teaching job or with my husband or friends or even sleeping. The fact that I'm on the phone much of that time isn't something I ever would have chosen. In fact, I've always had mild phone phobia; talking to disembodied voices makes me anxious and prickly.

Prisons generally don't welcome access or communication. Theirs is a sequestered world, and to most people an unknown place, constructed in the mind and scripted by bad TV, sloppy journalism, and tired Hollywood films. It suits most of the public to see prisons as institutions built to keep people in and keep people out.

Prison didn't come into my life because I had been incarcerated or was visiting a family member or friend inside. It didn't come into my life because I was especially concerned with prison or issues surrounding our punitive systems. It came into my life because I love to follow odd clues and seemingly random coincidences. San Quentin became so central to my life because of apparently chance introductions via two institutions I admire: National Public Radio and the United States Post Office.

I'm a visual artist and spend much of my time working in my studio, located on an inactive Navy base that faces the San Francisco Bay. It is a quiet place, filled with thirty years of work, as well as all kinds of items that interest me: collections of found objects, bottles of hair, piles of wishbones, shelves of books, and crates of old projects that mark the time I have spent working as an artist. I never wanted to be anything but an artist, and I've always been drawn to small details that others may cast aside as insignificant or worth avoiding. I've been that way since my first memories.

One of my earliest memories is sitting in a darkish room watching *Mighty Mouse* on our black-and-white TV. I was impressed by this character, so small and unassuming, who would always suddenly figure out how to save the day. My mom must have also read *Stuart Little* to me, and the two tiny heroes stoked my desire to find a mouse to be my friend. I looked for one everywhere, but no luck.

A year or so later, when I was about five, we moved to Maine. There was a big field behind our house. *Mice lived in fields!* That would be where I would find my little buddy. I spent days searching, and finally found a mouse hole. I set up my post and staked it out, waiting for a mouse to emerge, returning on multiple occasions, determined to meet my own Stuart Little. I was patient, and I always showed up. A few would scurry in or out, but they were always too quick for me. After several failed attempts, to my delight I finally caught one with my bare hands, but as soon as I grabbed it, the little thing sunk its teeth into my finger! Shocked, I held up my hand and just watched it hanging there. I didn't cry, but I was devastated by its reaction and rejection. Finally, it let go of its bite and bolted back down the hole. I told my mom and, shortly thereafter, I was at the doctor's, getting a rabies shot.

Though I failed in the vermin-befriending department, I had plenty of other small worlds of my own to explore. From a very young age I was a collector, someone who enjoyed picking up things from the ground and finding value in them. As soon as I was able to write, I began carefully filling and labeling shoeboxes to organize my various collections—stones, leaves, popsicle sticks, lost buttons, notes, and other miscellany—and stacking them in my closet. Always a shy kid, I found it easier to build imaginary worlds based on these assorted clues. Each one was a portal into something larger than what was happening around me. In them, I believed I would somehow find the answers to my questions about what it meant that the universe never ended, or why some people get so angry, or what really happens when we sleep. Though they never managed to satisfy that curiosity, I suppose that organizing those bits and pieces I found was a means of soothing my anxiety about all the unknowns. My impulse for gathering bread crumbs, cataloguing, and archiving only grew with time. Eventually, I would find ways to incorporate that into my art and life.

In addition to collecting, I always loved reading, writing, and exploring on my own. I was a confident young kid when it came to those abilities, but I struggled in school because I'm dyslexic. I never noticed; I just assumed everyone had trouble looking at numbers and saying them out loud. I wasn't aware that I wrote letters backward or read things incorrectly. They weren't incorrect to me, they were how I saw them. If an assignment was tough for me, I just figured out how to do it my way. I wasn't fully diagnosed until I was in seventh grade, when teachers wanted to put me in the "special classes" in the basement. "Wait! This isn't right—I don't belong here," I told them. I was allowed to stay in the regular classes, but these were broken up into three sections: achievers, middle of the road, and below average. For many years I was aware I was being placed in the below-average section. Of course it was demoralizing, but I remember thinking, *This won't last forever. I just need to get through it. In a few years this will be over and I'll be on to different things.*

Beyond my family, I was never particularly social during those years. I was always close with my sisters—my elder by two years, Aimee, and my younger by three years, Sarah—as we're so close in age. My brother, Stephen, is eight years younger than I am, so by the time he was a teenager I was out of the house. We didn't get to spend much of our childhoods together, because of our ages, but we've grown to share qualities and family traits—most notably that we're both introverts and have done a lot of work to get out of ourselves and learn how to be less socially awkward. We were instilled with the same tenet that extremely hard work pays off, and that's evident in our adult lives. We're both obsessive about what we do, and equally inclined to get lost in our work. He eventually took the science route (and today is a successful doctor and researcher) while I went in search of ways to survive as an artist, but we've always approached our investigations in similar ways: by looking at whatever problem we're trying to solve, and doggedly examining it until the answer reveals itself.

So, I had my family and I continued to get by in high school, but I always saved my real self for independent, out-of-school exploring. When I finally got to college in Vermont, I felt like *Fuck yeah—this is where I'll finally fit in.* And I did.

I studied photography in college. Initially, I only took pictures of places and things, because I was too shy to point my camera at people. I wanted to try, so eventually I set a task for myself: three days a week I would go to downtown Bennington and set up my camera on a tripod on the same corner. I would stand there until someone came up and asked what I was doing. Then I would explain my project, telling them I was doing a portrait series about people who lived in town. We would chat for a little while, and I'd ask them little questions about their lives—mainly because I was interested, but also because that would generally loosen them up and they'd let down their guard. The photos were rarely of them smiling; they'd give me something better, more real or just more intriguing to look at. I'd take their picture (it was film, not digital, of course) and the next time I returned to the corner, I'd have a print to give them. I was consistent, I was patient, and I always showed up. Eventually, people started to expect me. In time, they would bring friends to be photographed and it turned into a nice little project. Occasionally, I ended up spending more time with a certain group. On one occasion, when I met a bunch of high school students, I eventually got permission to photograph different groups at the high school. I was interested in photographing the cliques that formed there. Throughout the whole project, though I might not have identified it at the time, I became much more comfortable engaging with strangers.

In graduate school, I worked at the Harvard Museum of Comparative Zoology in the entomology department. Part of my job was to pin insects, creating organized collections of the specimens brought back from research trips. Working there gave me access to the back rooms of the museum, where I could freely roam and open any drawer I wanted. It was a dream, and reinforced my belief that collecting and archiving was indeed a valid way of problem-solving and better understanding the world. Portraits, objects that people have discarded, strands of hair, dryer lint—these are all markers of the human story. To me, these items have always been worth preserving, to examine all their intricacies.

After finishing graduate school, I was at loose ends. I came to visit my sister Sarah in San Francisco, and—as many do—I fell in love with the city. I went back to Boston, packed up my possessions, and drove across the country. Somewhat to my surprise, my dad said he would drive with me. I rented a U-Haul and off we went—it took about a week, and was the most amount of concentrated time we have ever spent together.

Along the way, we hit every kind of crazy weather: sudden, pelting rain; a small tornado; a freak snowstorm. We encountered no shortage of personalities, as well. In Tennessee, we stopped at an odd dinosaur park, got talking to the hard-luck woman running the place, and by the end of the conversation, she wanted to leave with us. In Texas, we got barbecue in a small town and learned, after eating it, that the man who made it was also an undertaker. We bought a ton of fireworks in the first state we entered where they were legal. (I have no idea why we did this, nor did I know what to do with them when I got to California.) Our trip overlapped with Thanksgiving, which we spent in Bakersfield, California. We ditched the ceremonial turkey and stuffing. Instead, my dad had nachos and I went for the buffet. Before leaving town, I took this little cactus I had brought with me as our driving mascot and planted it in the desert, conscious that I was leaving my old life behind and moving on to new territory.

I didn't know anyone in the Bay Area other than my sister. I didn't have a job, and my only plan was to be an artist. It was 1992, so the region wasn't yet ridiculously expensive. San Francisco at that time felt like a quiet, kind place, one that suited my temperament. (Those aren't the words I would use to describe it now.) The whole Bay Area was so different from where I grew up in New England, and it felt like a freer place—the kind of place where people came to be themselves. I spent a lot of time—years, actually—walking around the city, looking. It seemed okay to just let things unfold.

My first year in San Francisco was still tough. I couldn't get a job, and I kept wondering if I had made a mistake by leaving New England and all my friends and contacts. I expressed as much to my dad, who told me, "You have to give it a year—you can do anything for a year—and if you still hate it, come back. But don't give up before you give it a real chance." So I did. I landed a series of unimpressive jobs to pay the bills, but I knew the jobs didn't define me—they allowed me to do what I wanted, which was to make art. I tried to get jobs that allowed me to work four long days, like ten- to twelve-hour shifts, so that I could dedicate three days to being in my "studio."

At the time, that studio was a space I had cleared out in the corner of my bedroom. Given my tendency to collect and amass, I eventually gradu-ated to the table in my kitchen. It would be many years before I could move what most people might regard as junk into a real studio, but for me my studio was always a frame of mind more than a physical space. And I al-ways needed to have some version of a studio, because I never wanted to be anything else but an artist. I didn't know exactly what that meant for a long time, and I didn't have a plan. I just pushed forward. I don't remember anyone telling me I could be anything I wanted to be, nor do I remember anyone telling me I *couldn't* be something. Being an artist felt right. Need-less to say, that meant I went through stretches of not having much money. At one point, money was so tight that I thought I would have to leave San Francisco. My dad stepped in and did a very kind thing: he told me that for six months he would buy one piece of my artwork per month, for five hun-dred dollars. I was grateful at the time, but with hindsight I can appreciate just how supportive the gesture was—he wasn't just giving me money; he was supporting my work and, in doing so, expressing that it was worth something and that my desire to be an artist had value.

I continued enduring spans of feeling down and directionless. Dur-ing one of those times, I decided to just walk until I found something that would interrupt my sadness. I walked and I walked, for a few days, going home only to sleep. On one of those days, I ended up at a place called Friends of Photography—a nonprofit center. I asked if they took on interns and they did. From there I met other photographers and artists, got in-volved, and became part of the local photography scene. Walking, thinking, and looking for unexpected connections has always moved me forward.

I spent twenty-plus years teaching and working as a visual artist, exploring ideas through solo work in my studio. That's where I was when my life's trajectory started veering toward the San Quentin parking lot. Whenever I'm working, NPR is on. I find it soothing to listen to the sound of voices, and often get ideas from the fragments of stories that make their way into my thoughts while I'm otherwise engaged. One day a story about Kresty Prison in Saint Petersburg, Russia, caught my attention. I paused and turned up the volume to listen as the prison was described in terms that made it sound like a Dickensian workhouse or an institution detailed by Dostoyevsky. Built in the nineteenth century and still used today, it is ter-ribly overcrowded, violent, and lacking in funds. The piece went on to report that Kresty was being opened to tourists as a source of revenue. Tourists would be invited to view the prison, walk by cells, and end their experience in a gift shop, where they could purchase objects made by the people incarcerated there.

The shocking story was described in incredibly visual terms, and I couldn't stop thinking about what it would be like to be incarcerated there and have it become a site for tourists. I became determined to visit Saint Petersburg, not to tour Kresty but to try to understand a country that would allow this to happen. It took some time, but once I fix my sights on an idea, I tend to be relentless until I make it happen.

While visiting my sister Aimee, who lived in Sweden, I managed to make it from Stockholm to Saint Petersburg for a few days. It was not an easy place to travel around: you need a visa to visit Russia, and visitors needed to be escorted by guides—roaming freely was possible, but was neither easy nor encouraged. I asked everyone I met about the prison, but no one seemed to have even heard of it. I started to wonder if it was possible that I had simply had some delusional daydream and cooked up the whole thing. Had I conflated this wild story to suit my imagination? On my final day, reluctantly resigned to let it go, I packed up and my husband and I left for the train station. We arrived early, so we took a short walk. To my amazement, our aimless wander landed us directly in front of Kresty Prison.

Unlike most prisons in the United States, Kresty sits in the center of the city. There weren't any obvious gates and the signs were mostly in Cyrillic, so I couldn't read them. Anybody can walk right up to it, which is exactly what we did—so close that I reached up and laid my hand on the cold brick exterior. It was a huge, industrial, and imposing building. Craning my neck, I could see a series of small windows. To my surprise, I thought I saw a hand sticking out of one of them. In my memory, it was waving or pointing.

I walked around a bit, viewing the surroundings. I observed every rock, every industrial side street, trying to imagine what it would be like to view them from the different windows above. My eye was drawn to the ground, not far from those high windows. I walked closer to what appeared to be dozens and dozens of odd cone-shaped objects. They weren't deliberately or carefully laid there; they were scattered and haphazard, like leaves fallen from a tree. I reached down and cautiously picked one up. It was about eight inches long, made out of paper, and weighted at the point with a hard, brown substance that had clearly been worked by hand. We didn't have much time left, so I put one of the paper objects in my bag and we hurried back to the train station and left Russia.

As soon as I got back to the States, I pulled the cone-shaped object out of my suitcase and went to research what exactly was being thrown from those prison windows. The brown substance at the point was likely made out of chewed-up bread. During our travel home, I had begun thinking about it as a communication cone—an attempt by the people inside to correspond with the outside world. The method seemed ineffective at best, and futile, given the improbability that an intended recipient would ever receive the message. There were so many of them lying on the ground, undelivered. Nonetheless, I found the endeavor a deeply human, poignant, and willful gesture of survival. The cones were a way for the individuals inside to let the world know they still existed.

Sometime later, I ran into a guy I'd grown up with, and whose career path had landed him at the CIA. He told me he was going to Saint Petersburg, so I told him about my adventure there and the cones, and asked him if he knew what they might be. He said he would check. When he came back he told me what I had done was fairly dangerous: the police watch that area to see who picks up the cones, believing the men inside use them to continue illegal activities. I'll never know the truth of those cones—whether they represent a willful gesture of being or a form of nefarious communication. Most likely, it is a combination of motives. Regardless, those cones acted as seeds that would germinate into interests which preoccupy me to this day: how communication occurs within prison, how incarcerated people communicate with the outside world, and how those on the outside stay connected with their loved ones inside.

A few months later, a letter was delivered to my house from San Quentin State Prison. It was intended for a completely different address; not even the zip code matched mine. The envelope had an upside-down stamp on it, and the outside was heavily decorated with drawings. It was a gorgeous object in itself, and as much as I yearned to keep it, I delivered it to its intended address in San Francisco.

The crazy thing was that it happened several more times: intriguing, decorated letters showed up, misdelivered, in my mailbox, and they were always from the same sender, adding to the mystery. Each letter fueled my curiosity, but each time I reluctantly hand-delivered these pieces of art and correspondence through the addressee's mail slot. I never met the recipient, and the letters eventually stopped arriving at my house.

I don't believe that there is an all-knowing, invisible force that guides us toward a destination or destiny, but I absolutely believe that close attention and mindfulness can alter one's course. The misdelivered letters, like the communication cones, spoke to something that intrigued me and informed my work: how we share and understand (or misunderstand) personal, social, and experiential cues. Though I knew little about prisons, I started thinking about them regularly, wondering about how to interact with people inside.

San Quentin State Prison was not far from my home. I had driven by it many times on Highway 101 going north. It's not close to the highway, but the building is large enough that it's hard to not see it. From that distance, however, it just looks like some kind of factory—neither foreboding nor welcoming, just a large presence. I knew what it was, plus I had these two odd prison-communication experiences percolating in my imagination. I wanted to figure out how to connect it all, but had no idea how to do that, until I had my third chance encounter.

At the time, I was a professor of photography at California State University in Sacramento. We would frequently receive emails calling for volunteer teachers. It was through one of those emails that I first heard about an organization called the Prison University Project—a nonprofit organization that offers men inside San Quentin the opportunity to earn an AA degree. They were looking for someone to teach an art history class. At the time, this was the only on-site degree-granting program in California prisons, with all classes taught by volunteer teachers, professors, and graduate students from the Bay Area. It seemed like an ideal position. I could go inside with a purpose, meet the incarcerated men in an academic context, and use the tool I knew best at the time—photography—to form a connection and learn their stories.

In 2011, I started teaching the first history of photography class inside San Quentin. I taught the class for three semesters. Photographic images gave me and my students something to bond over, and became our bridge to conversation. Those conversations were the foundation for everything that came after.

San Quentin is situated on a peninsula surrounded by the beautiful San Francisco Bay. As you're driving onto the grounds, the 169-year-old prison is about two hundred yards straight ahead; to the left is the water and to the right are rolling hills dotted with pleasant housing, where some of those who work at the prison live. It's easy to be seduced by the calm setting and momentarily forget the structure ahead that holds some four thousand incarcerated individuals—some of whom don't belong there, some who do, some who will spend a handful of years there, and others who will perish within the prison's walls.

The parking lot is the way station between the inside and out. Correctional officers park there and so do prison administrators, staff, volunteers, and family members and friends who visit the men inside. It is the place where all those people merge, oftentimes leaving evidence of their time at the prison. The parking lot at San Quentin has become my hunting ground, a place full of intriguing abandoned bits and pieces that have helped me better understand life inside: a crushed tube of bright red lipstick, a Spitfire Skylander card, a flattened spool of string, underwire from a bra, Saran Wrap braided into a chain, a folded piece of paper covered with mathematical notations, one green glove, a tuberculosis test ruler, an exploded ballpoint pen, a tiny spiral-bound notebook wadded up and soaked by water, a CO_2 cartridge, a bent metal spoon, and a Post-it with a list of musicians and songs. Every crushed, crumpled, and discarded object I find out in the parking lot has an origin story. You can find a worthy story anywhere, it just requires being interested in what is around you, listening, and being attentive to what's said and what's unsaid.

Before you enter the prison, you go through the sally port, where they check your ID. There are two sets of gates ahead. After entering and closing the first gate behind you, you hold up your ID for an officer behind a secure window. He buzzes the second gate and you step into the prison proper. From there you pull open a large, heavy metal door, with worn areas. The first time I stepped in, I was surprised to be met by the sight of a large rosebush, various plantings, and well-maintained grass. After years of making this entrance, I'll usually see some gardeners I know. They're all incarcerated men who devote themselves to maintaining this area and take rightful pride in it. It all seems very pleasant at first glance.

To the left is an ominous building with the words "Adjustment Center" written on it, in nineteenth-century script. Next to that is another building, which houses the men on death row. Walking in, I can usually hear those guys' voices. It sounds very regimented—not necessarily aggressive, but militant. You don't see those men, you just hear them. Like everything in prison, the sensory messages are mixed: a beautiful garden and flowers to admire, set against the soundtrack of voices of men exercising on the row's yard.

The view is lovely, with Mount Tamalpais peeking out in the distance. I've grown accustomed to it, but it always used to surprise me that a prison had such a spectacular view. Walking along, the yard is usually filled with men working out, talking, and playing music. There are different areas for different races—it took me a while to distinguish who hung out where, but now I can quickly identify the landscape. I can walk through any of these areas as a volunteer, but the men inside respect the divisions. Most people are very friendly; I'll often hear my name or "Hey, radio lady!" called out. I always make eye contact and at the very least nod my head. If I have the time I like to stop and chat, but that means it will take me a while to get through the yard, because the guys like to talk.

Teaching the photography class gave me the opportunity to spend time in the prison, getting to know people and starting to understand how things worked inside. It also gave everybody inside—the men, the correctional officers (COs), and the administration—the chance to get to know me and my intentions. That was so important because, understandably, there are huge trust issues at stake. A prison is a kind of a cloistered society with rules and ways of being that were new and at times unreal to me. Understanding how to function as an outsider takes time. You have to learn to respect the racial divisions, the standards for how and when to deal with COs, and the all-important rule of minding your own business. Navigating a prison as an outsider requires politeness, patience, and persistence. Without those three qualities, you will spin your wheels and burn out.

Prison life is more complicated than I could ever articulate. If I'd gone in presuming I understood the lay of the land, I would have been tremendously misguided. In addition to needing to intuit unspoken rules and figure out how to get through reels of administrative red tape, you also have to figure out—quickly—who you can trust. The biggest mistake volunteers make is entering with arrogance, presuming they know best what people inside want or need. Pre-cooked assumptions get you nowhere.

Adjusting to such an environment suited me because I am, by nature, a quiet observer. I appreciate that real work takes time. I have spent years working on a single art project. And I trusted it would take a few years to understand prison, inasmuch as I could ever understand it while having the freedom to exit. I never could have foreseen precisely what those classes were laying the foundation for. Naturally, I hoped something would come out of all of my time at San Quentin, but I also knew I would have to pay attention for a while and let the end product reveal itself over time.

Despite having no defined agenda, there was much to be gained by hearing and watching my students engage and talk about their experiences. With time, I began entertaining the possibility of stepping away from photography and doing a project that somehow incorporated voice and audio textures. Photography frames an experience; it contains it. But there's always so much going on outside of the frame. I wanted to find the right medium to expand and detail everything happening within the frame, while also enabling subjects the freedom to step outside of it.

While teaching, I met several men who were interested in working on projects about life inside. I started talking with some of the film students about putting together a film, documenting life inside. In 2007, the Discovery Channel had come to San Quentin and set up a film school. Eight men were able to participate in a ten-week program in which they learned to write scripts and use film equipment. When the program ended, the Discovery Channel donated all the equipment (computers, cameras, and software) to the prison. That equipment, and the room in which it was set up, helped create the Media Lab, where I worked for close to five years. The first computers that we would use to do audio, however, were donated by the show *Criminal Minds,* which had filmed an episode at the prison.

San Quentin has long been unique in its uncommon encouragement of journalism. The prison's first newspaper (*Wall City News*) can be traced as far back as the 1920s, but it had a short tenure. A man named Clinton T. Duffy became the warden in the early 1940s, and revived the media program by approving the launch of the *San Quentin News,* which has run on and off ever since, but is still printed and distributed today.

Warden Duffy also started the first radio system within San Quentin, called the Gray Network. He installed radio access inside each cell, both as a means of addressing everybody and so that the men could listen to programs.

An inspired man who was incarcerated at the time brought together thirty men and they started a singing club. After a few weeks of rehearsal, they recorded a sample. When Warden Duffy took it to the networks in San Francisco, he was summarily rejected. Only KFRC—managed by a man named Bill Pappas—would entertain the notion of broadcasting a choir of incarcerated men.

San Quentin on the Air made its debut from the prison's mess hall in the early weeks of January 1942. By Warden Duffy's written account, within weeks the show had been picked up and was aired by more than three hundred stations nationally, resulting in an overwhelmed prison post office, which began to receive upward of four thousand fan letters per week.

Making a film inside the prison was daunting, but I believed it was possible. I came up with the idea of using "verbal photography" as its basis, and began by bringing guys down to the Media Lab. One example of an assignment was asking the men to remember an important moment in their lives and write about it as if they were describing a photographic image. They would take an experience, distill it to a single moment, remove any description of time passing or reference to what was happening outside the selected frame, and detail that moment as if they were holding an image of it in one hand.

Though the class was successful, and provided no shortage of rich, candid conversations, it quickly became apparent that taking on a film, and doing it right, was going to be overwhelming, and ridden with obstacles. No raw footage could be taken out of the prison, which meant that everything would have to be edited inside. I had never made a film before, but I knew how time-intensive editing is. So many of the elements started to seem insurmountable. The restrictions and unpredictability of it all made me realize that such an endeavor would take more years than I had to give to it. Audio made far more sense, and excited me. Although I didn't have any formal training with it as a medium, I was drawn to the intimacy and artistic possibilities of sound.

In the early stages, the group of men with whom I was working began a modest experiment, with a show called *Windows & Mirrors*. The idea was to have unscripted conversations, then air the results on the closed-circuit station inside the prison. I handled the interviews, and the production was technically crude. I didn't know anything about editing and wasn't concerned with a discernible story arc. I wanted to talk with guys about the specifics of their everyday lives, their observations, the small and the overlooked details, the minutiae, and their memories that hovered close to the unconscious. So much of importance can be gleaned there, but it takes the right environment, and the right combination of questions and questioners, to yield such responses.

While *Windows & Mirrors* was happening, more and more guys started expressing interest in getting involved. There were about eight of us working together in the Media Lab. Some were concentrating on film, others were drawn to audio. Don't let the name "Media Lab" evoke an image of something grand, clean, or digitally advanced. It is framed by concrete floor and walls, and ceiling tiles that have fallen out in places. Where the tiles are missing you can look up at the wooden rafters. Sometimes birds get in there, creating unique sounds. When it rains hard the ceiling leaks, so we have to be extra careful with our equipment. Though the entire space is probably around two thousand square feet, it's broken up into several areas. The *Ear Hustle* section is approximately ten by twelve feet.

The Media Lab was initially open from 7:00 a.m. to 3:30 p.m., Monday through Friday, with limited hours on the weekend. The hours were unreliable, depending on everything from CO availability to lockdowns, to whether the guy who ran the lab felt like showing up that day. Entry was never a reliable guarantee. The lab is situated in what used to be the old laundry building, so above us were these clanging pipes, which contributed to the unpredictable and uncontrollable noises. It is a very busy place, with people coming and going at all times, and loud conversations happening all around. There's no soundproofing, there's no quiet room. It's prison, and from the start we had to get creative about making it work.

Our conditions were far from ideal or professional, but we didn't need to meet those conditions where they were, which is to say that *we* could be professional, even though our surroundings were not. As more people—both those incarcerated and the volunteers—got interested in audio, we expanded the program and got everyone involved with interviewing, scriptwriting, editing, and story development. That all required training. Holly Kernan, the news director at local public radio station KALW, heard about what we were doing and offered to help. That led to an

exciting time of learning and moving forward, as a group of men and I worked together to produce radio stories. In 2013, we launched on KALW's show *Crosscurrents*. I was still a full-time professor, but I spent all of my free time volunteering with the radio project. It was collaborative and challenging and I gave it all the attention I could, hoping the show would continue to develop.

For over three years I worked on the radio project, meeting people and building a greater understanding of day-to-day life inside. There was a ton to negotiate with the space, the administration, and interpersonal relationships. Like all work environments, there were many personalities involved, and—as in all work environments—I found some of them easier to get along with than others.

Some of the men were quite extroverted and boisterous; others were quiet and slightly retiring. There was one guy who was always there, quietly helping out. Friendly, but shy. He had a gentle presence, and never demanded or required special attention. He was always present, and always willing to lend a hand with whatever needed to get done. At group meetings, he was mostly silent until something important or difficult needed to be said. At that moment he would speak up, say his peace, cut through the bullshit, and engage in frank conversation. He seemed especially observant of everything going on around him and, consequently, possessed a better understanding of the group dynamics. He was a slow reveal, not someone who has to tell you what he's all about the first time you meet him. He was kind, thoughtful, and paid unique attention to his surroundings—just the type of person to whom I respond best. I grew increasingly curious about him with each conversation we had. His name was Earlonne Woods.

CHAPTER THREE

EAR HUSTLE

EARLONNE

When the bus pulled into the gates at San Quentin, it looked like a college campus. I'd done time in a few prisons at that stage, but this place looked totally different. I could see guys playing tennis, jogging, and just chilling on the yard. I saw a number of geese plucking away at the grass on the baseball field.

There was also a group of guys standing in front of R&R, trying to see if they knew someone getting off the bus. When they took the chains off of me and stripped me out, taking the paper clothes, the first person I ran into was my ex-cellie "CC" (whose full name is Cleveland O'Neil Campbell—I used to tease him by saying his mom gave him the last names of her three exes). We'd been cellmates during my prior prison experience. He was an R&R worker, and the guy whose job it was to hand my naked ass a roll of clothes. He told me who was there that I would know and what San Quentin was like. All of us were placed in different holding cells. CC brought me all kinds of extra chips, cookies, and sandwiches. He also brought me new clothes that actually fit. It's always good to know people.

The next morning, I ran into all kinds of cats who I had met in prison over the years, as well as old gang associates. But it was two guys in particular I wanted to see: one was my friend Kenyatta Leal, from Centinela. He was an all-around good dude. The other was Troy Williams, who I wanted to ask about getting into the film school.

I eventually ended up seeing Troy in the shower area. He told me that unfortunately the Discovery Channel project was over, but they had left their equipment. He invited me down to the media center, where they had about eight iMac computers.

The Media Lab was the heartbeat of San Quentin—the best place to be serving time—and what had drawn my attention back when I saw that documentary. It was an atmosphere of creativity, ideas, respect, bickering, love, hate, creative vision, conflicts . . . definitely fertile ground for comedy. And even though we were a group of incarcerated individuals, we were a group of incarcerated individuals who were interested in learning about how we might change the narrative about our own environment.

Troy gave me the rundown: He and seven other guys worked for San Quentin Television (SQTV), and since Troy had been in the film school, he was able help other guys learn some of the stuff that he had been taught. I already knew my way around computers. I'd used Mac computers in Centinela, where I had completed a graphic arts trade.

Very quickly I recognized that even though Troy was cool, he looked at the Media Lab as if it was his. Like he owned it. That sense of possessiveness was due to the level of trust the supervisor gave him. He had the passwords to all the computers, and the power to go film in the institution whenever he wanted. I think—in his mind—the way to protect the program was just to retain all that control. But it got to the point where everything was all about him or his vision. During meetings, we'd have these grandiose conversations about production, and the best way to create good videos or PSAs, but there were no practical lessons imparted. I soon figured out that, whatever I wanted to learn, I would have to teach myself.

The Media Lab is where I first met Nigel Poor. She started coming in to talk about photography, and how to observe everything you see in a photo and map it, which means offering your thoughts and insights. I wasn't in the group initially, but I was always around, and Nigel seemed cool and professional. She was constantly having a meeting or working on something. Guys would share their visions with her, which would almost always be some story all about themselves. I'd see Nigel sitting there listening, her antennas up, trying to support and help guys bring their "all about themselves" visions to fruition. She'd tirelessly transcribe hour-long audio interviews, conduct crazy-long meetings, have endless, pointless conversations with the supervisor of the media center—and then, after all that, I noticed that she would often be treated like a secretary. I even saw volunteers hate on her *because* of how dedicated she was to her work there. San Quentin has a few thousand volunteers, of all varieties, streaming in and out every year. Guards come by occasionally to check in, but sometimes we would go hours without seeing them.

Nigel kept on bringing guys down into the studio and interviewing them. Our close friend Antwan "Banks" Williams and I used to help her with technical stuff when needed. After her show *Windows & Mirrors* started, people from KALW began leading workshops on production. I continued editing videos and assisting others with tech, but I was more and more present, curious about what they were doing, and eager to get involved and do a story. Troy wasn't having it, but he paroled in 2014 and handed over the reins of SQPR (San Quentin Prison Report) to a fellow incarcerated guy named Brian. SQPR was the group of guys who were interested in creating documentary pieces about life inside. They worked out of the Media Lab, making PSAs for the prison, but had originally focused on film work. Unfortunately, Brian tried to run the program just like his predecessor—like some sort of self-designated executive director. My friend Sha Wallace-Stepter was left in charge of the radio program. Sha did a cool job with radio, but both Sha and Brian were preoccupied with other stuff.

I kept my eye on Nigel, as it became evident that she was getting fed up with people's attitudes down there. Guys had her so pissed at one point that she was ready to walk away from the whole project and be done with San Quentin. I'd talked to her on several occasions and kept trying to convince her to stick around. I knew how frustrating the environment could be, with egos battling everywhere, but I was confident that I could change the dynamic with a few words and a bit of organization. I respected and responded to Nigel's drive and discipline; plus she was cool as fuck.

Guys would talk shit and gossip about why she was there; some even accused her of taking advantage of them, 'cause she had gotten a grant to be able to work with us while teaching. I could see she just needed them to respect her the way she respected us. She wanted it to be a professional environment, and I did too. When it seemed like she was close to her breaking point, I decided to take matters into my own hands, and asked her to give me ninety days to change some shit. She trusted me, and agreed to hold out for a few more months.

I asked all of the radio guys how they would feel if I took over radio for ninety days. Everyone was on board, so I went and got at Sha. He was kinda relieved that I'd be taking it off his hands for a while. But as soon as he agreed, I realized that I'd be going from sideline technical support to running the department. I knew how I *wasn't* going to do it (by using the iron fist approach or by taking on some lofty, meaningless title so that I could lord over anybody). Without much of a notion of what I *was* gonna do, I decided to allow more guys to explore what *they* actually wanted to do. Instead of trying to align a chaotic environment with one person's vision, everyone with a creative instinct was welcome to pursue their own project.

It was during this time that Nigel and I started talking about doing a podcast. Our first one was going to be for the institutional TV channel, and I suggested to Nigel that we should get Antwan involved, especially to create the sound—one of his many artistic talents.

That first conversation about what we were going to do, I believe, was a large part of what got Nigel to stick around. To be clear, I didn't know what the hell a podcast was, nor did I have any idea how to make one. But that seemed like an obstacle I could overcome, especially with the right partner.

People see things differently in this world. Some see no value in discarded things or people. Nigel looks more closely, sees the *what if*. Day after day, she showed up in the Media Lab and SAW everyone there. We weren't invisible to her. She saw us. As somebody who spends a lot of time watching things myself, I consider her a professional observationalist—and a constant, relentless note-taker.

NIGEL

When I was growing up, if I ever told my dad I was interested in something, he would tell me to take out a lined yellow pad and "write a damn list" of what I needed to do to accomplish my goal. He instilled in me some of my more obsessive tendencies, as well as the value of repetition and persistence. I remember shooting hoops with him, and him saying, "If you want to get better, you need to do this for hours and hours." I can't say he made it sound particularly joyful, but he definitely got his message across: if you want to understand something or improve at it, just keep doing it over and over and over, until you succeed.

Those lessons were essential as Earlonne and I began trying to figure out our plan for our podcast. Throughout those early days, I continued with my compulsive note-taking, which has since enabled me to re-create how our podcast came to be. My notes are ways of tracing threads that eventually commingle in a curious tangle. They are my maps; without them, the tangle might prove too hard to negotiate.

The process of figuring out how to transition out of the public radio project and into a more creative, innovative project took time and patience. It had taken a while for Earlonne and me to even come together to begin speaking about it. When he was part of the crew, he was more often in the background. He came and went without being noticed, often like a phantom presence.

But I was a frequent enough visitor to the prison that over a course of weeks, months, and years we got to know each other. If there was an issue with the computers or recorder, Earlonne, or "E.," as I came to call him, became the go-to guy. He *never* got flustered and was never a jerk about anything. If he couldn't answer a question, he didn't pretend he knew the solution; he pulled out the manual and figured it out on his own, patiently. If I ever started to get irritated, he provided a quiet, soothing presence. The more time I spent with him, the more impressed I was by his skills, in addition to his calm, humble nature.

Space is at a premium in the Media Lab. You can't just start something new and selective and assume that others are going to respect your space. Plus, working in an environment where resources are scarce means that, if you want to get things done, you have to find a work-around. That scarcity of resources usually leads to other problems: bickering, jealousy, suspicion, gossip, and the dividing of allegiances. What started as a wonderfully creative audio project began to feel less vital to me. It wasn't that the stories felt less important, but the way the shows were being made grew frustrating. Every few weeks there was a new argument or complaint—each person felt that the project he was working on was the most important. That's fine, but when time and space became a consistent issue, not everybody was ready to compromise or be reasonable. Then you had the egos: the guys that, as E. put it, needed to beat their chest and do the rooster dance. The power struggle became so toxic that people were actually firing each other . . . within the media center. It was so unnecessary. As the needless-drama quotient rose, I began to question why I was giving so much of my time and energy to an endeavor that was starting to feel unhealthy.

Earlonne recognized that I was growing tired of the negativity. He, too, got sick of being around all the infighting—it's just not his style. So, Earlonne being Earlonne, he had a plan. He asked me to give him three months to sort it out and improve circumstances. I believed in the possibility of what we could do, and we talked about what his plan would entail: while others continued fussing around or needlessly jockeying for higher positions, we would just get to work. I didn't want to walk away. I wanted to believe that everything from my college photography project to the communication cones, to the misdelivered mail, to teaching for the Prison University Project, to lessons learned trying to make a documentary in the prison was surely leading to something greater. I didn't hesitate to agree to his ninety-days pledge.

We first got together to quietly hatch a new plan for a more focused and creative project that would tap into the hidden, surprising, unexpected stories of life in prison. Neither of us needed to broadcast our intentions or ask for approval or attention; we would just work it out and prove ourselves through the results. We had a pretty clear shared goal from the start: Together, with Antwan's help, we would create a podcast that showed the commonality between those inside and those outside. We would help bridge the divide, and use voices and stories to bring people's humanity to the surface.

On October 5, 2015, Earlonne and I met at a table in a smaller area of the lab, telegraphing to everybody else that we were having as much of a private conversation as possible in that setting. We started jotting down how we wanted to structure the podcast, what we would need, and what we wanted to convey. A few things came easily. We chose the name *Ear Hustle,* which is slang for "eavesdropping." We liked it because we didn't want the name to be synonymous with prison. We knew we wanted to figure out a way to make photos or illustrations somehow be a part of it. We also knew we wanted a distinct sound design, and some kind of intriguing theme or hook to bind together each show. We wanted it to be surprising, and not just a replaying of the kinds of stories people expect to hear out of a prison.

By nature, we're both introverts, but we knew from the first meeting that we were going to co-host. We'd offer some banter and "yard talk" between segments to help relieve the weight of some of the tougher stories, while reinforcing the notion of inside and outside coming together to reflect on the humanity we all share. I took careful notes as we plotted out our vision, agreeing that we would always be the producers with the final say. By the end of our discussion, sitting amidst the chatter and energies of the Media Lab, our visions were aligned quickly. Now, all we needed to do was figure out where it would be recorded, who would air it, and how exactly to make a podcast. Somehow, against all reason, we walked away, confident and excited that we'd iron out such minutiae. And from that meeting came the first-ever podcast produced within a prison, distributed globally.

It would be generous to say that we didn't know a great deal about podcasts. But we had learned something from working on the radio project, and that would be enough to get us going. Plus, we both had plenty of ideas of where we could go with it.

To my mind, that mutual lack of experience worked in our favor. It meant neither of us was bound by expectations of precisely how things should be done. That, in turn, meant experimenting and bringing our own creativity and sensibilities to the project. I knew Earlonne was creative because I had watched the way he solved problems, and the persistence with which he did so. He doesn't give up until he gets it right. He thinks like an artist—meaning he is inventive, thoughtful, and creative about problem-solving. Though my work has almost always been solo, I knew instinctively that we would work well together, stepping into this unknown realm side by side.

There are very few people with whom one can truly collaborate. I often wonder and have frequently been questioned about why, and how, the two of us work so well together. It's a tricky phenomenon to articulate. From the start, we just trusted each other. There was never any bullshit or posturing. We showed up, treated each other as colleagues and equals, and it's never shifted from that. We also share a particular work ethic that's rooted in an ability to listen, to recognize and support the other's weaknesses, and to put forward the other's strengths without having to discuss it. He can do things I could never do; I can do things he cannot, and we roll with it. We created *Ear Hustle* as an unlikely pair in a very tough environment by laying out our dream from the start, and not letting go.

The obstacles to that dream presented themselves immediately. You cannot count on anything inside prison. Simple daily tasks that you do outside without a thought are never simple inside. Nothing can be done mindlessly. As important as we thought *Ear Hustle* was, when we started it wasn't a priority for anyone except us. There was no road map to follow. Earlonne and I had to make it up as we went along. That necessity, and our shared skills of improvising and swerving around problems, has been essential to our ongoing work.

Roadblocks became part of the process. We needed to print out scripts, but printers are hard to come by inside. Our sessions could be interrupted at any time by a prison lockdown—which would mean that I couldn't go into the prison and would have zero contact with Earlonne. He couldn't call me, I couldn't call him, and we would have no idea how long it would last. Could be days, weeks, months.

When we were recording, we'd try to have what were often deeply personal interviews in a space that was almost never quiet, and almost never private. Everything was a challenge. But whenever my tank was running empty on the essential qualities—politeness, patience, and persistence—Earlonne was there to level me out so we could get back to the work at hand.

When I'd leave, those heavy prison gates shut hard behind me, so our communication was nearly severed until I returned to San Quentin. Until he got out of prison at the end of 2018, Earlonne and I couldn't email each other. Talking on the phone was possible, but not easy, so we had to be super organized. I couldn't just call him with an idea. There were very specific times when we could reach each other, and always a limit on those times. Above all, we had to trust and rely on the other person to do what had been promised so that when we saw each other again, we'd be on track and ready to go.

Early on, a reporter writing about our relationship said, "Earlonne was a Virgil to Nigel's Dante." Poetic as that is, it misses the profound connection of our relationship and misrepresents the arena in which we work. While prison can certainly be a difficult place, we were interested in revealing more than the hell that prison can be. And while Earlonne is indeed a guide of sorts, the intricacies of the stories we tell have always required us to be partners, together exploring emotionally complex territory, each bringing our own experiences, sensitivities, and questions to the work at hand. We regularly find ourselves in completely unknown territory, but when we're approaching those situations together, that synergy provides the necessary light that allows us to get on with our job.

EARLONNE

As we were putting our podcast plan together, Nigel came to me and said, "Look at this brochure—we should enter." Radiotopia (a collective of independently owned podcasts) was hosting a "Podquest" competition, looking for a fresh, new idea. The winner would be picked up and become part of the Radiotopia network. I was down.

Telling stories from prison requires walking a fine line. We want to be as real as it gets when it comes to escorting the public inside. But that's also where it gets complicated. Having served decades in prison, I understand where the line is that causes eyebrows to lift, for prisoners and administrators alike. Together, Nigel (or "Nyge," as I call her) and I toe that line, but we respect that line.

We enlisted Antwan, primarily because he's very gifted, but also because of how some of the others treated him over the years when it came to him making music. The guys in the media center felt that computer time wasn't for making beats. But that's what Antwan loved doing, more than anything, so we enlisted him, in part to support his passion for sound. I didn't care that other guys didn't want him involved. We were determined to do this our own way, I was adamant that we include him, and Nigel was down. The three of us created a two-minute promo of what our show would sound like. Nigel gave Lieutenant Sam Robinson the promo and the Radiotopia brochure. Lieutenant Robinson is the public information officer at San Quentin, who is given the discretion to support (or not support) media projects. In time, he would become the man to listen to our episodes and give them the green light to let them out of the prison—which may sound easy, but if he made a mistake, he could have easily lost his job. He has seen it all, and would go to bat for us many times over the years. He's a straight shooter, and can smell bullshit from a mile away. When he first looked over the brochure he must have thought, *What are the chances these three are gonna win a worldwide competition*? So he allowed us to enter.

We submitted our application and promo, and quietly and anxiously awaited a response. About a month or so later, Nigel came in wearing a big Kool-Aid smile. Out of 1,536 contestants from 53 countries, we had made it to the Top 10. The Top 10 became the Top 4, and then . . . *Ear Hustle* won the Podquest.

Winning meant we were picked up by Radiotopia from PRX, and became part of their network. That was thrilling, not just because it meant our podcast would receive national distribution, but also that we'd be connected with an extended creative family. The people who had enough faith in *Ear Hustle* to give us a chance were a group of professionals who understood and believed in what we were trying to do. Even more, they were prepared to support our vision.

NIGEL

Over the course of the Podquest competition, we had come to know the executive producer of Radiotopia, Julie Shapiro, who corresponded with us throughout the process and would eventually become our executive producer. Given the unknown terrain we were entering, it meant so much to E. and me to have such a solid presence there to shine a light and encourage us down this new road. Every time an issue arose with *Ear Hustle*—which was often, especially when we were new to the medium and didn't know how it would all work—we knew we had an authentic, patient advocate who had our backs. Through all the bumps and tribulations, she never wavered in her support.

Neither of us ever took that support for granted. *Ear Hustle* was born of a shared willingness to leap in first, then figure it out from there. That's an attitude we both possess, but one that was made stronger when we cultivated it together. We were equally aware that if either of us had tried to go it alone, our podcast never would have left the concrete basement of the Media Lab.

Whenever we get on the mics, we warm up by singing "our" song, "Hello, It's Me." (For years we didn't realize that E. was singing the Isley Brothers' version, while I was singing Todd Rundgren's.) Our silly mic check warm-up routine had started with Lionel Richie's "Hello." It evolved over time to include other "hello" songs. But the routine doesn't just test our mics and sound levels; it also signals our presence to each other. It's a means of connecting, getting onto the same wavelength, and essentially saying, "I am fully here."

This adventure has moved us in unexpected directions. But no matter what challenge confronts us, no matter what story we encounter, we're always able to look at each other and say, "Okay, let's do this."

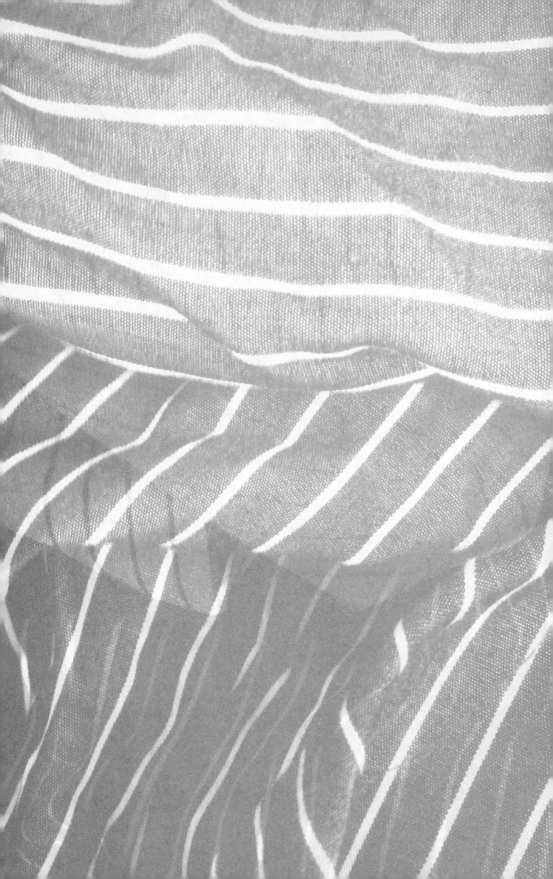

PART II

WE'RE GONNA TAKE YOU INSIDE

CHAPTER FOUR
PRISON 101

EARLONNE We're heading out to Santa Cruz, California, to check in with ole Mittens, aka Mr. Chayne Hampton.

NIGEL For our last few interviews we've had to travel.

EARLONNE Yeah, that's true. That ain't bad—you know how much I love the road.

NIGEL I do. And I like it. It's very different than what we used to do.

EARLONNE And that ain't bad at all.

NIGEL So, Chayne's going to tell us all about his first prison experiences. I have a list of questions to ask him. What are your first memories of going to prison?

EARLONNE I went from the youth authority and was kinda healthy, you know? When I got to prison I got sent to reception, for new arrivals. I bullshit you not, it seemed like all the people in the reception center were drug addicts on parole violations. Hella skinny.

NIGEL And you were like, What the fuck am I doing here?

EARLONNE Nah. I was just like, Damn, this shit is crazy. And I was young. 1991. I was nineteen, and I had a young mind. At the youth authority everyone is eighteen to twenty-five, but suddenly I was surrounded by grown men. I learned early that, in prison, size matters. If you're chunky and got muscles and shit, people leave you alone.

NIGEL So you were pretty big?

EARLONNE I was cool. In the youth authority, we lifted weights every day. I was in shape.

NIGEL None of the older guys gave you a hard time?

EARLONNE Nah, not at all.

NIGEL Did you see that happen to other people?

EARLONNE Oh, definitely. But it all depends on who you are and what you open yourself up to. A lot of time, individuals make room for bullshit.

NIGEL You don't strike me as somebody who would get picked on by people.

EARLONNE There were a couple of things I had going in my favor. I was involved in street gangs, which is pretty much a circle of protection. People knew I was aligned with the Neighborhood Crips as well as the East Coast Crips. So I only interacted with a specific part of the population. Also, I'm not a meddler; I'm not a dude who's trying to start some shit. I'm far from that dude. I've always been more kickback.

NIGEL Could you identify somebody who was going to have trouble—as in, was it easy to see the guys who weren't going to have it easy?

EARLONNE Sometimes you see how people respond or how they operate. Others, as soon as they get to the yard, are trying to borrow shit from everybody and gamble without money and all kinds of crazy shit, and that's when it goes bad. That's opening yourself up to a lot of people, and at the end of the day, prison is prison. You're going to run into some less desirables up in that joint.

　　I think, in prison, once you realize what's going on, what's beneficial, what's not, you can go from there. But in Chayne's world, that would have been a different ballgame.

NIGEL He would have been picked on. He's hyper. Very hyper, and he talks a lot.

EARLONNE He also went in using drugs. He cut that out early in his game. Today, he's still sober. This is the first time he's been clean and sober since he was a teenager. And he's really excited because he has his first apartment.

NIGEL Yeah. It's the first everything. He's learning how to live as an adult, or at least a responsible adult. I've had several exchanges with him recently, and he seems like he's doing really well. He's really proud of himself.

EARLONNE He's happy. He knows where he was at. He sees people living on the streets, doing the same shit that he was doing, and it's freezing, and they ain't got nowhere to go . . . Now he's got a place to go. When he sees people like that, he knows that he doesn't want to go back to that shit. Hell no, man. Not when you can help it. It's just getting over that monkey.

SANTA CRUZ, CALIFORNIA
December 2019

NIGEL Chayne, will you take a look at this photograph and describe what you see?

CHAYNE This is your fish kit, what they give you before you go in. So, a toothbrush, a spork, and a little bar of soap . . . maybe about two inches long and an inch thick. And fresh mint toothpaste. The first time I went to the county jail, I turned my back for a minute and mine was gone. So, you learn for next time: Don't fucking leave your fish kit out. The toothbrush is an inch and a half long; after one thorough brush, you'll blow this thing out. At that time, I was always kind of strung out—so it didn't matter to me; hygiene wasn't my main priority. But it becomes crucial once you're living in a small cell with somebody else. Or on any kind of like a lockdown, say, it's mandatory.

I first went to prison when I was thirty-two years old. It was a three-year sentence. Even before prison, when I was in county jail, I wasn't a youngster coming up, meaning there weren't any older guys who felt inclined to take me under their wing and say, "All right homeboy, when you get there, this is how this is going to work . . ." No one gave a shit—I was just some guy going to prison on some bullshit charges. Prison was not the lifestyle that I was used to leading. I wanted to do the time I deserved, but I obviously didn't want to be there . . . It was a learning curve for me.

I was jealous of the dudes who had been schooled about prison, younger guys that had an uncle or a relative. I'm the first person in my family to go to prison. I didn't hang out with dudes from prison. It seemed like another world. I was just as likely to be on Elon Musk's ship to Mars as I was to be going to prison. But there I was. I knew zero about the culture . . . other than what I'd heard in songs. So, when I went to prison, it was a big shock.

The first time I was strip-searched was when I left county [jail] at one point to go check out a rehabilitation center. They released me to my dad, but it was like a stay of execution—I had to come back that same day. While I was out, though . . . I mean, I couldn't come back empty-handed. So I took this patch of tobacco and decided, *I'm just going to hoop this thing*. It had been explained to me to "think of it like the biggest shit you ever took." That's how much could fit. I didn't want to, but it was only tobacco; it wasn't drugs or anything crazy. *No big deal,* I figured. So I went and got a pouch of it and put it into a rubber glove—but ended up looking like the size of a tennis ball! I'm like, *That ain't gonna work*. So I broke it down into three separate ones, then I did my thing and went back to jail.

This cop named Officer Hernandez noticed that I was acting sketchy in reception. I can't lie and I can't play it cool. "Hampton, get over here," he said. "Strip out right now. Bend over, squat, cough." I did what he asked.

"Hey, I see it. It's right there. Get that shit outta there!"

So I had to fish out one of those bundles and throw it on the ground.

"All right," he said. "Do it again . . . I see another one, get it out of there."

I pulled out another and he's like, "Hey, hey, Officer Gilmore, come here."

He was hella short, and he started checking me out too. I pull out the last one and at that point they're like, "Wait, there's another one." That's when I finally realized, these motherfuckers didn't see anything, 'cause they're telling me there's another one when there wasn't. So, I was just telling on myself.

Then they put you on potty watch and all. Who knows if they're even looking ninety percent of the time. They just seem so bored. They don't want to do it either, I assume. I think a lot of officers use it just as a form of inconvenience for the inmates. Then they make you shake out your hair and open your mouth and things like that. In prison, they take a picture of your tattoos when you come in, as a way of checking for affiliations or something like that.

The first time I walked into the block, there was all this freedom; it wasn't anything like reception. But then it's like, freedom to do . . . what? It was weird to go from lockup to night yard, because you suddenly don't know what to do with yourself. I tried to look for a homeboy, or someone from Santa Cruz, and there weren't any. So, I went to bed.

On my first night, I was just lying in my cell and it was kind of late, 'cause that's when they get you in there. Then I started hearing the "good nights"; you know, the sound-offs. The white guys are like, "To all of my solid white men, good night." Then they'd give shout-outs to . . . whomever. I was like, *What the fuck is this?* Then the pisas (whose home country is usually Mexico) will say something and then the Native Americans and the Blacks and the northerners . . . It goes on for an hour, 'cause there are so many different factions. The USOs were the scariest-sounding ones. I'm not really scared of anything, but theirs was like a battle call. Oh my God, I don't even think I'd ever even met a USO before. They're Polynesian, I think. And just *big*.

So I'm just lying on my rack and didn't know what to think. I guess I was reflecting on my life. Pretty bummed. Nobody comes into prison and sets up his bed in a super good mood. It's more like, *This fucking sucks . . . How am I going to do this?*

My first cellie was in West Block—this dude named Fireball (aka the Butt-Naked Brawler, because he fought this dude and his pants fell down). He was terrible. After a little while, we started getting loaded together. That was my mistake, 'cause I didn't realize how batshit *crazy* this dude was. I'd wake up in the middle of the night and he'd have all these newspaper and magazine clippings hanging from the wall with red strings connecting shit. And he'd be like, "Man, it's part of the algorithm." I wondered where the fuck he got the red string from . . . Anyway, he was crazy.

After that, I had a cool-ass cellie, Tom Lee. I was lucky; he was an older dude. He would tell me what time it was and be like, "Hey, hey, wake up, man." That kind of stuff. Then I was with another dude, who took advantage of our stash. We were getting drugs and he'd just be like, "Chalk me up for more of a debt." But then he started threatening me. I went to Medical one day and my homeboy from Santa Cruz was in the cell next to me. I told him about what was going on, 'cause I had a problem standing up for myself at the time. He went over there with another one of my homeboys and straightened it out. I think they just had a discussion with him, and told him to knock that shit off. I don't know the details of it. I just know that when I came back from Medical, his attitude was very different.

My first fight in prison came down to a money situation—this man's word against mine. Of course, it was drug-related. It was early on, when I had no intention to stop using. I needed to let people know that my money was good, so the next time they'd know I expected to get what I'd paid for. But I was trying to do what I'd been doing on the streets, in prison. On the streets, if I borrowed money off some guy, I could leave and never have to see him again. In prison, they always know where you are. They know, and they're coming for you.

Also, it was just such a fucking hassle. I was at the point where I was trading the sheets off my bed. I'd sell my whites for cigarettes. Pretty much anything that wasn't bolted to the floor I was trying to trade, 'cause I had a smoke habit and a drug habit.

Guys would give you a list of particular things they wanted for drugs. It was never simple. I might have two cases of soup, but the connect would want a meat log. So, I'd have to trade the soup, or find the guy who wanted soup for a meat log, but then he wouldn't give me full price if he could tell how badly I wanted it. I had to jump through all these hoops; go to different dorms or different cells, asking, "Hey, does anyone want this soup?" Then I'd have to deal with getting lowballed and bullshitted around. I might finally get it, but by then it'd be rack downtime and I wouldn't know why I'd bothered.

It took me talking to Miguel, a pisa who knew me from home. "Chayne, man, you look homeless . . . in prison," he said. Something about that made me think, *Fuck, I gotta get my act together.* I'd love to say that that was the tipping point, but it wasn't. It took more.

Bottom line: In prison, if you're using, you're more likely to get yourself into a wreck and less likely to be able to defend yourself. And you can't play like the lone wolf or try to stay out of the way.

I finally decided to stop getting high after my fiancée came to visit and told me the same thing I'd heard from Miguel: that I looked worse than I did when I was on the streets. On the streets, I'd been on 180 milligrams of methadone and a gram of heroin a day habit, plus a gram of crystal in shooting it up.

Hearing her say that I looked even worse was a loud wake-up call. It was a bad place to be, anyway. There were constant threats. My business was always out there. So, after twenty-five years of varying degrees of using, I was able to say, "I think I'm good." I started hanging out with dudes that didn't get high. After a while, I found NA [Narcotics Anonymous], and that helped a lot. But it wasn't easy.

The first week of not getting high was bad. Withdrawals, man. You're hungry, you're itchy. You're depressed, you're sad. But you're also in prison, so you ain't got time to dwell on that shit. I had to treat it as a day-by-day thing. I would wake up and my neighbors were all shooting dope or smoking weed. For me, as an addict, even weed's not okay. Same with drinking. If I drink a little bit or smoke a little weed, that's going to get me in a headspace where I'm going to go out and do what I *really* want to do.

My family was burned-out on sending me money. In the beginning, they'd send packages and then they'd come see me and be like, "Oh, you haven't been eating the food we sent you." It took a long time to rebuild that trust. I was in a pathetic place.

But I had a good buddy in there, Drew, and he was a big part of me staying clean. He'd never done drugs before. When I heard that, I was like, "You've been in prison seven years, and you've never even tried heroin?"

"No, I've never tried heroin—normal people don't just *try* heroin," he told me. I felt so stupid.

He was a normal dude. One time I came back from the shower, got to my rack, and was laying out fresh sheets and all that. I was just sitting there . . . about to do something bad. And all of a sudden my locker door flung open. Drew had been hiding in there, waiting for me to come back. He scared the shit out of me; I started yelling and shit, then laughing. It became an ongoing joke. Sometimes I'd come back and he'd be under my rack or something, waiting to fuck with me, but also to check up on me.

My fiancée kept visiting, and the more she came, the more change she saw in me. I told her I wasn't using. She noticed my skin getting a little bit brighter, then it just progressed. She also saw me being friendly with other men in the visiting room; I wasn't just hanging out with junkies. Telling her that I wasn't going to use anymore kinda kept me accountable.

My parents started visiting again as well, and I made amends with them—as one of the NA steps. I stopped asking for things. Every phone call wasn't a drama.

EARLONNE So, in prison, white boys can be some freaky motherfuckers. When was the first time you ever saw a fee fee?

CHAYNE A fee fee? Never seen one in my life. Honest to God. I mean, I've seen phones with an *exuberant* amount of porn on them, but that's it. And sex with dudes? Sex? I just don't like it. I've seen some men who are super gay, but a lot of guys inside understand it's just sex play . . . It's different. It's something you do, but you're just fucking around. Like this one dude that I was in prison with showered at the same time as I did. We'd be there in the morning, and he would do this thing when he was getting out of the shower where he'd pretend he was like Captain Morgan and put his leg up and go, "Oh, *heyyyyy*, Chayne." But he was just messing with me. I knew that.

So nah, I took care of myself. I worked in the sewage treatment plant, which meant that I had my own little trailer, with a shower. Every time I went and cleaned up shit, I'd go take a shower and rub one out. But then I started getting concerned, 'cause every time I cleaned up the shit, I'd rub one out. I got worried that I was somehow connecting the two too much. I didn't want to get out of prison and then not be able to get off unless I smelled shit, you know? So, I had to cool it. Especially because I do construction now. I don't want to be on a site and feel like, *Oh, man, it's going down.*

In prison, masturbating is more about maintenance. You're not gearing up or looking for anything. You're just like, *Yo, it's that time of the week.* But it's not a big production. And nine times out of ten you're going to have a wet dream. So sometimes you just hold out for that. Unless you have a visit and your lady is looking super hot. If she's kissing on you too hard, you gotta come back to your cell and just handle it, otherwise you're likely to snap on somebody.

NIGEL So what about the first time that you encountered or experienced race issues?

CHAYNE Prison was the first time I've engaged with so many different races. This is going to sound super ignorant, but before San Quentin, I had never seen so many Black people in my life. Santa Cruz is a surf town. There was one Black family when I was growing up, so it was just different. And overwhelming, at first. Like, for meals. In San Quentin, the cops tell you where to sit. If you're lucky, you'll be at a table with at least one other white guy. If you're unlucky, you'll be at a table with three Blacks. Not that there's anything wrong with that, but if there *was* a situation, you're fucked, because you're the only white guy at the table. And if you're a white guy sitting at a table with three Black guys, you're not in on that conversation. Unless you want to be a clown and entertain . . . but even then, you should probably just eat your food and pay attention to what's going on. Like, if these guys have problems with each other or are fighting or whatever.

While I was there, I was told not to be so familiar with the Black dudes—'cause I'd chop it up and joke around with them. One day, I was watching BET [Black Entertainment Television] in the dayroom, and this [white] dude was like, "Hey, come here, man. What the fuck you doing?"

"What do you mean?" I asked. "I'm watching music videos."

"Nah, man, we don't do that shit. What color is your skin?"

"It's white."

"Well, fucking act like it," he said. And this wasn't the kind of dude you argue with. I didn't want to fight. But he explained it to me as "Be aware of your surroundings."

NIGEL He thought it was his responsibility to save you if something happened?

EARLONNE Because he would get *his* ass whooped if they found out a white guy was in the proximity who didn't help a fellow white guy from being attacked.

CHAYNE Exactly. But I was never involved in racial politics. I didn't come out like a skinhead. I'm not some hardcore white power brother; I'm just white. There are peckerwoods and then there are gangs, like skinheads and Nazi Lowriders and shit. I'd never met individuals like that before. I had seen *American History X,* and that was the most I've ever seen of a Nazi. I didn't want to raise my hand to be a part of that. And there wasn't pressure to do so. There are just plenty of guys out there who *do* want to raise their hands.

It was one reason why exercising was so important to me. You'd be surprised how much respect you get from having a program and getting up and working out every day. Maybe it's the discipline, maybe it's the familiarity, but people notice. Then they also know what to expect from you. They know where you're at. They know what time it is.

Also, because I got in a fight early on, I at least wanted to be someone that dudes would look at and say, "Oh, I'm going to pick on this other guy instead." Shit could get violent. I saw this dude get removed from reception with his face rearranged. I didn't know people could bleed that much. It was gnarly. Really, really gnarly. And you can't run, you can't hide. It's just straight. Just a beating or a straight fight between two people. They could blow up at any time. You just get accustomed to that. Especially in a dorm. There are always people stirring the pot, people that want to see something happen. If for no other reason, than just 'cause they're bored.

There were a few crucial pieces of advice someone from a Level IV yard told me: Don't eat after other races. Don't smoke after other races. And don't hide during riots. In other words, if Earlonne had a bowl of food that looks hella good, I don't taste it. And if he's smoking a joint, a cigarette, whatever, that's not for me to smoke. No matter how bad I might want it. And if something cracks off, don't hide. Don't ever do that, because somebody's gonna see you over there balled-up hiding. That's some basic convict etiquette right there. 101. Follow those rules. And there's a few others I'd add:

Remember that mail takes three weeks. Don't wait two weeks, not receive a letter, get mad, and write to your old lady like, "Fuck you. I never loved you; anyways you forgot about me." Because then the next day (I'm speaking from experience), you'll get a letter from her telling you how much she loves you, misses you, and that she'll be here for you the entire time. And then you'll have to write a letter to counter your first response. So be patient with the mail. Your people have not forgotten about you.

Stay out of the way and work out every day. Go super hard all day long. Fatigue is the best sleeping aid in prison (if you're not using drugs). Whatever you can do to tire yourself out, do it. Then you'll have a nice, dreamless sleep. Working at something is the best way to do your time, because you get exhausted, you'll sleep, and before you know it will be the next day, and then the next. But as that time is passing, also try to have the best prison day possible. Wake up early, drink coffee, shoot the shit with the old-timer in the dayroom, watch a little *Good Morning America,* or whatever. As soon as they open the yard? Boom; get out there. I can't say it enough: Do whatever you can to be tired by the end of the day. Maybe it's the heroin-addict part of me that likes to get like a good nod . . . Whatever, it's effective.

Anyone going to prison for the first time should know that there are a whole lot of myths that just aren't true. At least from my experience. For one thing, you're not going to get raped. You can't be on a yard as a white guy with some white dude who's actively raping people. That's not going to fly. That dude will get stabbed. So, don't worry about that as much as it gets hyped.

Prison doesn't define who you are. It doesn't have to be the end-all. San Quentin is a nicer prison, as far as prisons go. Whatever anyone tells you about prison probably won't be your experience.

I miss the camaraderie—just joking, fucking around, shooting the shit. In prison, the days are long, so you can get a lot done. You realize that there are twenty-four hours in a day and there's a lot you can do within that time. Anyone who's ever like, "Oh, man, I don't have time for any of that," I'm, like, "Wake up an hour earlier—you'll have time for that." Also, when you're in prison you have a certain sense of security that everything's going to be taken care of for you. You have access to a shower; you have three meals a day. Out here it's like, *Oh shit, I have to make my lunch today.* I know that that seems weird, but it's true.

But out here, I obviously have creature comforts: my fiancée is not my cellie! I don't know if prison necessarily made me a better partner, but it definitely made me realize who I actually am. I still don't wash the dishes super well, but that's ongoing . . . I need classes, I think. I try to communicate and be as honest as possible.

People in prison who are trying to stay in relationships need to remember, no matter what happens while you're gone, dude, *you are gone.* That's where you're at. That's where she's at. Don't ask her shit that will drive you crazy. Accept where you are. When you get out, you can have another conversation about what you're doing from that point on. But while you're in? That visit, that letter, that phone call—they're great. They're perfect.

EARLONNE Prison seems to be the best thing that ever happened to you, man.

CHAYNE Prison was the worst and the best thing for me. It was an opportunity to pause and clean up my act. I'm almost three years clean off drugs. I did NA inside and now I sponsor other men, and I'm of service to my community. I live in a house. I've got a tacky little Christmas tree, and dishes that I bought, and just normal people stuff.

Prison had its traumatic moments, of course. But maybe I just assimilate quickly. I get somewhere, I think, *Okay, this is crazy. This is strange.* But then, boom, I'm like, *All right, let's do this.* Especially if it's only a short-term sentence, like mine. That made it easier to be, like, *I can't make time go by any faster, but there's an end.* I didn't have any particular goals. I wasn't on a spiritual journey. I didn't have grandiose plans. Until the day that I left, I even assumed that I was going to get more time.

Once you get comfortable with always assuming the worst, then you can get on with it, you know? Then the little things can start being positive. Like, *I'm going to have some fucking nachos later. It's going to be tight.*

EARLONNE Well, it's always good to catch up with ole Chayne. That guy made me laugh when he was inside, and it's no different now that he's out.

NIGEL He even makes talking about shit funny! Shit and sex—not something you really want to think about mixing . . . But he did have some good insights to share with people who might need to know about all things Prison 101.

EARLONNE That he did, especially if you're a white boy serving a shorter sentence.

NIGEL So, it would be good to hear from a few more people with different experiences than Chayne's.

EARLONNE Yup—and if I was still inside, you and I would have grabbed the portable recorder and headed out to get our yard talk.

NIGEL Right, our version of "man on the street" interviews. But since you aren't there anymore, we did something different: I got a group of guys to come down to the Media Lab to chop it up about their first experiences in prison.

EARLONNE You got a solid crew. Yahya, Rhashiyd, and Jessie—they're all at San Quentin serving long sentences. Between them they've got like over fifty years inside. And they've definitely had a different experience than Chayne's.

NIGEL And you spoke with Tyra. She's out now, but served something like sixteen years in CCWF (Central California Women's Facility) and CIW (California Institution for Women).

EARLONNE So we've got white, Black, men, and women to describe their first prison experiences.

NORTHERN CALIFORNIA
December 2019

TYRA As soon as you come in, they tell you to undress and take your shoes off. They take your shoes, turn them upside down, and hit them together to make sure that nothing's in there. Then they take your clothes. They check each garment, take your underwear, check your underwear, and put it over to the side. They tell you to move your hands behind your ears so they can see if there's anything there. Hold your hair up, shake it up and down, make sure you're not hiding anything in there. Then they tell you to hold your breasts up. Squat down, hold your butt cheeks open, and cough three times.

Turn around. Then they do the front the same way. They gotta make sure that the muscles contract, so they can see that nothing's in there. The first time, I cried. But I was mad at the same time. I remember wondering, *How can I get out of this? Do I really have to take my clothes off in front of sixty other people?* I was disgusted. It was very humbling, and very humiliating.

Years into it, probably around the halfway mark of my sixteen-year sentence, as soon as they'd say, "Come on, Woodson, we're gonna strip you out," I'd hurry to the front of the line, get it done, shake my tail feather, and get out. Just get it over with, you know? It took a long time, but eventually I was able to make a joke out of it. I'd laugh and say, "Shake it!" The guards would laugh and wouldn't pick on me. They knew I was just gonna clown around, so they'd be like, "Just let her go."

JESSIE The first time I was strip-searched I was probably fourteen, in juvenile hall. You get in and there's a small cell with a little drain hole in the center of the floor, but nothing else. You strip all your clothes off and they ruffle through them, then hand you each item back before putting you in a holding cell with a toilet and a bunk. Because of my age, they just touched my clothes. I wasn't bending over to cough and squat and all that. It was much more basic.

Going to juvenile hall was sorta neat to me. I was expecting it. My dad had been to prison before I was born. So, he was always (maybe purposefully) giving me the rundown on what was gonna happen inside. One time he took my mattress out of my room and just made me sleep on the hardwood bunk. He was like, "This is what it's going to be like when you get locked up."

My uncles had been to prison. I had friends that had been to juvenile hall. So it was kinda like graduating. It was a badge of honor, a rite of passage. A weird part of me couldn't wait to get there. I thought I was going to learn all this cool stuff, and then get out and look like all the guys I'd seen: They came back bigger, more muscular. They grew their hair long. They had a bunch of tattoos.

I assumed I'd just hang out, lift weights, get a suntan, and learn all this information that would make me some empowered individual. These guys came home with cool little hobbies: they made their own cigarette lighter covers out of wood, or their own leather belts, or just knew how the world worked—systematic things I didn't know. So, yeah. I associated it with the weights and food and being on the yard in the sunshine all day long.

But that was when I was a kid, before I really went away. I was thirty years old when I actually went to prison. There was no glamour, no shine. Prison was cold, gray, depressing, lonely. Nowhere to go. People are scared. You're not getting a tan; you're stuck in a cell. You look outside and see nothing but the gray sky.

RHASHIYD Reception was different for me. I stuck to the people that I had come in with on the bus. Everybody was scared. We didn't know what to expect. There were a couple of people who had been in prison before who took the lead. I just kind of stayed in the background. That first walk through the chow hall, the smell was like mildew, rags, and mops. There were people moving everywhere. It was very scary. I felt out of place; it was like extreme culture shock. At the same time, I was thinking, *Why am I scared?* I'd been in a county jail. But when you get to prison, it's like . . . This is *prison*.

But the first meal you eat in prison is delicious. Something about the anticipation and the fear, the what-ifs. You're starving and scared and emotionally drained. Food just tasted good and warm. My first thought about that was, *Okay, this isn't that bad . . . These noodles and beef broth are delicious.* Then you get used to it and it's like, *This is disgusting.*

YAHYA For my worst arrival experience, I'd have to go back to the first time I laid down in bed. I was twelve years old, and had been arrested for attempting to steal a bike. Needless to say, juveniles are the grossest incarcerated people there are. I remember walking into this cell and seeing this hideous cloth mattress that had pee stains and other kinds of stains all over it. I was like, *I'm not laying on that thing.* So I dragged it off. They had cement blocks underneath, so I decided I'd sleep on the slab.

It was filthy. The cells don't have toilets. If a counselor didn't let people out in time, they'd urinate in the corner. There were loogies all over the wall, where individuals had laid on their backs and had spitting contests. I was so creeped out. When the counselor locked the cell, I just stood there in horrific wonder. I banged on a door. When you do that, you have to yell out your cell number. The counselor got on the intercom, answering, "What do you want?" I told him there was no way in hell I'd sleep there without it being cleaned. He said, "Well, for recreation you can clean your cell out. In the meantime, make it your home. Welcome home." I stood at the door until daylight . . . so probably like four hours. The fact that the adults didn't care made me feel angry. Just very angry.

RHASHIYD The first time I went to lie down in my cell, the first thing I thought was, *This is disgusting.* So I cleaned up, but when I was done and sat down, the next thing that came to my mind was, *How did I end up here?* That initial sit-down in a cell is just like . . . *I'm a loser.*

It was a reality check. That's what it was. You start thinking of all those little things you got away with, but keep coming back to *How did I get here, what led me to this?* It was the longest night ever. I went to sleep, but once I woke up, I couldn't go back to sleep. I couldn't stop thinking, *How can I get out of here?*

When I woke up, the first thought was, *What's going on and where am I?* Then it hits you: *Oh, I'm in prison.* I'd have these dreams where I wasn't incarcerated. Waking up was heartbreaking, just traumatizing. The fear . . . and also just not knowing what's happening. The hopelessness when you remember, *They got me.* Then you get back into what-if questions. *What if . . . What if . . .*

TYRA The first room I got in prison was dirty, but we were blessed because we had a shower. But it was so nasty. I didn't want to take my clothes off in there and get in the shower, even though I was able to actually close the door. I would rather shower in the county . . . that's how dirty it was. County jail was a community shower, and sometimes you had to shower with two or three women because you had to rush out right on time. We had a full pod, so we had to hurry up and shower, often together. We only had one shower per pod, but we still had to get in that rusty, nasty shower— and the guards could always see us and our bodies, no matter what. So the first shower was horrible. It was hard. It was dirty.

YAHYA The first time I took a shower . . . nothing could have prepared me for that trauma. I was on a fifth tier at the time. The police announced over the intercom, "Shower time. Prepare for shower release." I was brand-new, so I asked how the shower program ran. This dude was like, "I can't even explain it to you." All of a sudden, I heard this loud, booming sound—the police lifting the bar. I heard a whole bunch of foot shuffling and rumbling. And I'm like, "Damn, what *is* that?" The noise kept getting closer and closer, slowly coming up. "Man," the dude said, "make sure you shower in your boots."

"Shower in my boots?"

"Yeah. And get there as fast as you can." When they finally pulled the bar, the door swung open and he shot to the right, to the left, then was gone. I ran down to the showers. When I got there they were already full, and all the guys were showering in boots and boxers. There were maybe four or five showerheads for a hundred guys. I thought, *How in the hell am I supposed to shower in this?*

We only had five minutes. For one hundred men. I was terrified. It was traumatic. I had the presence of mind to just watch how everything went. Guys were getting in the shower stall, soaping up and then getting out and letting another guy shower. Rotating. While I was there process-ing it, somebody said, "Hey, soap up and get the hell outta the way. You wasting time!" So I got out of the way before putting the soap on. I took this little bitty shower bar from the fish kit and rushed to put soap all over my body. I didn't know yet that I had to cut my bath towel and use half of it as a wash towel and the other half to dry off with. So, I just showered with the bar of soap and dried off. The whole experience was crazy. Pandemonium. I learned in time: Get in, get wet, step to the side, suds up. Then head back in and rinse off. If you don't make it in time, you have to go back to your cell covered with soap.

You need your boots because it's better to be prepared for anything that can happen. Someone can get drowned. Someone could potentially get raped. Someone can get stabbed with a toothbrush. There can be fights. You want to have some type of traction. I never encountered shower rapes personally, but I've heard rumors. Regardless, it's still a huge violation of privacy because we're packed in there like sardines. People touch you and you don't know if it's intentional or not.

RHASHIYD I didn't get to shower until maybe two days after arriving. They brought us some fresh boxers, T-shirt, and towel, but you have to stay in the orange carrot suit. We didn't have anything to use to wash ourselves. You can't just go to the store. You wash with the state bar of soap, you've got some tooth powder with that little bit of a toothbrush. It's like two inches long. You can't clean your teeth thoroughly. You can't clean your body thor-oughly. You don't have deodorant. I had dreads, but I still stayed in the shower every day as long as I could. You get wet to kind of wash the fear out.

NIGEL So what was it actually like once you settled in? Like when you met your first cellie?

JESSIE My first cellie, in the county jail, was *insane*. He was a Cowboys fan, and we could see the dayroom TV from our cell. So he'd watch the games and he'd beat on the door, shouting shit like "Cowboys up!" It was off the hook—he was taking all kinds of medication and basically behaved like he was on crystal meth, 24/7.

I moved in with this one guy who must have lived a really, really, really rough life. I was probably thirty-one or so. I got in there, and he's got all kinds of property everywhere. Typewriter on the desk. No room for anything. I had a toothbrush and toothpaste. All the other space was his. He was a lifer and had been down forever. He was never getting out, he told me from the gate. Then he said, "My only rule is that you sit down when you pee." I was like, *Look, man.* So he explained, "Well, just at nighttime . . . I don't like to be woken up."

"What?"

"I'd appreciate it if you didn't flush the toilet either."

"So, you want me to sit down on the toilet, pee into the toilet, and then get off it without flushing?"

"Yeah. I don't like the noise of the toilet."

Had that dude been my age, I don't think I would have done it. In most situations, I'd say that's weird. But because he was so old and frail and looked like he was going to die any minute, I decided to respect this dude and his space. But I didn't think it was cool. And the first time I sat down to pee was just weird. Awkward. Uncomfortable.

I'm in a dorm now, where they have stand-up troughs. But with other cellies, it was explained to me, "Look, it sprays everywhere, and I don't want to clean up your urine. You don't want to clean up mine. So for both, sit down and be cleaner." I also learned about squeezing your legs together when you flush. That way, it doesn't make noise. In time, it just became a normal thing—suctioning the sound.

TYRA The first person that I was in a cell with was probably a rat. That was my first cellie. A real rat. I was on the top bunk. He was crawling all over the walls, so it was, it was crazy. Needless to say, I was up all night.

YAHYA The first time I stepped out into the yard, I was in a Level IV prison, New Folsom; 1996. It was incredibly tense, and I had basically been orientated about how yard politics went; that Blacks had a specific area that they hung out in; same for the whites and southern Hispanics. And so you had these designated lines of demarcation where you could walk to an area and just be near the cusp of another individual's area. I remember wondering,

How close can I walk? Where's the danger zone? When will somebody stick me? When would there be a riot? I was still just scared. I still remembered being free and not having these severe restrictions on movement. But even more so, I hadn't realized how much you are watched in Level IV prison yards. Everyone is preoccupied with what the other race is doing or what he's going to do. There was always this sense of scrutiny that I felt at that level.

I was on Level IV for sixteen years, so I saw countless stabbings. Some went on for one or two minutes, which is an awfully long time. I once saw a guy get shot. I still remember his name: Victor Flores. I had just arrived at New Folsom. There was a riot between the South Siders and the Blacks, and Victor got shot in the buttocks, but because he got shot from halfway across the yard, and due to the velocity of a bullet building up when it hit him, it hit a bone and eventually killed him. He was in the process of trying to stab somebody when he was shot by a correctional officer from the tower. I just remember thinking, *These people play for keeps. This is not a game.*

My thinking changed. It became, *Please don't let me get shot while I'm trying to defend myself. I want to make it home to my kid. I want to make it home to my mama. I want to have a life outside.*

TYRA The first time I stepped onto the yard was like a breath of fresh air, because in county we never got to go outside. I mean, there was a lot of people fighting. It was kind of hilarious. I thought these girls was hard! They're not, they wasn't. It was just a whole bunch of hair-pulling and scratching and talking. But just to have real sunlight, to be able to walk around and see people. So I was so grateful to be able to go outside for the first time and see other people.

NIGEL Yahya, I know you're too much of a gentleman . . . but do you remember when you first saw a fee fee?

YAHYA I refuse to incriminate myself. But I did have a cellie, whose name shall go unmentioned, who was the first person to ask me if I had ever seen a fee fee.

"No," I told him.

"So . . . you don't want to make it?" he said.

Out of curiosity, I asked, "What do you do?" He told me that everyone has their own unique way. For him, he grabbed a huge bath towel, some cardboard, rubber gloves, and string. He took the rubber glove, put it in the bath towel, and rolled it up. Wrapped the cardboard around that and tied it with some string so that it wouldn't move. Then he put lotion in [the glove].

"This is how you do it."

"What the hell is this? Is this what you use to have sex with?" I thought it was the craziest thing. "But . . . the hand—it'll work," I said.

"Doesn't work like the fee fee," he said.

I was unconvinced. I never used it. I mean, my thing would be discretion. And that didn't look discreet at all. I couldn't see you land down in a bed with it. It looks like a kaleidoscope! So I'm like, "Dude, this looks so impractical."

RHASHIYD People use different pictures, too. "Asians tonight . . ." That kind of thing. Crazy.

TYRA I made sex toys in jail. I used to work in Dental and we'd use wax to make the moldings for teeth. So, I'd use wax to make moldings of penises. We make it, it gets hard, and it stays like that. And I'd sell strap-ons. Make them for the girls. They went for thirty dollars. We had any color. Well, the colors you want was really pink and white, and you could get like a porcelain one made too. We couldn't make a brown one or a Black one because you'd need some food coloring or markers or something. You don't want markers.

YAHYA Jessie, you're the official guy I come to for all things white in prison. Okay. Why is it that white guys, out of all of the incarcerated people, sexplay each other so much?

In a lot of prisons, you can go to a chow hall and sit where you want. But in most maximum security prisons, the COs arrange it. When you come in, you have to get in a single-file line, and fill the tables as you come. Sometimes you'll have three white guys and one Black guy in a line, so if there's a whole table, they'll be sat together. This happened to me once, and I had the unfortunate experience of sitting with three white guys. I say unfortunate because of the unpleasant conversation I had to hear.

It was a Sunday, and I was really looking forward to a grand-slam breakfast: toast, jelly, sausage, hash browns, fried eggs, milk, juice. Right after I sat down, one of the white guys picked up his sausage and said, "Hey, Brad. This is about the same size as your pecker. Small, isn't it?" And Brad was like, "Yeah, well, why don't you show him how you suck on it when we're in a cell with each other?"

What the fuck is this?! I thought. *Who . . . Who does this? At the break-fast table?* And these guys kept carrying on back and forth like, "Well, why don't you tell them how you let me stick my finger up your ass." I was to-tally repulsed by the conversation. It was just their casual banter; there were no issues whatsoever.

Meanwhile, it just ruined my grand-slam breakfast and made it . . . not so slam.

How can you make sexual banter so easily in a prison? In this male-charged environment?

JESSIE I think it's a lack of better words and communication. Sex play be-comes anything flirtatious that you would say to the cutest, most beautiful girl you ever saw . . . but it's a dude in here and you just exercise all that game you got on him, and you're doing it in front of a group of people to entertain them, to make them laugh like crazy. It's like a male bonding thing. It's just normal, regular, everyday shit.

YAHYA But these aren't the kind of guys that you would think would be having sexual banter with other men. They're like six-five, tattooed with Viking symbols and lightning bolts and all kinds of tough masculine things. So, I'm always surprised when I hear them engaging in sexual banter so freely. I wonder, do you think it has something to do with being in prison?

JESSIE When you take anything and compress it and pound it down into almost nonexistence, it's going to come out in some form. Human beings are sexual. We're supposed to have sex. We're supposed to procreate. There's an appetite and a hunger for sex, *especially* when you're in prison and you're not doing it. That's going to creep out however it can, and whites are especially inclined to talk about it, for whatever reason. It's accepted terminology. If you don't engage with it, you're looked at kind of weird. Like if you don't respond to their sex talk, they're gonna want to fight you—because then you've offended them, you're disrespecting them, you're judging them.

RHASHIYD I've known you for a while, Jessie. There's no shame when you talk about this stuff. It's like candy—that you don't mind sharing it with us.

These topics are taboo in most places, in most situations. But you touch on something with it being a rite of passage. It's interesting . . .

EARLONNE Well, Nyge, we know they could keep going, but I believe we covered the basics of what Chayne's, Tyra's, Rhashiyd's, Yahya's, and Jessie's first prison experiences looked like, smelled like, and, in some situations, felt like.

NIGEL I'm wondering if there's anything they left out?

EARLONNE Oh, definitely. For one thing, none of them really got into the violence that can occur at the drop of a hat.

NIGEL Can you fill in the blanks there?

EARLONNE I remember a situation where we hadn't had yard in a few weeks. The day we were finally going to get it, the officers had to search all of us. So during the group strip search, an officer took a tiny pencil from someone and threw it in the middle of the floor. When he went to pick up the confiscated items, the pencil was gone. He asked where it was and, obviously, no one said shit. The officer then instructed half of the line to go back into the housing unit, and the yard for that half was just canceled. When the other half, who were able to go to the yard, came back, the cell doors opened and a riot ensued because people were so mad that they had been unable to go to the yard.

NIGEL That's all it took? A riot over a pencil?!

EARLONNE Yup. One tiny-ass pencil. I mean, Nyge, people wanted their yard time! People couldn't accept that the person who took the pencil didn't speak up or his race didn't make him throw it back in the middle.

NIGEL That's wild. Or, like Rhashiyd said, it's interesting . . .

EARLONNE Indubitably.

CHAPTER FIVE

OBJECTS

Joseph Krauter served fifteen years in prison. We spoke to him while he was still incarcerated, as well as shortly after his release. Joseph, who is on the autism spectrum, was fixated on a couple of boxes—and the objects within—that were being kept at his mom's house.

His parole restrictions did not allow him to leave the county. We offered to go retrieve the boxes, interview his mom, and be with him when he reopened those boxes from his past.

He had only one request: "Can you bring a heavy hammer with you? Or a five-pound sledgehammer?"

SAN QUENTIN
November 2019

NIGEL Your hair's longer.

JOSEPH Yeah. It's a note of fire. Whenever my hair or my fingernails get long, it triggers an angry reaction within me. I start growling at people and getting very reactionary.

It's part of my autism. Dealing with my hair is a delicate balance. I only have one person that I trust to cut it. I've been with him in other prisons, and we've got it down to a science: short enough that I feel comfortable and not awkward; with the first signs of it becoming snarly, cut it again. It's not about looks. It's about wellness. When I'm snarly, I'm snappy . . . and it can escalate from there. I don't like being hurtful towards people.

NIGEL I've known you for at least a year, maybe a little bit longer, and over that time, I feel like you've become much more friendly. Maybe your guard has come down a bit? Or am I imagining it?

JOSEPH No, that's true. You've moved closer in my circle of awareness—past the defense mechanisms and prompts that are in place to keep me guarded and distant. In my life there are multiple circles of awareness. I'll draw them for you.

FACES

NEAR FRIENDS

Nigel

BeST Friend Mesko IN The WORLD

HOLLY

There's one circle; then, within that circle, there's another circle; and then another within that. It starts to look like a target, with a bull's-eye. Outside of the circle, there's just a big mess, a bunch of squiggly lines all over the place. That represents the world for me: Loud. Jangly. Chaotic. Most of the time, it makes no sense.

The outer circle is called "Faces." Within it are people's faces I recognize. Do I really know that person? No, I do not. Do I care about that person? More than likely not. But I recognize them. Within it might also be a dangerous face; one I know to stay away from. Moving inward to the second circle are near-friends—people closer to me, who are friendly.

You're in the near-friend circle. But there are gaps between the circles, so there's room for movement. I'm constantly assessing and reassessing the world around me. Like a computer that's always calculating. When I assess people, they're moving around my circles of awareness. So, if I hang out with someone for two weeks, he moves closer to my near-friend circle—but if I don't see him for a few months, he moves outwards and becomes a face again.

Everything's in flux. For social interaction, I have an uncontrollable assessment process. When something loses importance or value, it becomes erased. I lose all memory of it.

NIGEL Can you describe your first day in prison?

JOSEPH I was scared, to the point of being numb. But I had coping tools. With autism, there are good tools and bad tools. There's one I learned as a child called the "hallway," and I use it to disassociate from pain and stress.

When I was young, my father used to whip my hands with metal rulers. One day he hit me, and a picture appeared in my head of a car. Behind the car was a hallway. And at the very end of the hallway, there was a metal door; it didn't have a latch, it would just swing and bang against its door-jamb. I [was] in the driver's seat, then got out and walked, but could only walk backwards.

I'd take a step,

a step,

a step.

After enough steps, the sound of the meaty smack of my hands being hit went away. Then the pain went away.

Then the sense of the impact went away.

The hallway is how I've endured the majority of my sensory overload—especially in prison, because I don't like being touched and I don't like weird smells. I'm continuously in the hallway.

It's about twenty-five, maybe thirty feet long, with blank, eggshell-white walls. It smells like fresh rain, and has hanging glass-flower light fixtures and a Mexican-style paved floor. It's quiet except for the tick of a metronome. There are file boxes with random papers in them, and a met-ronome about ten feet away from the back door. The door has a screen-door frame, with sheet metal covering it. There may be a little bit of a breeze pushing the door open and closed, but that's about it.

I can't go *too* far down the hallway. At the very end, past that door, is a field where a tornado is. An F5 tornado that just spins and spins and spins. It's terrifying; it's the finger of God; it's destructive power.

I've had the hallway for so long that it's a part of me; a comforting place. I call it going away inside, and it's where I go to think about or pro-cess something. It makes it easier to endure and survive. Over the years, it's evolved and is not just used to disassociate anymore. Even right now, as I speak to you, I'm in the hallway. To not have access to it would be fairly terrifying. But if I go too far away inside, I just blank out; the lights turn off.

There's always that threat of danger in it. There's a term called "au-tistic catatonia," when autistic people withdraw so far into themselves that they don't come back. I fear going away inside and not being able to get back. I've gone very deep. Sometimes, I've been gone for as long as ten days; then I come back and don't know what happened or where I've gone.

Another tool of my autism is mimicry. I can mimic patterns, sounds, and movement. I've developed masks, building them out of interactions and sounds and movements that I've seen people do. One of the ways I can make eye contact is by putting on a mask. Then I'm able to hide myself. I don't like being noticed. But I have tools that allow me to focus on the ob-ject rather than become distressed, angry, or afraid. When I have to look at somebody in the face, I touch my own face, near my eye, on the cheekbone—right near the orbital socket for my eye. It's a physical prompt.

NIGEL Can you tell me about your other coping tools?

JOSEPH When I first got here, and prison was really hard, I made myself a bunny rabbit out of socks. I was starting to regress to escape the pain and terror, and needed something to comfort me. And so I built a stuffed animal. In my childhood, one of the things that protected me the most was my stuffed Grumpy Bear, the Care Bear. I didn't have the knowledge or means to build a Grumpy Bear. So, I built a bunny rabbit . . . it basically looked like a bloated tube sock. I balled it up in different ways and filled it with other socks so it had lumpy impressions of feet and little impressions of arms and then two socks sticking out the top: the floppy ears. Then I used a permanent marker to create a crudely drawn bunny nose and stuff like that.

NIGEL Would you sleep with it?

JOSEPH I kept it between the wall and my pillow, so it just looked like rumpled-up sheets. I would put it right close to my face and then pass out and go to sleep.

NIGEL Did anyone give you a hard time about it?

JOSEPH Not until there was a search. The cop was like, "What the fuck is this? Are you having sex with this thing?" And I was like, "What are you talking about?" Then he told me, "You can't have this," and he took my bunny and threw it in the trash.

NIGEL What did that do to you, to have him throw it in the trash?

JOSEPH That ignited—I was gonna say "rage," but rage is temporary. I felt fury. It was deep in the roots of my body, it was smoldering, and it just wouldn't let go. I couldn't believe this person felt the need to be so uncaring, so unfair, and so cruel as to throw away something that had no meaning to anyone but me.

NIGEL Did you make a new one?

JOSEPH No. Now I have this cube. It's made out of glued-together chipboard. Early on, I knew that I needed something to fidget with, because prison is so dank, dark, with no fresh air and nothing to distract you. The very first cube I made was out of Scrabble tiles and it worked to distract me. When that one wore out, I made more. Of all my senses, touch is the strongest; the one I use to navigate. When I have the cube, I can spin it, squeeze it between my fingers, roll it in my hands, or just hold on to it.

They help me keep it together. Another symptom of my autism is intrusive imagery. Which means my imagination gets hijacked, blasted with images of brutality and violence. This happens pretty much every waking moment that I'm conscious. It's horrible stuff. I've probably seen ten images since I've been in this room—just random terrible stuff. Like you picking up that pen, stabbing him in the eye, and then breaking the pen off. When you pulled bits of paper out of the spiral of the notebook, I thought about you pulling veins out of an arm. That kind of imagery stays in my head, which then becomes clogged like a toilet, keeping me from sleep. It's one of the reasons I have insomnia. My brain won't turn off. There's a lot of imagery stuck in there, and it becomes more and more horrible. It gets really rough. But it's been that way as long as I can remember.

NIGEL Prison is such a chaotic place; it's so loud. And so physical, right? It's all about reading social cues. Facial expressions, body language, the emotion in the room?

JOSEPH Correct. And that's something I can't do. I mean, I can hear sincerity in your voice. But it's very difficult for me to read people. To do so, I have to access a stockpile of pattern recognition from things I've seen. That comes from anywhere from television to cell fights, to riots, to whatever has been imprinted in my memory to know that this is important. But I still make mistakes.

I get lied to or taken advantage of. But once the realization is made, my brain replays the tapes, as it were. I'll pick out the parts that offer enough pattern recognition to say, *Okay, this person is a liar* or *This person is violent* or *This person is sincere.*

I've figured out these ways to navigate in prison. It hasn't been easy. Every day, the rules change—and I love rules. I love structure. I live it; I breathe it. When the rules change, and there's no reason and no logic, that's physically painful to me. Nothing makes sense. To survive prison, I had to carve out a routine: [I go] from my cell, to the library, to the yard to exercise, and back. Doing the same thing over and over and over again.

I primarily hang out with the gamers. I became a gamer on the streets and continued in prison once I found out it was permissible. But I'm also a storyteller—a creative writer. That's another soothing tool, or a coping tool, that I have.

EARLONNE Just curious, when you get out are there things you're gonna miss about prison?

JOSEPH Yes. For a week or so, I contemplated sabotaging my suitability. I mean, don't get me wrong, I hate prison. I hate that it is jangly and I hate the illogic. But I have lived with it long enough that it has become a routine I endure.

SAN FRANCISCO BAY AREA
June 2020

JOSEPH I still have my cube. I said to myself, *She's gonna want to see this.* It's had the crap beat out of it. It's been painted and sealed. It was one of the only things I brought with me when I left prison. This and three little mini dice that are about a quarter of an inch by a quarter of an inch. I drilled holes through those suckers and made a bracelet so I could wear it out.

When my dearest near friend, Holly—a trans woman in prison— paroled, I went to the hardware store and found a stainless chain and put them on a chain and gave them to her, hoping that they would bring her the same luck they'd brought me.

This soothing tool is about two and a half years old. When I'm touching my cube it activates a sensory thing because I'm hypersensitive; my sense of touch is pretty powerful, and tactile things calm me down. They take away my focus from the world and allow me to think about my present rather than what's going on around me. Like, the woman behind Earlonne— who's probably about thirty feet away—is crunching wrappers and eating a candy bar. The gentleman behind Nigel is making scuffle sounds. The cars, the vans, the lights are all winking. These things only become peripheral because my sense of touch is forcing me to focus on the cube in my hands.

EARLONNE What did you leave behind for others?

JOSEPH Some hair clippers for one of my closest friends (my barber—that one person who could touch me without me freaking out). I also left behind all my Magic: The Gathering decks. I gave my *Jurassic Park* dinosaur deck to Mesro. My artifact deck to my friend Richie. Ninja deck to my buddy Wolf.

My pride and joy, the most feared deck on the yard—Pat Sajak—I gave to Holly. Everybody wanted the Pat Sajak deck. I kept telling them, "You cannot handle it. It would be like giving a baby a shotgun!" I named it Pat Sajak because it has a specific card called the Wheel of Fortune, and that card causes the mechanic to wreck everyone at the table except for the person playing it.

Everybody knew about the powers they were inheriting. They'd been stomped out by them so many times. They knew. I asked Holly to keep hers (just like the Ring of Power from *The Lord of the Rings*) safe, secret, and hidden, in a clear box with the words "Table Killer" stamped on it, which she did. Actually, she put it in a box that says, "Herein Lies the Most Feared Deck on the Yard."

It was emotional to give those to people that I cared about and knew I was going to miss wholeheartedly. And I do miss them. Those people from prison are slowly (or sometimes quickly) becoming strangers. They've moved to my outer circle. Eventually my memory of them will be discarded and erased, like they never existed in my life.

I miss how San Quentin helped shape me to become the person I'm supposed to be. But the rest of it—the sewage and the poison that came with it—I don't miss that at all.

EARLONNE When you went to prison, where did all your stuff go?

JOSEPH I was so completely unprepared, my mom took charge of everything. Everybody else was still in shock. When I was fighting my case, I thought about my stuff, but it was more in a retrospective way. I spent more time thinking, *What happened with my life? What brought me here?*

So, my mom kept the boxes. They're ominously called Christmas boxes, because each one has a giant Christmas emblem on the front. Inside one there's a dagger that I bought from my first job—it had a cool name: "the Sorcerer." There are three Zippo lighters; one is the very first lighter I ever bought, when I was sixteen. It's super faded, and little pieces of it are missing, but it has a picture of a blond bearded wizard with a blue hat with white stars on it. There's another Zippo, a birthday present, that's stainless steel and engraved with the words "Because it's funny." That was one of my catchphrases. Anytime I'd be like, *Why is this happening to me?*, the only answer was often *Because it's funny*. The third lighter is matte black, with three hour-glasses on it. One is silver, one is dirty brass, and the last one is wooden and says "Tabasco."

There are skeleton keys of all different sizes, and a bunch of marbles, including a giant green cat's-eye marble. Couple of stainless-steel ball bearings, and a blue incense burner. The rest of the knickknacks in the boxes are just odds and ends: little toy riverstones, incense burners, pocketknives. I'm most excited about seeing the wizard lighter. It's been fifteen years since I've seen any of those objects. The person who owned those is dead and gone—I mean that person who I was.

NIGEL Who were you then? If we had met you then, who would you have been?

JOSEPH You would've met a kind but very bitter person. I was stoked to the point of . . . obsession. My second year of therapy at San Quentin, I was diagnosed with a hero complex. I would strive to help people, take care of people, "rescue" people all the time, until I'd self-destruct.

My hero complex revolves around self-loathing. When the terrible stuff in my head is directed inwards, I feel worthless, undesirable, unwanted—all the horrible things you can think about yourself. And when my self-image is in the toilet, it triggers my hero complex to rise up and strive to be more than I am; to put the cape on and go do something to get approval from others.

Though that person is no longer here, I still want the stuff in those boxes. They're all beautiful, neat, cool objects. But they're bound up with a lot of angry demons and old memories of striving to be this person; this protector; this good person who failed continuously.

When you offered to go get them I was like, *Yup, it's time.*

EARLONNE Just curious, man: Do you think you're more powerful than all these objects? They don't have any remnants of the person you used to be?

JOSEPH Part of the challenge of healing and moving forward is how I'm gonna feel when I see them. I know I'll remember the good times . . . but definitely the bad times as well. I'll have those attachments. And I know it's not healthy to keep triggers to old memories that could in turn trigger old patterns of behavior.

When my whole reality got shattered about being a hero, it left me with a sense of loss—a void. I drove myself to a disaster; I sacrificed happiness, love, all kinds of stuff. And then to be arrested and have my life destroyed trying to do what I believed was the right thing . . . I mean, my whole world turned inside out.

NIGEL We don't usually ask about crimes, but since you brought it up I'm going to ask.

JOSEPH I was asked by one of my closer friends at the time to help him kill a rapist. And so, long story short, that's what I did. As the hero I wanted to come and . . . save the day. I went to a town I'd never been to before, to help kill a man I'd never met, to save a girl I had never seen. To this day, I still don't know whether or not he was an actual rapist.

I regret it every waking moment of my life.

There were so many different ways that that could have been worked out. Instead, we took the law into our hands and did a revenge killing. I had never been in trouble before that night. The only other thing on my record was a speeding ticket, which I paid for immediately.

I worry that those things in the box are still tied to my desperation, and that all these nasty associations might affect other people. That causes anxiety and strife. You can put belief in anything—you could put faith in a Pop-Tart, and if you have strong enough faith, that can have power over you and other people. Belief is a very powerful thing; I don't take it lightly.

There have been times when I've forgotten my cube and I've panicked, just outright freaked out. I've become agitated and almost like a drug addict, looking for a fix. There are other days I haven't even touched it, but as long as I knew I had it on me, that was all I needed.

NIGEL In the story of your Christmas boxes, what's your role?

JOSEPH Probably the wounded person asking for help, and you guys are the heroes. If *I* were going to get them, I'd be the hero. Since I can't, I'm a secondary character.

Truthfully, I might keep the wizard lighter, because it's the very first thing I bought right before I started becoming a bitter, angry person. And I think some of [the objects are] going to transfer over to Earlonne.

NIGEL For me to deal with for years to come?

EARLONNE Nyge, you're the one who wanted to go get this Pandora's box!

CENTRAL COAST, CALIFORNIA
July 2020

CARMELA My name is Carmela Frank. I am Joseph Krauter's mother.

In my eyes and in my heart, Joseph is still twenty-three, because that's how old he was when he got arrested. Today he's thirty-eight. I brought out Joseph's baby books so you can see some of the pictures and how he grew into such a different person.

When he was an infant, I insisted to the pediatrician that something was wrong. I noticed it immediately. When he was nursing, he started pulling away at four months. He didn't want to hug, and he never wanted anybody to hold him. He would tear up and push them away, from a very young age. In 1982, "autism" meant one was not functional. He was always functional and made normal sounds, so it was dismissed. They thought I was just a crazy, overbearing mother.

It was very stressful, because he *did* want to be loved, but from a distance. I built lots of tents where he could hide out with his objects. Joseph was actually a very happy little boy. He was happy with his solitude and his belongings. But as he got older, he became more and more withdrawn. In elementary school, he was almost as tall as the teacher. He was big, so of course kids picked on him, and that became a problem. With age, I had to just watch him climb into a shell.

He never shared how hard it was for him. He was always trying to take care of someone else, but that's what got him into trouble. The hero complex only got worse in high school. He wanted to become a counselor. He organized a group of people who—in my opinion—were all autistic in one form or another. That was how he survived, by finding a group of friends who were just like him; plus a wonderful high school teacher who got him into the arts. That saved him for four years.

NIGEL That's what he did at San Quentin: he found a group of people who were on the spectrum, and who were very artistic. They created this world for themselves there.

EARLONNE Were objects important to him growing up?

CARMELA Very much so. I had three children—two girls, one boy—and they had to share a bedroom. Joseph was *very* protective of his things; whatever was his, was his. He allowed his younger sister to look at them, but she could *never* play with them. He had a special little mouse with a drawstring that his Grandfather Krauter sent him when he was young. He would pull that around all the time. But when his sisters tried to play with it . . . oh dear, that was a no-no.

He rarely slept as a boy. When we were in bed I'd hear him get up and start playing the piano. Then he would turn on the TV and eat. It was very strange. From about four years old he slept no more than four to five hours a night. He was terrified of sleep. Even when he grew to be six-foot-one and weighed 403 pounds, Joseph was always scared. He never told me of what.

NIGEL You know how he has these soothing tools? A little die that he plays with all the time. Did he have something like that as a kid?

CARMELA Yes. A huge green marble. It was his toy, but also where he found his comfort. And he always had to have keys; lots of keys, lots of chains. That was comforting to him. He's also very interested in hourglasses. I don't know where it came from—he just always had an hourglass. When he got through the minute he would flip it over, again and again.

I never, ever imagined he would end up in prison. Never, ever, ever. Hearing about what happened was a nightmare. I was watching the evening news and I saw my son's picture on TV with his two friends. I just screamed and screamed. I couldn't believe it. I had gone out to dinner that night, and when I came home I had [missed] a collect call from Joseph, which was rare. I thought he must have run out of gas or something and that he would call me back. Then I sat down to watch the news and . . . well, it was horrible; just horrible. He was already in Redding [in the Shasta County jail]. That had been his one and only call. I was beyond devastated. I wanted to see him so badly. I still worry about that collect call; that I didn't get it. It weighs heavy, right here, I carry that burden right here.

To find out about it on the news: *Three Bakersfield men arrested for murder* . . . They claimed it was a gang hit. He wasn't in a gang. None of them were! They were the three nerdiest guys you've ever met!

When he was sentenced to fifteen years to life, I mourned his loss like a death. He was so far away. Then it was so difficult seeing him in prison; it was like a death and then a brief rebirth. We were all scared to death, but he was so scared he became a person that I had not seen in a long time. He was Joseph and he was going to survive this. He didn't want to die in prison. He decided he wasn't going to do any "stupid things," like get involved with gangs. He claimed religion as his gang affiliation. He always brought that up, and I think it saved him. Going to prison pulled him off the streets and gave him a chance to find himself. What a hell of a place to find yourself, I know. But it's also the place that identified him as having Asperger's, which would not have happened out here.

When he was arrested, he had been smoking two packs a day and was four hundred pounds. Heart disease, diabetes, all that runs in our family so . . . do the math. After years of praying and praying and praying for his safety, I've come to realize that prison saved his life. He quit smoking and started losing weight.

But the fact that there's a mother out there without a son will always be my nightmare. I thank God that Joseph was able to survive prison, but, as I keep reminding him, she doesn't have her son. "I have you, but she doesn't have that."

NIGEL Obviously, when Joseph went to prison he left everything behind. How were his possessions gathered?

CARMELA Joseph moved around, so he would bring stuff to store at my house for safekeeping. I collected his things and kept it all: paper notes, notebooks, books, the baby stuff, and his toys and special marbles and things. I put them in boxes, then shoved them in the back of the garage. Having his things around when he went to prison was so hard. It was hard to keep his belongings in the garage because if I ever needed to access that area and saw them, I'd just cry and cry. They smelled like him. He always reminds me of a fresh loaf of bread that had just been baked—like a good nut bread.

But he was gone.

I always kept his baby book out, and that train that was so special to him. It's still in my house. It travels with me. When he was younger, Joseph needed to be able to see it at all times. It became important to me because I knew how much it had meant to him. It was such a part of him. By keeping it near, I kept him close. My husband thinks I'm crazy, but it's a life.

For fifteen years we wouldn't be able to make memories. And the most recent memories I had were not the happiest. I kept all his letters, of course, but as far as childhood items it was just his book and his train. I never had a day when I forgot he was in prison, and I wanted to move ahead from that nightmare period, put it aside, then start rebuilding my life with him a year before he was to be released. I started to feel like I needed to get into those boxes, but I never wanted to. Those were from another life, and not one I wanted to relive.

When he got out of prison, that was just . . . awesome. That's the first time I've ever seen him break down and hug us (our family) with no fear. He held on to us, just hung on for dear life. It was so good to feel that. It was never easy to get close to that boy—emotionally or physically. He never liked to be touched. It was so hard for me, as a mom, not to be able to touch him. Whenever I did, he flinched. He's getting better, though. He'll hug me and we can go to three Mississippis.

Since he's been out, I know he's been trying to bond with people. He's still very selective, but I know he's connected with more people and is more open to conversations about sensitive, personal issues. This is a test that he's going through right now. He was saved, and now he's being tested to stay strong, change his life, and make it a better one. I have to thank the prison system for identifying him and giving him the services that they did. I could tell the way he was changing when we had conversations on the phone. He was very impatient with me at first, and he could only say so much and then he would want to get off the phone. It got better through the years. He's reborn. And I'm just hoping for the best.

EARLONNE In some instances, people need to get away and find themselves. They might find similar people or be able to discover new things and have different conversations. Prison takes you out of certain environments and puts you in one where you're able to create your own place.

CARMELA He made the best of it, but was also able to blossom because of the services. I mean . . . it wasn't all ice cream and cookies, but those services would not have been offered to him otherwise. So, I'm grateful.

EARLONNE The day his parole allows him to walk through that door, what's gonna happen?

CARMELA Well, I owe him fifteen birthday cakes.

EARLONNE We don't want him to be four hundred pounds again . . .

CARMELA No, but I always told him, you just come in and stay here with us. Come visit, have a meal, and stay if you'd like. I want to prepare a meal with him under the same roof and sit in a safe place and talk about whatever he wants. We haven't had a chance to do that. He can sit down, and we can just talk and eat and talk.

NIGEL What's different about these boxes? Why have you kept them separate from other items that seem to be associated with his childhood?

CARMELA Joseph asked me to keep these special Christmas boxes, but told me not to open them, ever. He was *so* insistent that I never touch them; it scared me. It still does.

When he opens them with you . . . I still don't want to know what's in there. I hope he'll look and realize that it was such a difficult time in his life. [Those objects] don't define him anymore.

EARLONNE What do you think he should do with them?

CARMELA I hope he'll get rid of them. If Joseph wanted these boxes just to destroy his past, I'd tell him to go for it. He has that opportunity. He's always worried about other people and how his things will affect them. I say get rid of the crap, then start over. He's got it in his hands. If it's negative, get it out.

EARLONNE Do you have anything of his you think you should get rid of?

CARMELA I think I want to get rid of the prison history; the letters, even. But I'll wait to do that with him. When I got a divorce [from his dad] I had a bonfire—best thing I could have done—it just cleansed me. It was *my* bonfire. *I* made the choice of what to get rid of, and that was great. I made it a ritual for myself. Had a little wine. I believe in putting the past in the past. Keep the good memories, get rid of the crap. Move on.

NIGEL If you had to pack a box of your objects, what are the items that you would want to keep safe for yourself?

CARMELA It's interesting you should ask—I have things that I keep, mainly from family members who have passed. If they had a special item, I put it in my box. I have a special box for my parents and my brothers who have passed. Maybe that's where Joseph got it. He knew I kept my special things in a box and that no one was to touch them. Stuff like my mother's little ivory elephant and my dad's little ceramic dog. It's worthless, but it was his little dog. I look at that little dog and it brings my father back, in a way.

NIGEL So it's all about the power of memory.

CARMELA Memory, memories. That's my box.

NIGEL I have a similar thing: just a box, and if anyone looked at it, it would just be . . .

CARMELA Junk.

NIGEL Yup. But I can't let it go.

CARMELA No, no.

NIGEL E., I'll show it to you someday.

OUTSIDE NIGEL'S STUDIO, SAN FRANCISCO BAY AREA
July 2020

We met Joseph in the studio's big parking lot—a vast open space right near the Bay. We had taken everything out there: the boxes, a bunch of blankets and towels to contain the wreckage, and several large Tupperware containers that Joseph had filled with water from the Bay.

JOSEPH I'm looking at the three Christmas boxes—the storage containers for the last remnants of my old life.

NIGEL How's it feel, seeing them?

JOSEPH As soon as I saw them I was just like, *Oh, my God. It feels like I just came home again* . . . But at the same time I got that salmonella cramp before you crap your guts out. That's what it feels like.

NIGEL Are you ready to open them, or is it going to be too much?

JOSEPH That's what I'm here to do.

EARLONNE You've got another bag; says "Husky" on the side.

JOSEPH Yeah . . . So I have a tool bag that's got a bunch of tools in it. Because I'm going to systematically execute everything in those boxes.

EARLONNE What tools are you going to use?

JOSEPH I've got a crowbar and a sledgehammer.

EARLONNE But you're on parole.

JOSEPH I got permission to have these things.

NIGEL Can we look at what's in there, or do you just want to go right to destroying them?

JOSEPH No, I'll show you. First, this is a list of songs that are integral to the memory of these boxes, you know, like infusing the memories with what's in the Christmas boxes.
    Song One: "Bones and Joints," by Finger Eleven. That song was a sad version of knowing that your life sucked, and you gotta either get back up or lay down and die.
    Two: "The Red," by Chevelle. It's about being overcome with anger and trying to push past it and feeling ostracized and criticized for what you feel and you believe in.

Three: "Vitamin R," also by Chevelle. One of the phrases that stands out for me is "because levitation is possible." Back in the day, when these boxes got filled up, I believed anything was possible, and that any accomplishment could be done by force of will and the power of your soul.

Four: "Name of the Game," by one of my favorite groups, the Crystal Method. It's an industrial rock/techno song; a calling-all-cars type of song. People started to like my philosophy and hang out with me, but I preferred to be by myself. As the stuff in the boxes grew, so did the number of people who wanted to hang out with me.

Five: "Hero" [by Nickelback], from the Spiderman soundtrack. That's when I really started to go for this hero complex, though I didn't get the diagnosis until prison.

Six: "Vindicated," by Dashboard Confessional. It helped me strive forward to be a hero, but also inspired me to lie to myself that I was doing the right thing. It was toxic for me.

The last one is called "Home," by a heavy metal group called Sevendust. That song was hardcore. It's a marching song . . . like to march off to war. That was the final choice for me. When I heard that song I made the wrong choice: dig down, dig in, and go . . . until I died.

EARLONNE So when you're going through these boxes, those are the songs you're hearing? That's the soundtrack in your mind?

JOSEPH Yup. Okay, so now here we have six scented candles. Each of these were made by hand.

EARLONNE By your hands?

JOSEPH No. They were made by hand by the love of my life. Her name was Misty. She was a massage and aromatherapy student. She made these for me; it was very sweet of her at the time.

NIGEL The smell when you open the box is so intense, it's a very sweet, earthy smell. Like aromatherapy. I'm amazed how potent that is. What kind of memories does that smell bring back for you?

JOSEPH The first word that comes to mind is "hate." But underneath that are some good memories.

NIGEL Why hate?

JOSEPH I hate what I became as I collected these things. I hate what I allowed myself to become. I thought I was becoming a hero, but I ended up becoming a monster. The way villains think that they're doing the right thing, and that's how they're able to do terrible things, no matter the cost. All right, here we go.

I'm pulling out three hourglasses. One is sterling silver, one is brass, and this last one is wooden. These are tied intricately to one of the fascinations, obsessions, of my autism. I'm very time-conscientious, I try to be exact. When I found them, they spoke to me, so I collected them.

NIGEL Your mom said when you were little you liked hourglasses, and that you would just watch them.

JOSEPH Yep. Love the hell out of them.

Well, this is interesting. I believe this here is rose quartz. When I first got this, it was clear. There were no cracks in it. Now it's heavily damaged internally; there's a lot of mess inside it. When this was given to me, it was clear and see-through. I put it in my pocket and carried it around for two months. The damage, according to witches' stuff, means this thing is fucked—it's the equivalent of poison.

NIGEL I was going to say it looks like a cancerous lung.

EARLONNE Okay, let's keep going . . .

JOSEPH I found this stone at the Kern River. I think it's lava glass, but the Kern River is nowhere near volcanoes. When I found it, I was like, "Hey, you don't belong here! You're coming with me."

Fuck. Now I'm holding three rings. There should be six. There were six rings total: three for each hand. I'm holding two chains with two skeleton keys per chain. There's one set of rings on one chain and one ring on the other chain. So there were six rings total—three for each hand—and it went thumb, pointer, and ring finger.

EARLONNE What are the keys for?

JOSEPH I've always been fascinated with skeleton keys. Skeleton keys are representations of the soul.

Now, I just pulled out feathers from three birds: an eagle, two hawk feathers, and a peacock.

EARLONNE What else?

JOSEPH So we've got four ball bearings, two cat's-eye half marbles—though there are supposed to be four. This was an incense burner given to me on my twentieth birthday. And this is a cork from a Hennessy bottle . . . which I think I took from a gangster hip-hop club I used to bounce at.

Now we're on to the second—box number two. Going in succession, from largest to smallest.

This box holds all my music and movies, like *Bill and Ted's Excellent Adventure*. Music is integral to my life, and these were CDs that I made. Everybody has a soundtrack to their lives. You know when you hear that one song that just makes your head perk up? That's on your soundtrack.

Let's see. Anybody want a Snoop Dogg CD? And here are some old bills from before I got arrested; there's an income tax form from 2004.

EARLONNE Hey, what's that thing?

JOSEPH That's one of my original gangster fidget tools. Back in the day I used to wear a lot of bracelets, and every once and again I would hold the bead in my hand and turn it and twist it and manipulate it whenever I was stressed or angry or frustrated. Like this . . . Okay, that felt gross. I'm not doing that again.

EARLONNE Seems like just pulling it on irritated you.

JOSEPH Yeah, that triggered some good memories. And by "good," I mean shitty—

EARLONNE Nyge, you okay? You keep coughing.

NIGEL Sorry, yeah, I'm okay.

JOSEPH Nigel is an extremely positive person, and everything I'm pulling out of these boxes is infused with rage, despair, and defiance. Those are extremely negative emotions. So you could say that she's having a visceral reaction to a poisonous clashing of energies.

NIGEL No, I'm okay. Really. I can actually look at these and come up with lovely interpretations of each of these objects . . . but I realize that's not how you look at them.

JOSEPH Nope. But I get it. One of the things about my old life is that I took wonderful things and twisted them out of shape with my misperceptions and beliefs. Okay, our final box is the smallest box. Oh shit, that makes me sad.

NIGEL What does?

JOSEPH The bottles. One of them broke. They're cool, and antique, and had collected river stones in them and pieces of jade and things like that.

EARLONNE Does that one have a letter in it?

JOSEPH It's a message to myself in the future. A crude drawing of myself in the sun with the words "Good Fortune" over it. This is, like, thirty years old. They say that when you burn these types of messages and things, you release whatever's haunting you.

And do you know what I'm holding in my hands now? This is a thirty-year-old Zippo lighter. It is the first object collected that brought me on the journey from then . . .

EARLONNE . . . to now?

JOSEPH It's probably going to be the only thing I'm going to keep.

NIGEL What's on it?

JOSEPH It's a very scuffed-up picture of a wizard in a blue hat with stars and moons on the hat. The wizard has a blond beard. Most of the face is scratched off and missing.

EARLONNE Why would you keep that one?

JOSEPH Because this isn't the Zippo's fault. It was my fault, my decision that led me onto the path that I went down.

NIGEL How does it feel to have gone through it all?

JOSEPH I was expecting to be more afraid, more worried—like when Earlonne joked about whether I should even touch this stuff. Like, what if it goes all *Lord of the Rings* and I try to destroy it and it's like, "No, you cannot destroy me; I am yours." What if I had run off with a backpack full of nonsense and instead of just looking at old ghosts and old bones it turned out they still had power over me? But they don't.

EARLONNE Okay, so you have a crowbar, a sledgehammer, and pliers. Should we step back? Everyone have eye covering? Hey! A piece is rolling away—he's like, "Shit, he ain't got me."

JOSEPH Why are you rooting for this stuff, Earlonne?

EARLONNE Can't you just let some of that shit roll to the Bay, like, "He's gone"?

JOSEPH Like it earned his freedom, as it were? Never.

This is the second ring I ever had. My mom bought this for me when I was young.

NIGEL Does it still have to go?

JOSEPH Yes, remember? We talked about it—beautiful things that were twisted out of their purpose with a little burp of rage and defiance. They all have to go.

My mom liked this one, here. One day on the phone I heard her say, "Oh my God, that's beautiful."

"What is it?" I asked.

"It's a giant marble."

I was like, "No, no, no, put it away." But she didn't. She liked it and kept it by her bedside for like fucking ten years! I know she wanted to keep me close, but she could call me or write a letter instead of holding on to that stuff. Instead of keeping a metaphorical rage grenade beside her. Doesn't matter how beautiful it is.

The glass marble is the focal point. That's where the anger began. That will be the last to go, the big marble: the last piece of a dead man's bones.

After cleansing the objects in saltwater, Joseph arranged them very deliberately on the surrounding rocks, almost like an altar. Out of his tool set, he primarily used the sledgehammer. He was very methodical as he started smashing each one, working to keep the growing pile of varied debris in one place.

Some objects were surprisingly tough to destroy. The dagger and the green marble were probably the most difficult. The dag-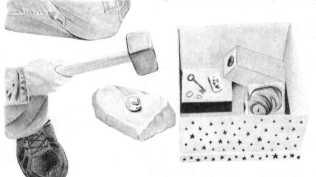ger just would not break. After several tries, it finally broke into pieces and became part of the pile, but it was clearly a real effort for him. He's a pretty big guy and was kneeling on concrete. The whole ceremony took a while, long enough that at one point we went to get a blanket for his knees. The feathers required special effort. After letting them soak in the water, he tore them apart—not too much a hammer can do to a feather—but he still laid them down on the pile and whacked at them until satisfied.

For the candles, he used the crowbar to break them in half and then crumbled them up. He'd pause every once in a while and make vague little mumblings like "You're gonna be gone," "You're out of my life," and "You're done," but it didn't seem performative. It was more like he was talking to himself. This was something he needed to do on his own. He was sweating and breathing heavily. It was clearly a workout for him. It wasn't just the physical labor; it was also the emotional work.

The green marble, or "rage grenade," also didn't want to go. Every time Joseph tried to crush it, it would skitter off. He refused to let anything roll away, least of all that piece. He'd stand up, go get it, bring it back, and get back on his knees. He eventually had to put a towel over it, then just kept smashing until we heard it break.

When he was finally done, it looked like ashes after a fire. The green marble was maybe the only recognizable color, with the odd fleck that popped out; everything else was just black, white, and gray. You couldn't tell what had been the dagger from what had been an hourglass. It looked like what's left after a cremation. Joseph carefully took the blanket and wrapped his rubble into one big bundle. We offered to throw it out, but he didn't want that. He insisted on putting it in his backpack, so he could distribute it into the Pacific Ocean.

NIGEL How's that feel?

JOSEPH Scary. That is real destruction—whatever was inside just disappeared.

But this was the mission, this was the purpose. I don't have to worry about this crap anymore. It had to be done, because every day I mentally look over my shoulder, wondering if I could have made better choices.

NIGEL Could you have?

JOSEPH No—think of it like functioning heroin addicts or functioning alcoholics. *No, I can do this. I can do this. I can do this.*

This is the proof that I'm never going backwards. I can't even look over my shoulder anymore, because there's nothing to look at. This was always a purpose; always a decision that had to be made. This is a goodbye, a farewell, a fuck you.

But now what? Now I'm scared. Once again, I'm stepping one foot forward into an unknown. What's next? What's the purpose now?

NIGEL Is there some strength in what you just did?

JOSEPH If there is, it's a gift from God. The only reason I survived jail and prison is the faith and resolve and the inner strength that He gave me.

NIGEL Well, you survived. I'm sure a lot of people didn't think you were going to survive prison, and maybe you didn't even think you were, and you actually did. You even thrived in some ways.

JOSEPH Yeah. By God's grace and dumb luck.

NIGEL Can you take some responsibility for it?

JOSEPH Probably the dumb-luck part.

NIGEL I see such a difference in you since you've gotten out of prison. It seems like you've already made these huge steps. I got a lot of faith in you.

EARLONNE Indeed. But I'm curious . . . What's that one thing you're holding on to?

INSIDE NIGEL'S STUDIO, SAN FRANCISCO BAY AREA
September 2020

EARLONNE What is all this junk, Nyge? I don't want to call your collection junk, but . . . Nigel, what *is* all this?

NIGEL It's from a project I'm working on about the San Quentin parking lot. Whenever I go to San Quentin I always try to find some kind of object that was left behind in the parking lot. I'm really interested in how inanimate objects are imbued with memory and history, and how through time and disuse they become more interesting than their original intent. Also, knowing that everything here has something to do with prison gives them an extra layer of meaning.

What do you think is my prize possession here?

EARLONNE Out of all of this . . . stuff, on the table? I'd say this right here. This object is for the common criminal—it's how you break into cars and locks. And these right here represent different anatomy sizes of women; those are the bra underwires.

NIGEL We've talked about these a lot, because I find them all the time in the parking lot. I have three, four, five, six, seven . . . I don't know, I must have twenty of them, in all different sizes. The first time I saw one I thought someone was just having crazy sex out there and somehow the underwire came out. After I started finding more and more, I entertained the idea that it was happening for a reason. Then we started asking questions.

EARLONNE And that's your most prized possession?!

NIGEL I mean, those are interesting—but this is the thing I love the most. It's a little spiral-bound notebook about the size of my palm. It's been run over many times and rained on, so now it's just a cluster of paper held together. When I look at it, it seems like a little nest that's holding somebody's information that's obscured—because all the pages are welded together. I imagine it contains a lot of secrets, never to be known.

And then there's this thing . . . It's string that was once on a spool, but now that it's been run over, it looks like intestines.

EARLONNE Why does this stuff pique your curiosity, Nyge?

NIGEL The stories. Trying to figure out the stories behind the objects. They're like beautiful sculptures, little things that somebody held and cared about. They had a purpose and then they got left behind, whether by mistake or just tossed away and forgotten.

This one kind of breaks my heart—it's Superman, from a kids' coloring book. This was just crumpled up in the parking lot.

EARLONNE The kind of thing you give to kids so they have something to do while they're waiting.

NIGEL Then there's this paper bag that says, "Must be consumed within four hours."

EARLONNE Yeah, that's on there so you won't be accumulating state-issued food and so it won't spoil on you. That note covers their asses, because they can say, "See, we told you to consume it within four hours."

NIGEL Okay. So there's one more thing I want to show you.

EARLONNE Shit! Those are the clamps that held my six volumes of trial transcripts together. Those transcripts were from 1995 to . . . I want to say 1997 or 1999. I would go through all four corners of those trying to figure out any angle that would undo some of the wrongs inside those transcripts, until I came to the realization that, man, this is some bullshit. I marked up all of those pages—highlighted, underlined, just trying to figure out different ways to get out of prison. And these little pins you're holding bound those transcripts together.

NIGEL How many hours do you think you spent going through that paperwork?

EARLONNE Shit. Years. I spent years.

NIGEL I can't believe that you shredded them—weren't you worried you might need them?

EARLONNE Hell no! Once they commuted me . . .

NIGEL . . . there was no going back?

EARLONNE That was a wrap. That was over.

NIGEL How does it feel to see these?

EARLONNE I'm like, *This is over. This is done,* you know? Those held oppression together.

NIGEL Yeah, but they're also your history.

EARLONNE Nyge, you keep *a lot* of shit.

NIGEL I know there's that bullshit side, but don't they also represent hope? That in a situation that seems utterly hopeless you went back to that transcript over and over again to find something, because you're that diligent? That says a lot about who you are as a person.

EARLONNE My tenacity?

NIGEL The tenacity of Earlonne. That makes these valuable to me. Can you see that? Or does it bother you that I kept them?

EARLONNE No, no. I can definitely see that, and I appreciate that you care. I definitely appreciate that, Nigel Poor.

NIGEL So, what do *you* have to show me?

EARLONNE Let's go out to the trunk of my car . . . These are two shirts from my past. My father held on to them for twenty-two years. I got them back after he passed. This one was like a Versace knockoff, I think.

NIGEL Oh wow. This is an intense green. It's like fluorescent, but a gorgeous color and one hundred percent silk. It would be beautiful on you.

EARLONNE Back in the day I had a hookup and I used to get all these shirts and suits in bright colors. So, I had to have the shoes.

Over here are my lipstick-red alligator shoes from Italy. Probably got these in 1997. Me and my friends had an R&B and hip-hop club, so I used to dress up a lot. I think I spent about five or six hundred dollars on these shoes. They were probably the loudest shoes I ever had, the rest of them were like black, dark blue, you know. But these were the ones.

NIGEL They'd be like twelve hundred now. They're from a different era. Like you said, red alligator leather, not pointy but pretty tapered in the front. They're slip-ons, but they also have a part over the top of the foot that ties, so there are red laces that have tassels on them with a little gold bead. I'm not going to say they're subtle . . . You would definitely notice somebody wearing these shoes.

EARLONNE Yes. I remember the one comment I got from this older lady, she said, "Brother, I don't see too many men wearing black and red—you make it look good!"

I probably had six or seven different pairs of alligator shoes. I used to love to wear them around my homeboys 'cause you know my background was the Crips, which were blue, and I'm wearing these lipstick-red shoes and no one's gonna say nothing to me about it. So, I had fun with that.

I usually wore a mock-neck sweater with a white suit or an all-red suit. I had all kinds of stuff. I knew I would stand out. When I was running the club, I used to try to dress better than everybody else.

NIGEL How'd you feel when you dressed up in this?

EARLONNE Dapper Dan–ish, you know, you feel suave, you feel . . . great.

When I was in custody, we were going to trial and I said to one of my partners, "Man, I need some clothes for the trial," so they brought me one of my red mock-neck sweaters and my white suit. When I got into the trial, my co-defendant was looking at me like, "Bro. Really, bro?" I'm sitting there all bright red and white and they're picking the jury.

NIGEL And what do you think the jury was thinking?

EARLONNE They probably was like, *These arrogant motherfuckers.*

NIGEL So if those clothes made you feel great, how come you always dress down now?

EARLONNE Well, this is sad, but a lot of that stuff I bought with ill-gotten gains, so I didn't really care about it. You know what I'm saying? Today, I would never buy a five-hundred-dollar pair of shoes.

NIGEL So are you saying those clothes and expensive shoes represent something that you don't care about anymore?

EARLONNE Yeah, this represents easy money, you know? I can never really see myself in these again. But when I go back down to LA, I'm going to take them to this shoe place called Chambers and have them restored. Then I'll put them somewhere on the mantel or a glass case or something.

NIGEL Does that have something to do with you, or with your dad?

EARLONNE More of my dad; my time is gone. When Pops was wearing my clothes and shoes, he was styling. He probably felt like I felt when I had them on—*Nobody fuckin' with me right now.*

NIGEL So if these are *always* in the trunk of your car, seems like you believe in the potency that objects have—and how memory lives through them.

EARLONNE Definitely, definitely. And one day when we go out, the shoes may just have to come out too.

CHAPTER SIX
ALLIANCES

NIGEL The first episode we ever created was aired on June 14, 2017, and was called "Cellies." We were very intentional about our first episodes, knowing they would set the tone for all the stories that followed. We were not going to make the show people might expect to come out of a prison.

EARLONNE We also wanted the subject to be something that everybody could relate to—whether they were in prison or in society.

NIGEL Exactly. People assumed *Ear Hustle* would be about crime, about our unjust penal system, about wrongful convictions, or we would cover salacious stories about the intense violence that happens in prison. We wanted to offer a different narrative. Before anyone had even heard the first episode, there were questions, reactions, and criticisms: How can you do this from within the system? How can you possibly use humor? And why is there a white lady involved?

EARLONNE Yeah, I remember thinking, *Damn, they're basically saying that everyone in prison is Black?*

NIGEL It irked the hell out of me. But it didn't matter. People who weren't involved in making *Ear Hustle* might have been confused about the stories we were going to tell, but we sure weren't—we always knew we wanted to share the everyday stories of life in prison and use them to reveal the connections between those inside and outside. So the first episode had to defy expectations and set that standard.

EARLONNE That's how we came up with "Cellies," because everyone has to figure out how to find companionship and live with others. We all have roommates at some point in our lives. So, we picked a range of folks. We

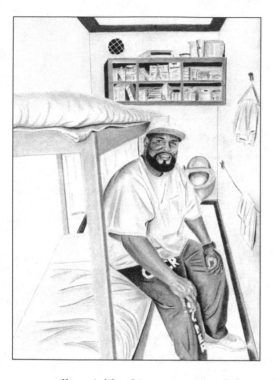

talked to a tough Native American man who had been through the military but was scared for his life due to his cellie's attitude; to two brothers who had nothing but love for each other but did not belong living in a cell together; and to Black, my cellie of three years.

The moral of the story? In prison, it matters who your cellmate is. The cells in San Quentin are five feet by ten feet. If I had my back on one wall, I could touch the other side. Within that space there are two bunks; a toilet and a sink, side by side; and two lockers—one above the top bunk, one in the back of the cell.

I'll put it like this: you can't walk by each other. One person has to sit on his bunk and the other person can walk by. It's like a little public storage locker.

NIGEL And we highlighted our own alliance and rapport. We weren't cellies, obviously, but we were colleagues, and we used humor to show that.

EARLONNE Indeed. Even though you were trying to tell me that finding a cellie was like dating or something . . .

SAN QUENTIN
June 2017

NIGEL You have a new cellie that the prison put in with you, but you're still going to be looking around. Right?

EARLONNE Actually, it's a trip, because the cellie that I have now is temporary. He's about to leave. I don't want a cellie, but I got to go find one, because if I leave it to Custody, they'll just throw anybody in the cell with me, somebody that I'm not compatible with. So, I have to find someone that I'm compatible with. And then, on the other hand, you don't want to tell somebody that you want to move them into the cell, and then you change your mind. You know what I'm saying? Like, you tell a person, "Hey, man, you want to move up?" And then, you'd be like, "Oh, I'm gonna go get this dude over here."

NIGEL It's really like dating.

EARLONNE It's not like dating, Nigel.

NIGEL There are a lot of similarities.

EARLONNE There's . . . I . . . I can't even look at it that way, Nigel.

NIGEL I knew you wouldn't be able to. That's why I hesitated.

EARLONNE No, but it is, it's a relationship. It is a relationship.

NIGEL Yeah, and so that's why the comparison to dating comes up, because there isn't any other time where two adults are expected to live in such close proximity. So, like, tell me what you're doing now. Like, are you looking around at guys? Are you checking people out? I know this all sounds like dating.

EARLONNE Yeah, especially the checking people out.

NIGEL I know! So, what are you doing now when you're walking around the yard?

EARLONNE Well, there's one cat. He's laid-back. He's older than me. Probably like forty-nine. Cool dude. You know, he's out of the way. He's been locked up like twenty years. A person that's been locked up for a long time gets it. You know, it's—it's a professional prisoner.

NIGEL So, what would the conversation be like with this guy?

EARLONNE What do you mean?

NIGEL When you pop the question.

EARLONNE So you're saying, will I court the guy?

NIGEL Yes. How are you going to court this guy? And then, when do you move to asking that really important question, "Will you move in with me?"

EARLONNE I be like, "Look here, man . . ." Put my Barry White voice on.

NIGEL Yeah!

EARLONNE It's like, I'm gonna look at him, get on one knee, and say, "Hey, you wanna move in with me?"

NIGEL Exactly.

EARLONNE Nah. It's more like, "Hey, man. Look here, man. My cellie's fixin to bounce, man. You good where you at . . . or you want to move up?" You know, that's it.

NIGEL The "Cellies" episode had everything we were looking for in a story: varying emotions, surprises, looking at the details of life inside, showing the connection between those inside and out, and revealing the potential of professional relationships between those incarcerated and those who are not.

Companionship is an essential human need. That certainly doesn't change simply because you are in prison. Connections happen for many reasons: friendship, association, and sometimes for protection. It's often assumed that inside prison, race and gang affiliation are the primary alliances that are formed. Sure, that happens, but of course things are always more complicated and surprising than one would assume . . .

NIGEL'S AND EARLONNE'S HOME CLOSET STUDIOS/ SOUTHERN CALIFORNIA (TOMMY)
August 2020

TOMMY I'm white, and I affiliated with the whites in prison. There were only whites in the neighborhood where I grew up in Texas. There was the Black side of town and the white side of town; those lines were drawn deep. But then my family moved to Los Angeles and we ended up in a very Hispanic neighborhood.

It was confusing, because we came with that Southern attitude that we were white, and that [different] races don't live in the same neighborhoods. But I'm kind of a darker-skin white guy, so a lot of people mistook me for Hispanic, which made it easier for me to fit in. White people get abused too when they are a minority in a neighborhood. They get beat up and have to fight a lot. But I used my darker skin to my advantage.

NIGEL When you were growing up, what did you imagine your life was going to be like?

TOMMY I never had a clear direction. No aspirations, no dreams of what I wanted to be. I didn't want to be a cowboy, I didn't want to be a firefighter, none of that stuff. Remember those commercials of the egg frying that ran on Saturday mornings with the cartoons? That said, "This is your brain on drugs"? One of them said something like, "Tim's a junkie. Nobody wants to be a junkie when they grow up." I said, "I want to be a junkie when I grow up." My dad hit the back of my head and told me to shut up, [saying] that I didn't know what I was talking about. Years later, when I was sticking a needle in my arm, getting high in prison, I thought back to that moment, to that memory burned in my mind.

EARLONNE Was it easy to transition from the streets to doing drugs in jail?

TOMMY I was in LA County jail for about a year, and the opportunity to do drugs just wasn't really there. If you're white in that jail, you're a very slim minority. I was a teenager, just trying to survive. I kept my mouth shut, tried to get in the least amount of fights and not get my things taken from me. Drugs were not on my radar.

Once I got to prison and was around older guys—like my cellie, who was doing drugs—I tried heroin for the first time. He was like, "This is how we do it here." That was the first time I stuck a needle in my arm. When I was on the streets, the idea of sticking a needle in myself was disgusting. It wasn't going to happen. When I got to prison, all of a sudden I was in a world I knew nothing about. I had to trust the older guys around me, which is a very psychological game. Gangs and race in prison, that gets very psychological, especially if you're young.

NIGEL Were you easily manipulated when you first got to prison?

TOMMY Oh yeah. Looking back now, I can see that. Back then, I would have said "Hell no," or would tell you that every decision I made was my own. But the truth is, I was heavily influenced and manipulated. By a lot of people.

NIGEL What's a typical way people get manipulated?

TOMMY Let's say you're young, you've been on the yard for a couple of months, and you've seen violence—especially white-on-white violence. You know, prison politics. White guys aren't going to accept someone who's been labeled a sex offender or a snitch. And you're just a young guy trying to stay above ground and be with the cool guys, 'cause that's where it's safe. So, they'll take a kid around the yard and tell him, "You and your cellie take turns cleaning the house every day. Mondays it's your turn; tomorrow it's your cellie's." Then they'll say, "See that guy over there? The cops told us he's a child molester and they gave us paperwork on him. We'll lure him out, and when we do we'll give you a knife and you're going to take care of it." That's how it goes.

NIGEL What role did race play in your life before prison?

TOMMY I'm from a white family, one with traditional Southern values. We didn't live with other races. Moving to California changed everything for my generation in my family; we were like refugees in a whole new world.

When I first moved to LA, some guy drove up in a Cadillac with his wife. They were just an old white couple asking for directions. I was with my brother, who's really pale, and I was thinking about how to direct this guy. He turned to me and asked, "Do you speak English?" I was so mad that he just assumed I was Mexican. I'm white. Everybody else in my family is white. Why couldn't he see that? You know?

It bothered me that I was dark and they were all light-skinned. That was huge to me when I was a kid 'cause I wanted to be like my family. Just wanted to be white. Fitting in was huge. And when I went to prison, I wanted to fit in and show the white guys I was just as white as they were. That influenced a lot of the decisions I made going through the prison system.

EARLONNE Tell us about the first day you went to the yard.

TOMMY The first time I walked out onto that yard, me and my cellie had come from Delano Reception Center [about thirty miles south of Bakersfield]. We were in orientation for days and didn't really come out of our cells. High Desert, the prison we went to next, is like an alien landscape. There's no grass; it's just straight dirt. All concrete, nothing painted. And when the doors to the yard open, it makes this eerie creaking sound. Those buildings are designed to be like cattle shoots, meant to herd you into an execution chamber. All the guards have rifles; it's very in-your-face—like, "We will kill you."

These are the type of guards that would kill you for a fistfight, just shoot you with that Mini-14. My cellie and I were rolling into the yard for the first time and this guard asked me, "Are you white"? I said, "Yeah." He goes, "Oh. We'll see how long you last." He was serious—because whites do not have a long shelf life there. In my first five weeks, five white guys got stabbed on the yard by other whites. They were like, "If you're not one of us, you're not staying."

So, I wanted to be tattooed. In time, I got racist tattoos. I wanted to show everybody on the yard who I was with; that if you got a problem with them, you've got a problem with me. I used it as an excuse to hurt other people.

NIGEL What was the first racist tattoo you got?

TOMMY I got a swastika put on my chest. A huge swastika. I was allowed to get it, because I'd earned it.

EARLONNE You're saying you couldn't just get the tattoo because you liked it? That you had to . . .

TOMMY I'm saying if you had a swastika tattoo, especially on high-level yards, and you hadn't earned it by putting the work in, then chances were you're going to get checked, hard, because it's not acceptable. If a white guy has a swastika at a Level IV prison, he commands tremendous respect. It says, "If you do something to me, I'm willing to do something to you."

A year or two after I got it, I went from a 180 yard to a 270 yard [in a 180 yard, the housing units are sectioned off and there's a guard in the tower with 180 degrees of vision; whereas in a 270 yard, there are no sections and the guard has a U-shaped, 270-degree view]. Some older white guy told me, "You're going to regret having a swastika on you." I was maybe twenty-one and was like, "Fuck you, fuck what you said, you're just a fucking piece of shit who's lost his way." He had tattoos all over him and obviously had been in prison for decades. It didn't matter how I responded, he was like, "Nope, you're gonna regret that." It took a long time, but I did regret it. I mean . . . my wife's Jewish.

I hate to say this, because it makes me sound bad . . . but the level of hate that a white guy has in his heart for other races is not determined by that symbol. Having that symbol on my chest was about status, about having membership in a club, and going through rites of passage. I put in the work to become a member. It's like a gang member having their symbol tattooed on him. You can't just go get a gang tattoo. You gotta put in the work.

NIGEL Who gave it to you?

TOMMY My cellie. Took all night. I asked, "Is it going to hurt?" And fuck, it was painful as hell. I woke up the next day and I looked at my sheet, and it was imprinted on my sheet.

NIGEL In blood?

TOMMY Yup. A reflection of my tattoo, on my white sheet, in blood.

EARLONNE Did you want everybody to see it?

TOMMY Like I said, it was a membership card. I'm here, I'm part of this club, and you're not going to just run me off the yard. (Which is what they were doing when I got to High Desert.)

NIGEL When did you first feel any shame, looking down at your tattoo?

TOMMY San Quentin. It took a long time. I got very into the Norse religion and would point out that it wasn't about race, it was a symbol of our culture. I wrapped myself in that ideology. I'd talk about "Thor's Hammer in Motion." Even wrote a big research paper on it. I distanced myself from who I didn't want to be anymore . . . but I wasn't completely ready to let it go.

I went to the [parole] board, who brought it up and made a big deal out of it. But it really escalated when I got out and was home. If my wife and I were in a public space or on the beach, I couldn't take my shirt off. If I was with her family, I obviously didn't want them to see it, because they are really Jewish. I was still trying to justify it—you know, talking about how it had gotten subverted by the Nazis, insisting that it was other people's issue with the symbol. But it was me, trying to justify it to myself. That's probably the biggest revelation I've made since I've been home.

EARLONNE If it's one hundred degrees and you're at the beach, you still keep your shirt on?

TOMMY I got it lasered off.

NIGEL Is the skin all burnt?

TOMMY It's just blank. You can barely make something out, but it used to be like wings that went across my chest, with a big swastika in the middle.

NIGEL Was it a long process?

TOMMY Yeah. It took about a year.

NIGEL Before you had it removed, did you feel judged?

TOMMY Every time I took my shirt off, I felt judged. So every time I went to a doctor, or got acupuncture or whatever, I had to have this conversation.

EARLONNE In prison, when was the first time you saw something gang-related that made you realize, *This shit is real, this shit ain't no joke?*

TOMMY So, LA County jail is kind of a scary place. I've got a little bit of a chip on my shoulder, but I'm not that much of a fool that I've ever thought I could take on the world.

It's a dorm setting, and very overcrowded. There weren't enough beds, so everyone was given a mat. If you were white, you were not going to get a bunk because Mexicans and Blacks take care of their own. Everyone was looking to see the fish come in, right, see who they know, and look for their homeboys and stuff.

I'd been in there for a little while and had gotten comfortable with some Southsiders from Norwalk. We had a lot of conversations going on, we grew up together and stuff, but there was this one Southsider who was punking everyone for their grapefruit juice; these little cartons. He didn't give a shit, he was just taking people's juice. It caused problems with other races, and they started saying, "Fuck this. We're going to war; we don't care." So there was a lot of tension in the dayroom, and the cops saw something was going on. They pulled us out and made us sit facing a wall in this empty room, like sixty of us guys who were in this dorm. We were all just facing a wall, sitting Indian style while the guards went in and tossed the dorm, looking to see if they could find out what was causing the tension.

About thirty of those guys were Southsiders, sitting there facing the wall. For about two minutes, nobody said a word. Then one of the Southsiders jumped up, so they all had to jump up, and they just beat the crap out of this guy, just beat him to death. A few minutes later, the guards came back and everybody was sitting down again, except this guy was in a puddle of blood. Not one word had been said; it was all done in silence.

NIGEL Like they just all knew that was gonna happen?

TOMMY Yeah. We were all in our boxer shorts. No shoes, no nothing—just boxers. They did what they had to do and just sat back down. They killed that guy for making problems; stealing little cartons of grapefruit juice.

At Level IV prison yards, violence doesn't happen in a moment of chaos. Extreme violence happens in silence. Everything gets quiet and still. It's like the eye of a hurricane.

EARLONNE Do white guys get more favors than Black guys from correctional officers at places like High Desert? Because High Desert is the spot where you have trucks out in the parking lot, probably with Confederate flags and shit.

TOMMY There were definitely officers that were friendly to white guys. Like I said, they give paperwork to white guys on sex offenders or snitches—there's stuff like that.

NIGEL So what was the advantage of being white in prison?

TOMMY I don't see any. You're a minority in there. I think it's like being Black on the streets.

EARLONNE What would you do today if somebody thought you were Mexican?

TOMMY I wouldn't care. But if I went back to prison today, I'd still run with the whites, just knowing everything I know today, whether that's a racist decision or not. I mean, you have to make that decision. It's survival, and there are limited choices.

When I got out of prison three years ago, I got in trouble and was back in the parole office within three weeks. I was raising hell about the program they put me in and they said, "Look, we'll send your fucking ass back to Donovan. If you keep fucking with us, that's what's going to happen." In that moment, I realized I didn't have any social capital. I didn't know how the world worked. I was in another alien environment, like when I was nineteen years old in jail. So I was like, *I better slow my roll, take a look around me, and keep my mouth shut.* I was scared.

But if I went back to prison today, I know I would be okay, 'cause I would pick white again. That's what's familiar to me, and that's how I would survive.

ALAMEDA COUNTY
August 2020

EARLONNE Why did you get your tattoo?

DREW I used to hang out at a tattoo shop, and one day my buddy said, "You want to get this tattoo? I got portraits. Do you want to do one of them?" It was Eazy-E, Snoop Dogg, and Dr. Dre. So I was like, "Sure, I'll do Eazy-E." I'd heard his music, but I wasn't a huge fan. If anything, I was more of a fan of Snoop Dogg and Dr. Dre. I just thought he'd look cool, and it came out nice.

On my second day in prison, one of my neighbors, Deuce, went by. I believe he was from LA; he was the rep of the Blacks. He saw my tattoo and he was like, "Oh shit, you got Eazy-E!" He said it out loud, you know, like he was impressed. That quickly spread around the whole dorm and everybody wanted to come see it. They're like, "White boy got a fricking Eazy-E tattoo! That's bad!" They were really excited. I'm pretty sure it was kind of like, "Okay, this white boy is cool. He's with us, he's not racist, he's got a Black guy tattooed on him." It was like a hall pass.

So it didn't cause any issue with them, if anything they were excited. But it did cause an issue with the whites. A few days later, somebody pulled me aside and told me that there was talk of some of the guys wanting to stab me because of my Eazy tattoo. He told me I couldn't say anything because he could get stabbed just for telling me—because you're not supposed to warn people. So, I'm like, "What the fuck am I supposed to do?" The next morning, somebody pulled me up and said, "Hey, man, we're gonna go down to the table and have a meeting."

At the table are all the main guys, plus the rep and my bunkie. "What's up with the tattoo?" they asked. I told them, "It's just a tattoo. It doesn't mean I'm Black—you all know I'm white!" They asked me what I wanted to do, so I said, "What are the options?"

"You have two options."

I already knew what one of them was. So they told me, "Option two is you cover the tattoo up, and it'll be a dead issue," meaning it won't get brought up again. Basically, they told me to blacken it out. In prison, they don't really have tattoo guns. They have a pen with a staple and then the staple has yarn wrapped around it, so it doesn't go too deep. They burn a candle, collect the soot in a bag, and make ink out of it.

I never wanted a prison tattoo, but that's what I got. When it was getting done, I saw all those Black guys that had given me praise looking like, "Okay, man. We see this." And it's not like I could go explain it. They just had this sad look on their faces like, "We thought we had a cool white." But I didn't really have a choice. I was in prison, I was new, facing another six years, and other whites were already talking about stabbing me on my second day, over this tattoo.

NIGEL Seems to me that you have to be extra careful about who you hang out with inside. Because everything you do with other people reflects on you, right?

DREW Yup. Say you hang out with this guy all the time and he has a hundred-dollar debt and he's PC'd up. [Protective Custody, for people who are inside for sensitive crimes, or have left a gang, or snitched, or maybe were a cop.] The people he owes money to will come to you and be like, "That's your homeboy, so you gotta fix it." It puts you in a situation, worrying about some other guy's debt. And your *family* is going to be paying for that, because they're the ones sending money. So I picked my friends carefully.

AR When I first saw Drew, I was unloading my stuff on my bunk. He looked like a preppy white boy. I looked at him like, *Okay, he's cool.* I can automatically tell the rowdy types from the tweakers—he wasn't one of those. No neck tattoos; he just looked clean, like a college student. *So* clean. He's the only person I know that had a floor mat by his bunk. You gotta wipe your feet before you walk near his bunk. So I was like, *Okay, I'll keep my eye on him and see what's up.*

DREW I remember when AR first came in the building. Anytime someone new comes into your area, you just watch and see what they're about. He had his dreads, and is a big guy, and he was moving onto the top bunk in the back. I was like, *Damn, that's a shitty bunk to move into.* It's right next to the showers. Anybody taking a shower is in your peripheral vision.

NIGEL How did you start to become friends?

AR It started off just like regular casual conversation.

DREW But we really bonded over a television show we both liked to watch.

AR That's right: *Big Brother.*

DREW We were tough into *Big Brother.*

AR We used to bet, like, soups on that show. If your person got sent home, you owed a soup.

DREW I won, betting on that blond girl!

AR Yeah, she was badass.

NIGEL What does "AR" stand for?

AR Always Ready! You can count on me for anything. When I was younger it was for stupid things—making bad decisions—but I always showed up. I never let anybody down.

NIGEL Drew, can you think of a time when that name showed itself to you in your friendship?

DREW If I ever ran out of food, he was always ready to give me a packet of something. Our friendship started building when he moved into the dorm. It was like any relationship started slow, exchanging "What's up," but we were there for each other, and the friendship grew.

NIGEL Were there any challenges to having a white friend in prison?

AR Oh, yeah. We had to be careful. I didn't want to get him in trouble.

NIGEL What do you mean?

DREW Well, the white guys are the ones that have more of an issue with it. Mostly the Blacks would be cool, but we still had to pay attention to the structure. For example, AR cuts hair, and there were so many times in there that I couldn't get a haircut because the white guy who did it didn't even know how to cut his toenails, you know?

AR I know. I'd see you and be like, *I really wish I could cut his hair.* That beard needed help!

DREW And the rules around food, that was a big one.

AR Yeah. My boy Drew is an extravagant cook, man. He makes something out of nothing all the time, right? And he's the one who usually does the cooking, due to the political situation, right?

DREW So, if he gives me a package of food or whatever . . .

AR This is pouch food—mackerel, salmon, whatever. I'd take it over to him still sealed in the pack, because it's okay as long as I give it to the other race sealed. So, it's not tainted. Right?

DREW He couldn't help me. The Blacks can't help you cook it. It just doesn't work that way.

AR We'd talk about how stupid the rules were, but you can't really do much about it. Sometimes we'd get sneaky and be like, "Oh, man, taste my fried chicken." And remember the fried Oreos?

DREW Oh, man. The fried Oreos.

EARLONNE Who made the fried Oreos?

DREW *This* guy! He took pancake batter from the kitchen and rolled the Oreo in the pancake batter and then rolled the Oreo in Frosted Flakes. Frosted Flakes! Then he deep-fried them. Amazing!

AR That's right. But I loved the fact that you would open up with me and share stuff about your family and children. He'd get new pictures and he'd be like, "Man, look at my twins." People in prison don't just share pictures. They keep that stuff to themselves.

DREW When we were in visiting, I got to meet his family, and he met mine. That's a big deal, because in the visiting room you don't want just anybody meeting your family or your kids, because you don't know their full story. There are a lot of creeps in there. But when AR had visits, he'd introduce me and I'd introduce him. It was really cool.

NIGEL How was it when you had to say goodbye to him?

AR That was hard for sure. I was like, "Damn, man."

DREW He had about two years left. So that was hard, you know? But we kept in contact.

AR Yeah, we kicked it all the way up to the end. I got up early that morning to say goodbye.

DREW We had a big hug.

AR Then I watched him walk out the door, and when he left, I cried like a motherfucker.

DREW I was sad too, because I was leaving somebody who I had really connected with.

AR We talked every day, hung out every day; we created a bond. So, when he left, it was hard.

NIGEL And did it take you a while to adjust to him being gone?

AR It sure did; I'd think to myself, *Oh, yeah, I gotta go ask Drew a question.* Like, I'm terrible at math, right? And he's basically a mathematician. But then I'd remember he was gone. After he left I started hitting the workout hard, just trying to take my mind off the actual pain, like the grieving part. I really missed him.

NIGEL Drew, I know you were happy to get out, but was there also some sadness for you?

DREW I had waited for that day for five years and fifteen days. So, getting out felt awesome. I couldn't wait. But, of course, there was also sadness, because I was leaving behind people I care about. I wanted him to know I wouldn't forget him, and that when he got out, I'd be there.

NIGEL Now that you're both out, do you feel like you have a special bond that you don't have with other friends? Because of what you went through together inside?

DREW Oh, yeah.

AR Definitely. It's like we have a secret language; we just understand each other.

DREW He's got my love, like always, for sure. If he ever needed something, I'd be there.

AR Drew is my first authentic white friend, like, definitely. For real. I never had asparagus and I never had a white friend until Drew.

EARLONNE At San Quentin, you aren't allowed to have pets, but some guys get creative, like Rauch.

NIGEL You could always find Rauch in the yard, sitting on the ground without shoes.

EARLONNE When I'd see him, he'd always be sitting cross-legged; drawing something. He'd have extra pencils between his toes—his reds, his blues, his greens—like they were pencil holders.

To me, Rauch looks like the original Jesus Christ. He's got the dreadlocks, he looks like he's from the earth, and, if he could, he'd probably just be wearing a leaf. He's got this thing that he does: he sniffs on his dreadlocks. He said that he likes that they smell like he just came out of the dirt, hanging out with roots and stuff.

NIGEL When he was a teenager he was homeless, and lived in different people's houses in the rafters, secretly, and he felt like a roach. His friends knew that he was there, but their parents wouldn't necessarily know that he was. And that's how he got his name. But he changed the spelling of his name because people thought it was insulting to call him a roach.

SAN QUENTIN
Summer 2017

RAUCH My name is Ronnel Draper, but I go by Rauch. My relationship with people is . . . strained. From early on, they've been a source of pain for me. When I was a child, before I was removed from my mom's custody, she tried to drown me a couple times. One time she stopped and left the bathroom, crying. She was sad at something I did. I wanted to comfort her, but I didn't know how. I don't remember her face, and I haven't seen her since.

I do not call animals pets. I call them critters. They're my friends. I hang out with them. I love animals and can communicate with them better than I can with people. Sometimes I can see or know what an animal is thinking, how it's feeling, when it's depressed or unhappy . . . even when it's on TV.

The first critter I had in prison was a moth. I only had it for a day because my cellie came and killed it when I went to the yard. Since then, I've had tarantulas, a lot of grasshoppers, beetles, snakes, slugs, crickets, gophers, rabbits. I had four swallows, a toad, a praying mantis, twenty-one snails, a frog, a red-breasted finch whose arm broke, pigeons. I had a desert vole that was partially paralyzed. Teddy bear hamster—just really lazy, with an attitude. A centipede who was a bad little monster. Two fish that had babies twice. I had a tarantula who broke out. My cellie just said, "Yo. Spider got out."

I had a frog who was not cool. Everywhere I moved in the cell, it would move to watch me. I'd move over to get out of view; he would come and look at me. He was letting me know, "You know what? You go to sleep, I'm gonna pee on you, dude." I ended up letting it go. Then I had a black widow and I'd feed it insects. I'd be out in the yard being pimped by a spider, and I'd come in with bugs, bees, and crickets. I'd put them in a container and let nature take its course. The bees would fly around in there, but not for long! They'd get caught in the web, and there she'd be, spraying them with the webbing. Then she'd wrap 'em up and eat 'em. Action. Comedy. Theater. It was better than watching TV. You never knew what was gonna happen.

I had four swallows at once and they ended up dying. I lost maybe ten that year. They would always fall down along the building and people would come get me, saying, "Hey. Rauch. Got some more." I'd smuggle them into the building. They looked really strong, but I left and came back and one was down; two was down. I found out that they were dying because they needed to be touched and to feel a connection with some other; with a parent. So when I have to take care of another baby swallow—oh, it will happen again—I'll keep it in my shirt pocket, on my person, so it can hear my heartbeat and my voice and feel connected and nurtured. I take care of animals because they teach me what I can't learn from people: unconditional appreciation and love.

Sometimes COs are cool about it, but I recently lost twenty-one snails. They threw them in the trash. So, it depends on the officer. Some don't mind. Others see it as a health violation. If I'm in a cell and a mouse wanders in and says, you know, "I'm going to hang out here," it's cool. I'd be willing to take care of it, hang out with it, chill with it. I wouldn't chase him out. I'd let 'em stay as long as they wanted and be my friend.

NIGEL We all have that urge to nurture, one way or another, whether it's kids or taking care of pets. We wanted to find out what other guys inside do to nurture.

EARLONNE Except guys aren't going to call it "nurturing." They're gonna say "looking out," or as guys on the yard explain it:

> Sometimes they may need some hygiene or some food and, you know, it feels good to be able to actually help out my peoples.

> There's not really too many things to nurture. When I had more time, I kept lizards. That's how I satisfied the need to take care of some-

thing. I spent hours every day catching flies to feed it. It was like a kind of meditation.

I used to feed the geese, and help them with the babies and stuff. Just check on them and give them advice: where they could teach them to fly; where to hide from people. I enjoyed watching the parents raising children, corny as that is. Getting nurturing vicariously. It felt good to see that, because I've been away from that kind of stuff for so long.

NIGEL E., if you could be an animal, what would you be?

EARLONNE Uh, beluga whale. There's no rhyme or reason for it, but it just sounds cool. Let's ask guys on the yard what type of animals they would be:

I'd be a penguin. Super cute in tuxedos, the coolest animals ever, and they slap-box like crazy.

I would want to be a panther. I like the sleekness of the animal.

Dog, because I know that someone would adopt me.

Galapagos turtle, because they live to be over 150 years old.

Lion, because it's king.

Marmot, because it's misunderstood. Everyone thinks they're weasels, but they're not.

Water buffalo. It's diligent and says very little.

I would be an eagle, because they can fly. So, I'd always be free and always be safe.

Tiger, 'cause they love their independence.

A jellyfish, because it has no natural enemies.

RAUCH If I could be any animal, I would be a wish dragon that would only appear when a kid needed it. Based on my experience with imaginary friends, they're needed. But dragons eat meat, and I couldn't do that. So, I'd have to be a vegetarian dragon; a thin dragon, because I'd spend a lot of time looking for food. That's a ton of carrots, apples, oranges. Lots of vegetables. Unless I was a tiny, baby dragon. Then I'd just need, like, a little slice of cheese.

SAN QUENTIN
Spring 2020

Juan "Carlos" Meza has been incarcerated for almost twenty-five years. He started off in a maximum security Level IV prison. But when he transferred to California State Prison Solano, in Vacaville, a Level III, things started to change for him. For one, he got a prison job.

NIGEL Earlonne, what do you call a correction officer? What do people in prison call COs?

EARLONNE Five-Oh. Hot Water. Slaps. Turnkeys. Rollers. Gilligans, you know, Goop Troop. Cluckheads. The P-I-G: Police-in-Green. Uh, Citizens. I call them officers when I talk to righteous ones. Correction Officer, sir. They call 'em a lot of things, man, but they just police, you know what I mean? They just police.

CARLOS My personal rapport with officers was basically, I didn't talk to them, they didn't talk to me. No trust between me and the officers.

I worked for two officers: Officer Overstreet and Officer Hunter. They were my bosses. I worked as a porter in the block. Every day, I came out and did my job. There was never any argument. Then one day, this officer pulls me into the office. "What's going on? What did I do wrong?" You know, everything goes on in my head. Like, *Am I going to get beat up?* Because you know, all these stories we tell ourselves in prison, like, *It's about to go down.* And I'm scared, sitting there, looking at these two officers, and they took a good second to pause. And then Overstreet goes, "Calm down, nothing going on." I said, "What is going on here?" He's like, "Meza, do you not like working for me?" I said, "What do you mean, do I not like working for you?" He goes, "Well, you don't ever talk with me." I said, "Well, no, I don't talk to cops. I don't trust you. You know, y'all set people up in the past." He looks at me, he goes, "Well, not all officers are like that." And he goes, "Well, just give us a chance. You know?"

NIGEL So Carlos did give him a chance, and after a while, he began to develop a rapport with Officer Overstreet.

CARLOS I know this may sound silly, but if anybody ever seen like *The Simpsons,* where the bully kid's like, "Papa!" When he'd go by for count, me and my cellie would yell, "Papa!" But as much as we joke, he was really like that figure in my life, 'cause he was older than me. He had a bald head and a handlebar mustache and he looked like Yosemite Sam in so many different ways.

I had this paint set, and one time I found this cutout of a Cap'n Crunch hat. So I painted it all blue with a nice gold big *C* on it, right? It was about two feet wide, maybe two and a half wide, this big ole blue hat. I handed him this bag, and he's like, "I don't know what's in there." I said, "Just take it man, take it," and he's like, "What's in the bag?" Eventually I insisted. "Take the bag. It's nothing stupid." So, he takes it and he pulls out this hat and he's looking at it, then looking at me. Finally he goes, "Man, get outta here, fool."

Not that day, but the next day, this officer came out when he was doing count, and he was wearing his Cap'n Crunch hat. Oh man, I fell out laughing. I didn't ask for it, but this officer, he like got me into who I am today. And I think he, he really . . . Well, I don't know what he saw in me. Maybe he saw how I joked with my cellie or how I interacted with other people and he felt like, *Why do you only put that in one place?* But he nurtured and brought out this side of me that I now use everywhere I go. And I really thank him for that, because he got me out of the idea of an "us" versus "them."

NIGEL So this just sounds like normal human interaction, but there's a lot of risk in any kind of friendly relationship between the CO and the guys inside, because even the appearance of overfamiliarity can lead to a problem, both with the administration and with guys on the yard.

CARLOS I used to get really scared, anxious about other incarcerated people seeing us, but then I would say to myself, "I'm not doing anything wrong!" The idea is that if I'm talking to an officer, I must be snitching. Right? That's why I didn't want to talk to them to begin with; because of what people might think. I don't want to get stabbed. I don't want to get beat up. I like my face. I don't want it rearranged.

I ran into problems here and there. There were guys like, "Hey man, you sit in that office too much." I would tell them, "You wanna come sit with me? If you want to be there, you could be there." I have nothing to hide. A lot of good memories. In fact, when I left Solano to go to Soledad, you know, the weirdest thing was he shook my hand and then he pulled me in for a hug. It was a surreal feeling. Like, I never hugged a cop before and it was just a weird thing. He was like, "Man, take care of yourself, and be safe." It was a really profound thing for me right then and there, because growing up the way I did—from house to house, city to city—I never had any real substantial relationship with men like that. He cared, and it was life-changing.

SAN FRANCISCO BAY AREA
Summer 2020

NIGEL I want to ask you about something you told me, maybe in 2015. I've never brought it up, I've just held on to it, kind of pondered it and never asked you to explain. But now I'm gonna. Do you have any idea what I'm talking about?

EARLONNE Not at all. Nyge, we've had fifteen million conversations since then.

NIGEL I know, I know. Okay, remember when we were having a lot of problems inside the Media Lab, and you were always so good at negotiating with people? I asked you why, and you responded that when you were on the outside, your job had been to say who would "get fucked off," and you couldn't make a mistake. Do you remember telling me that?

EARLONNE No, but that wasn't just on the outside. That was also on the inside.

NIGEL I never asked you to explain exactly what that meant.

EARLONNE It means you're in a position of influence. Say there's ten of y'all on the yard, and one is messing up or getting into stuff and word comes to you that this one person is in violation. If evidence is given, and the evidence is valid, you have to make a decision: how you want to get that person removed. Getting them socked out is an easy removal. But you have to think, in trying to get rid of one person, will you end up getting rid of two or three? Your decision has to be based on facts, not someone's emotions. That's what I meant. Sometimes people make decisions based on some reactionary homie shit like, "Man, fuck that fool," you know? That ain't based on anything—just words—and whatever was said might be some bullshit. He might have just not liked the guy. If you decide to remove that person violently, that's going to come back to you, if it was faulty or not based on facts.

NIGEL The way you told me, it sounded ominous. "Fucked off" sounds pretty final.

EARLONNE People might get stabbed, people might get beat down. You influence why and how. As I think the saying goes, the object of war is peace.

NIGEL Do you think that deciding who gets fucked off is a kind of power?

EARLONNE That is an ultimate power; it's influence.

NIGEL How did you get to the point where you held that kind of influence?

EARLONNE Well, it usually goes to older individuals. When I was young and in gangs, I would listen to the older guys. They got the floor, until you started seeing flaws. You'd get to the point where you're like, *I'm cool on that*. I don't want to say you get more followers then, but you get more support if you notice you're being led in the wrong direction and you take a different course.

I've always been the dude laying in the cut. Quietly. Even on the prison yards. Everybody tries to get a name by being the loudest dude on the yard—that was never me. I'd sit back and observe, to better understand the structure.

NIGEL E., you know exactly what I mean—it's what we do! I'm trying to get the story. When did you realize you didn't have to follow; that people would actually follow you and come to you to make really tough decisions?

EARLONNE When I was seventeen, my brother went to jail for kidnap-ransom. He had always looked out for me, so I felt obliged to gather his bail money and lawyer fees. I devised a plan with a couple of homies to kidnap this guy, Mr. Christopher, to finance that for my brother. Even older dudes (they were probably nineteen or twenty) agreed to roll with me. We went and did the same exact thing that my brother had done. Same exact result.

NIGEL Someone ended up going to jail?

EARLONNE We all went to jail. We ran inside this guy's house and tied him up. There was no money, so we took him to a different location and demanded a ransom. It was all about the money. Money is leverage. People in the community follow the money.

NIGEL Is that the skill you brought to gangs?

EARLONNE Yeah, probably money-making. My brother used to be out robbing drug dealers, and sometimes they'd come back with ten, forty, fifty kilos. Piles of this shit. As the little bro, I was in the game. When the homies came through to buy shit, they'd want an ounce; I'd give them two. Make them happy. Easy come, easy go. I was looking out for the homies, and the individuals made money.

NIGEL How much money do you think you made over the course of your time?

EARLONNE That's a good question—we didn't have financial literacy. Every dollar I made, I spent, you know? Just buying shit, changing how I looked. But I couldn't say exactly how much.

NIGEL What'd you do with the money?

EARLONNE Did what kids do: went to the mall and bought some clothes. Got me some cool Nikes.

NIGEL How did it make you feel about money?

EARLONNE It made me feel that money was easy.

NIGEL What drugs did you end up selling?

EARLONNE Mainly cocaine.

NIGEL But you never used it?

EARLONNE Hell nah. I seen what it did. I watched strong people, real strong, smart people, go down. That shit took over. It became people's God, seriously.

NIGEL I mean, you were selling it to people. You didn't feel like you were contributing?

EARLONNE No. I had my rules. I didn't serve pregnant people. I didn't serve none of my friends' parents. They'd say, "I'm gonna go get it from somebody else anyway," and I'd say, "Well, you can just go get it from somebody else, then. 'Cause I'm not doing it."

Sometimes you look back and see what your imprint was on a neighborhood culture. And I was part of the destruction, you know. It wasn't like weed—where people may lose a job if they don't go. Instead, they'd lose a job because they chose to sell everything in their house and steal from work to buy this stuff. I had homegirls who started smoking that shit in junior high, and they never came back. When I got out of prison the first time, I saw people who were still on that shit. When I had left, they had jobs, they had cars, they had lives. When I got out, they had baskets. They were gone, like *gone:* hair gone, teeth gone, everything. They fucked up. And I was like, *Aw, that was due to that shit.*

NIGEL Did that give you any remorse?

EARLONNE You don't think about it like that. You can't think about it like that. You don't think you've harmed people because even with crack cocaine, you know, everybody thinks you sell the shit. You don't. You're not broadcasting it. You just hold the shit; customers come to you.

NIGEL So you were just about the money.

EARLONNE I was just about the money. I wasn't no badass dude. I was just . . . more of a thinker than other people, you know? I wasn't the gang member out to kill you. If I went on a robbery I wasn't taking the dudes that I knew were wild, because I'd learned: there's no pulling some people back. I wasn't one of them badasses.

I probably got into more violence in prison than the streets, because when you're in a gang on the streets you can move. But in prison you're in one spot.

NIGEL What changed about being in a gang in prison?

EARLONNE It was more disciplined. You had to make sure you weren't doing anything faulty. Don't gamble. In prison you just have to be ready for whatever; you have to be ready. My dedication, or what I was willing to do in prison, was more than what I was willing to do in society. In prison you have a whole different mindset. People are coming to get you and you cannot just disappear. On the streets you can bend a corner, you can go where you want, you're not obligated. In prison, it's an obligation. It's real when you get into a situation where it's like, "We're beefing with the Mexicans. Let's go get them."

That changed over time. If I see someone getting stomped out, that's what it is. Especially if it's gang related. If it's race related, that's a little different. Look, I'm in prison. I'm gonna protect myself. I'm not going to start no shit; I'm not going to initiate a situation.

The thing about prison—and this is probably life in general—you can't let shit get to your core. You can't let people get to your core, because once people do, they are actually controlling your emotions. They can get you mad.

When it comes to fighting? Yeah, I have prison fights. Shit happens. But when it comes to the violence . . . I went to the SHU [security housing unit] twice. Got into fights with officers, pushing the line. It was me bringing this shit upon myself. I've stopped responding in those ways. I know how to refrain. As I said, I have to protect myself, but I'm just gonna do me. You have to get out of that lane of pretending to be somebody that you're probably not.

NIGEL Tell me about a decision you had to make in prison about someone getting fucked off, to use your expression.

EARLONNE I was in the highest-security prison, Corcoran, Level IV, and all my homies up there had life without parole. I got ten years, with probably a year and a half left on my sentence. I said, "Let's go stab these Mexicans."

NIGEL Why?

EARLONNE Because people were breaking into the package room and stealing shit. That's like a cardinal sin in prison—stealing shit from other people. Even though packages might be insured, it's still stealing. Your family member took the time to go and buy stuff. It could have been your grandma, or your mama, who might be ninety. People felt disrespected, and that turned into a riot. The Mexicans dealt with their people, but the Blacks didn't discipline any of their people for breaking in, so the Mexicans attacked.

The war began. And it went back and forth for months.

NIGEL All over packages.

EARLONNE Yup, over packages. So, I made a declaration. And once you make that declaration, there ain't no turning back. At all. Like, you should've shut the fuck up.

NIGEL Wait—you're saying you led that?

EARLONNE Exactly. Basically, you call out that you're going to lead that front. Once you put it out there, people aren't gonna be like, "Nah, I'm good." Nope. They are in, and you gotta lead. So, I was pumping everybody: "Let's nip it in the bud. Let's stab the shot caller." There's no bigger statement than stabbing someone. If you get their shot caller, that's the biggest statement you can make. Declaring that this is what we're going to do. We're gonna run up on the guy and end it, because the Mexican shot caller was directing this shit.

We went to the spot on the yard where our knives were buried, but the ground was too hard and we couldn't get them out without being detected. So, we ended up putting water all over the area, trying to soak into the ground. Corcoran is the desert, and our shit was dried.

NIGEL All the knives were buried under the dirt?

EARLONNE Yup. At the time they were buried there had been some moisture, but it had hardened. There we were out in the yard, trying to be discreet, bringing out little jugs of water to dump on the area to loosen the dirt, hoping it would soak in. But when we came out the next day, there was a hole right there.

So either they did a sweep, or somebody gave it up. One way or the other, it was one of the happiest days of my life. Because it saved me from either dying or from possibly killing someone. It didn't take the pressure off—something was still going to happen—but not that day.

NIGEL Do you think somebody who was helping you plan it didn't want to do it either?

EARLONNE I never wanted to speculate, or say somebody dropped a kite on the stash.

NIGEL What ultimately happened to the shot caller?

EARLONNE Well, some other shit happened, and a bunch of guys and I went to the hole for thirty days. By the time we got back on the yard, they had negotiated a peace treaty. The war was over.

NIGEL Okay. So back to my initial question: Why do you have influence?

EARLONNE Maybe because I'm reserved and not out there. People who are bullshit and always doing the talking ain't never going to have that. It's a different caliber of person who decides he or she isn't going to be the loud-mouth. They might be the fighters, but they're not gonna be talking shit all the time. They're going to be the dudes who are at least a little bit smarter than the rest; who can think and make a sound decision.

I told the homies, "I'm done when I get out," and I was serious. I still hung with the hood, hung with the homies, but it wasn't on the same principles or the same philosophies of that gang shit. We had a different relationship. We all grew up together; we still hung. But when I went back to prison, I didn't go with the gang shit.

NIGEL How did that play out?

EARLONNE When I got transferred to Soledad, I ran into some of my homeboys from my old gang, who were perplexed about why I wasn't fucking with them. Usually when someone is new to a prison, they check in with the gang or people that they affiliate with. My old gang wanted to find out why I wasn't associated with the East Coast Crips anymore.

I was thinking all of this through, strolling around the yard, when two reputable cats from the East Coast Crips—LumberJack and Tiny Ice Man—suddenly pushed upon me and asked to talk. LumberJack was an OG and well respected within the neighborhood East Coast Crips. They started asking questions: "Why don't you run with the hood no more? Do you know the homie Too Cool? Tone Capone? The hood is for death doe." I know when I hear cues indicating violence, so I was real with them.

"Look," I said, "when I joined East Coast, I was a kid. I'm a grown-ass man now—it would be stupid for me to continue the same juvenile ideologies. I had to walk away. I didn't get kicked off the hood. I made up my mind." After our conversation, they respected my point of view. And I understood theirs: they wanted to make sure that I wasn't a liability and wasn't straddling the fence, meaning only being a gang member when it's convenient. If I had still been active, I would have investigated myself as well. Most people don't willingly walk away from the protections of a gang.

But I'm not most people.

NIGEL No, my friend. No, you are not.

CHAPTER SEVEN

MEMORY

NIGEL Recollection and reverie, meandering through one's own history and bringing back stories to share with others, is an essential human impulse. It is a way of saying, "I am, I matter, I was here." Of course, *Ear Hustle* tells stories with words; using questions to prompt memories.

To sit across from someone in a studio, being recorded, and engage in the types of conversations we have requires a lot from everyone involved. Time, trust, and patience are prerequisites, as is knowing when to push a bit harder and when to be sensitive about having gone too far. Even when conducted in a crowded room, each interview aims for a kind of intimacy, a personal connection. When it's achieved, it is a gift and a privilege to share.

But words are not the only ways to tell a story. The photographic image is also a generous communicator. During my early years of working at San Quentin, once in a while I was allowed to bring in my camera, usually when we were moving around the prison to record. One day we were in a housing unit, North Block, which is huge: five tiers; all concrete, metal, and wire; and with approximately seven hundred guys living there. There is a bank of pay phones and I took a portrait of Earlonne leaning up against one of them. This was before we really became friends and colleagues. Later, when I was home, I was struck by the image. In the portrait, Earlonne is a solid but relaxed presence, with a sort of golden glow highlighting his frame. There is a curious vulnerability in his expression, one I hadn't noticed in our limited interactions in the Media Lab. Seeing him through this photograph connected me to him in a different way. It was a turning point, because after seeing that vulnerability, we started talking more.

Photographs communicate; they also help trigger and populate our memory. The image encompassed within the frame reveals its own narrative. It can be as complex as any conver   , and—like a story—also carries a point of view, characters, plot, ai   subtext. Part of its power is its capacity to mean something a little different to each person who views it.

Memories are jumbled and chaotic, difficult to assemble in a way that allows access for others. A photograph can both prompt and help anchor recollections, while allowing viewers to drift back into their experience and find the story they want to share.

In 2013, I gained access to a large, unexplored collection of negatives taken at San Quentin State Prison between 1938 and 1980. Most likely taken by correctional officers, the photographs document all facets of life inside the prison. Over several years, I have been archiving the collection and using it to further explore life inside, and the legacy held within the walls of San Quentin. One method of exploration has been showing the images to men inside and asking them to describe what they see.

SAN QUENTIN
September 2018

BONARU The broken glass. So the picture's a bunch of square frames, small frames with glass in the middle of them. There's a hand pointing at a hole in between, where one of the panes of glass has been broken. It's like a rock or something got thrown in the middle of it.

It's strange. I don't know why this photo was taken. Actually, if this is a prison, I do know why it was taken: because people could take a piece of that glass and use it as a weapon. Maybe the picture was taken to identify that this particular glass is broken, so if they find the glass they can identify where it came from.

NIGEL How many weapons could be made out of that broken pane of glass?

BONARU Oh, I'd say about ten, maybe twenty, depending on how small you cut the knives.

NIGEL That's a lot. I mean that window isn't very big; it's maybe five by seven inches.

BONARU You don't need much to make a weapon. People are very creative. This picture kind of makes me think of the glass at Tracy. Tracy's a prison in California, and in our cells at the back there was a window frame, kind of like this, with glass. You could hit the glass with your hand. So if somebody wanted to make a weapon, they could just break the glass, take it out, and make a weapon without the correctional officers knowing. Eventually they'd come to your cell and do a search and find that the glass was broken.

My first time in prison, I went through Tracy. Tracy has a reception center, right, so a lot of people go through there. I was there in the summer and it was very hot. Like over a hundred degrees, easy. It's an old prison and there's no ventilation in those cells. A lot of people break those windows not for weapons, but just to get some air. It's terrible. It's so hot, people just lay on the bunks in their underwear and don't move all day. It's that bad.

NIGEL When you break a window, what changes in the cell?

BONARU You can get some air! I wouldn't say much, but any air in that situation is good. So, I'd hear people yelling across to the other building, "Break another window, brother, break another one, brother." I'd hear that all day long. Anyone who's gone through Tracy knows that term, "Break another window, brother."

Once that window is broken, you try to get as much air as you can, because eventually the COs will come and cover it up.

NIGEL What's the punishment for breaking a window?

BONARU You're definitely going to get a 115. That's a disciplinary write-up that adds time to your sentence—if you do it a lot, you might get sent to the SHU.

NIGEL How many windows did you break?

BONARU Who, me? I didn't break any. It was my first time in prison, so I was scared . . . scared half to death. I mean, I'd rather just sit up there and sweat.

NIGEL Earlonne, were you ever at a prison that was that hot? Where you had to break the windows?

EARLONNE Yes, yes, yes. It was Chino. It's one of those areas of California that's hot as hell. The buildings were built so long ago, there's no air-conditioning or anything like that. We didn't have windows in the cell but there were windows across from the cell like maybe ten, twenty feet away and most of them were broke out. You get a little air, you get some circulation, you know what I'm saying? But it's still hot. It also let in bugs and mosquitoes, and in the winter when it was cold you see the frost coming out of your mouth.

NIGEL Did you ever break any of the windows?

EARLONNE I probably did. I threw apples at the windows.

NIGEL Apples?

EARLONNE You don't have anything hella hard. You got to find something you don't have, but if you throw that apple at the right velocity and trajectory? You could hit it. And that was a hot-ass prison. When I got there I was a kid, just nineteen years old. I was like, *What the hell is this shit*. You know what I'm saying? I didn't know about these warehouse prisons! It was horrible.

You know what else was crazy about Chino, Nyge? When I was there they were filming the movie *American Me,* and they used my unit, which was called Sycamore. We called it "Stickamore" because people got stabbed so much in there. Anyway, when the production company came in they painted the unit to look like it was 1933. I'm serious. The way they painted the walls, they had it all looking like we was doing time back in Prohibition days.

Yeah, their paint scheme looked like the paint had been peeling off the walls for decades, so it was extra drab. Even though you knew you weren't in that time, it made you feel like you were.

NIGEL Were you an extra in the movie?

EARLONNE I wasn't an extra, but they did kick me out my cell and used it. They took like five cells and made them the cells for the movie. They paid us in cigarettes—we each got two packs of cigarettes a day.

NIGEL What'd you do with the cigarettes? You didn't smoke. Did you?

EARLONNE Oh, back then everyone was smoking. We were happy smoking.

NIGEL And what's the craziest weapon you ever saw somebody make? Or at least the craziest weapon you ever saw?

EARLONNE So this one dude named Monster Kody—that was his handle—

we used to get into these conversations. He was a crazy-smart dude who had this way of wiggling out his door late at night. I don't know how he did it—he had a funky mechanism on his door or something—but somehow he could slip out and would come talk to me. He taught me how to make a spear out of newspaper.

NIGEL Come on now . . . How do you do that?!

EARLONNE You just need three things: newspaper, sugar, and water.

NIGEL Okay, you know I need to know how to do this.

EARLONNE Of course! So you mix the sugar and water, lay out your paper, and wet it with your little sugar concoction. Then you start rolling it, almost like you're rolling out bread dough, you know what I mean?

NIGEL Like with a rolling pin?

EARLONNE Exactly. And you keep rolling sheets of paper, wetting it with the sugar water and rolling. Now, it's important you roll at an angle, so one end gets to be a sharp point and the other end gets thicker. Can you picture that?

NIGEL Yup. The sugar makes it hard, right?

EARLONNE That's right. And when you got the right length, you let it dry and harden. Then you just sharpen the point. It's strong enough to puncture skin. I mean you'd probably only get one shot, maybe two. But yeah, I learned how to make that.

GREG So they're deep in a kiss, this man has his hand around her shoulder and around the back of her neck. She's holding his chin. It looks like she's visiting him in prison. In the room there are metal chairs, the walls are cinder block, there's a metal light switch on the wall, and there is what looks

like a window with blinds and a curtain . . . but if you look more closely, there isn't actually a window.

The man is wearing a denim jacket, a thermal shirt, and denim pants. His hair is black. The woman is wearing a blouse with a fur coat. She has on pearl earrings and a watch. In her left hand she is holding a photograph, it appears to be a family photo with an older lady, two younger women, and two younger men, who seem to be couples.

The couple is very classy; the guy right here takes care of himself, and the woman does too. They're so in love and so into the kiss.

NIGEL When do you think the photograph is taken?

GREG You know, I'm young, so I really don't have a good read . . . but I would guess it is the fifties?

NIGEL What makes you think it's the fifties?

GREG Because the woman is dressed like my great-grandma used to dress.

NIGEL The kiss is really potent.

GREG Yeah, they're deep into it.

NIGEL It's clear they don't care that someone's photographing them.

GREG They're so relaxed. They're just feeling it. You know? It reminds me of a picture that I took with the only girl I ever fell in love with. We were young, like sixteen. Her name was Amber and we were just crazy in love. I still have the photograph and everything is exactly the same; just different people, different things, and a different background. My hand was on my knee, her hand was on my chin. My arm was around her. Our eyes were closed. Our mouths were together. And, uh, yeah. I just remember feeling like, *This is just so right.* I felt so relaxed, so in love. I just wanted to be lost in that moment right there forever.

NIGEL What happened to that love?

GREG Well, a few years later I ended up getting in trouble and I went to jail. I ended up catching a ten-year prison sentence. I knew I couldn't hold her down while I was away for ten years, you know? So, I told her, "Just move on."

NIGEL How was that? What was it like to have to tell her that?

GREG It was rough. She had invested all this time in me, and I had made promises to her—and I couldn't fulfill my obligation. I felt ashamed.

I didn't actually reconnect with her, on a prison pay phone, for a full seven years. When you make a call on the prison pay phone you only have fifteen minutes. I remember she sounded exactly the same . . . just a little bit older, a little more mature.

So, I just tripped out seeing this picture right here because, like I said, it's exactly like the only photograph I have of us—it's really shocking how similar it is. Seeing that just brings all this back to me.

When I talked to her, I didn't even know what to say. It was like, "Wow, it's been so long. How are you?" And this and that. She said, "I have two baby girls." I could hear them in the background.

I imagined what it would be like if those were our kids, because we used to talk about what our kids would look like. I wondered what she looked like now. There was so much I wanted to say, that I couldn't possibly say in fifteen minutes. I could hear it in her voice, too. She was lost for words. She wanted to say so much and I wanted to say so much, but we only had fifteen minutes. Then the phone said, "You have sixty seconds left."

NIGEL What were the last words you heard from her before the phone call ended?

GREG The last thing that I heard her say was "Take care and be safe." And then the phone went dead.

In my head, when we were talking, I was sixteen years old and I was everywhere we were back then: hanging out at parks, meeting her friends, camping, renting out hotel rooms behind her mom's back. It really took me to a whole other place. But when the call ended I got up and looked around and the first thing that came to my mind was *Fuck, I'm back in prison again, with a bunch of crazy people around me, yelling and screaming and doing what they do.* I just wanted to go back to my cell and cry.

There's a part of me that wants to know if she still thinks about me the way I think about her—because I still love her.

EARLONNE When I first went to prison, I was young. I had a childhood love, Cynthia. And when I got served so much time, you know, she was still in high school. I was seventeen, so I knew that a ten-year sentence was serious.

When you're in prison, you can't expect other people to be there. You know what I'm saying? And even though I did want her there, and I wanted her to support me or whatever, I knew I had to let her go.

NIGEL What did you tell her?

EARLONNE I told her, "I want you to find somebody that treats you well, and I want you to find somebody that loves you, because I'm not going to be there." It's too much to ask somebody to wait. Ten years is an eternity for a person in high school or college. That's the longest time. But, man, it was hard.

Years later I still thought about my decision. Like, was I on some crazy shit or was I protecting myself from being hurt later? From time to time we kept in contact. I'll never forget, I got a letter from her with some pictures. She told me that she had found a new friend and that he was really nice to her. She said, "You probably don't care anyway, but I just wanted to let you know." And I was like, *Damn.* I really tripped out. It was like, *I can't believe I did that.*

It made me think about my actions and their consequences. You know me. Committing that crime changed the trajectory of my life, especially in the love department. Because even though we were young, I just knew that she was the one to marry, because she was so down to earth. She was the right one.

And my willingness to help my brother, you know, going to commit crime to try to help him get out of his situation . . . I got myself into that. I messed up my life trying to help him. If that hadn't happened, Cynthia and I probably would have been married.

MESRO Centralized in the frame is a blood spatter that something's been dragged through, probably someone's body. There's a bunch of blood and then a crudely drawn chalk outline, with no real definition. It was drawn very poorly: they literally just outlined the body, dragged it out of the way, and then took the picture. It looks like it's on a stone floor, maybe on a tier because I see part of a staircase on the side. There's a couple of people standing around just looking at it.

Whoever's standing there has on shiny black shoes, so that lets me know that they haven't done a lot of moving yet. Meaning, it doesn't look like they've had to kick up any real dust or anything, and cell blocks are not clean. So this was sometime in the morning, probably at chow time, right at breakfast. You cannot maintain shiny shoes all day.

The outline was done with very little care. If it was supposed to be for documentation purposes, they did a real piss job of that. They would have made a better picture by just leaving the body in situ, and then taking the picture. The fact that somebody took the trouble to trace this thing out and then turn around and, add insult to injury, do it kind of terribly . . . it just sticks in my craw.

NIGEL I noticed on one hand they attempted to make fingers, but the other one looks like a mitten.

MESRO Yeah, I guess it was too much of an effort to draw out the fingers of this poor soul who got stabbed in the morning.

NIGEL Can you tell me a story based on this image?

MESRO When I was in reception, I used to hang out with this white guy named Shred. I never knew his real name. He was a 1488, which is a skin-head variant. I'm not really up on gang things or Aryan brotherhood stuff, but he had a lot of Norse tattooed on him—iron crosses and the like.

But Shred was hysterical. He was one of the funniest guys I've ever met. He had jokes all day. And despite what people think about racism and racial politics, we hung out. We always used to meet up with each other, going to and from chow, and we'd always be cracking jokes and talking crazy to people, laughing. He was a really cool guy.

One day we were coming back from dinner, just talking shit about how terrible the food was or something. Then he saw someone and just started screaming, "Eighty-eight!" Then he pulled out a couple of box cut-ters and cut this guy to ribbons, right in front of me, the cops, God, and everybody else.

He's going to work on this guy and the cops are reaching for their canisters and they're blowing their whistles and telling him to get down. He's not listening. He's stabbing and slicing this guy with these box cut-ters. So one of the cops let loose with his Mace canister. And I remember that brief, slow-motion moment of knowing that the spray was going to hit me across the face, 'cause I was standing right next to the guy when he did it.

It was a horrific thing to see someone get sliced up with box cutters. But growing up, I used to do a similar thing with single-edge razor blades that I kept in my mouth. It's something that came from Rikers Island in New York, where you walk around with razors because you don't have to worry about metal detectors and can go and get at somebody the way you need to, then dispose of the evidence quickly.

But in this case, Shred had two real box cutters just in his pockets. And so when he ran up on the guy, he sliced him the hell up. We all had to just sit there while they were trying to secure the scene. I was looking at this guy and his face was turned towards me with his dead eyes, which hadn't been closed yet.

It made me feel a little guilty. I didn't know that this guy was going to get sliced up, and it felt like he was looking at me saying, "Why didn't you stop him from killing me?" But there was nothing I could do; it happened so fast. I still have dreams about that dead gaze.

NIGEL Were you surprised that your friend did that?

MESRO Yeah, I was. Even though we had spent a lot of time together cracking jokes, it wasn't like we had really bonded. We hung out based on humor. I didn't know him all that well; I guess his name, "Shred," should have been a giveaway . . . but I just thought it was a cool name. I didn't realize that he actually shredded other people.

EARLONNE That makes me think of how quickly things can change in prison. You know? Like at a drop of a dime or a flick of a wrist or flip of a light switch, shit can change. That change can be real.

NIGEL What does it do to somebody to have to get used to living like that? That at the drop of a hat, you can go from laughing to a dead person staring at you?

EARLONNE It affects you, of course. It makes you take shit seriously if you want to survive. You learn how to stay out of people's business and how to just get on with your own life.

But in that particular situation, I assume it was white gang stuff, because it didn't escalate from those two people. If it was opposite-race stuff, then others would have been involved. What that story tells me is that the guy that he was stabbing and slicing was another white guy. If it had been a Black guy, even though Mesro was his partner, Mesro would have been somewhat obligated to do something.

Being in a prison environment demands that you stay aware. As this shows, the craziest shit will happen, and happen quick. You might have no clue what's going on or why, but you have to assess the situation immediately. See who's doing what to who, and evaluate your surroundings, within a fragment of a second. You might not know why, but you learn to heed it, 'cause in those situations, there ain't nobody playing.

NIGEL How long does it take after you get out of prison to stop assessing the situation like that all the time?

EARLONNE You never stop; that instinct is in you forever. It becomes ingrained real quick. We can be going somewhere and I'll look at something that might seem normal, and I'll see some shit. You might not even be paying attention to it, but I'm reading it like, *That looks fishy. That don't look right. They're getting ready to rob that place.* I look at body language, I look at movement. Which is a trip, because in a prison like San Quentin, you'll take some college course that you never thought you would take, like psychology. Meanwhile you're learning how to read people's behavior in real time. It might be a conversation you overhear; it might be somebody's mannerism. If you're talking to someone and they get hyper or his lip starts shaking, whatever small detail it is, you learn to pay attention and to understand what's being communicated.

NIGEL Can you ever relax?

EARLONNE I'm always relaxed. I be chill. I be cool. Because even in prison I wasn't the dude who was like, "I'm going to bring it to you." But if there was a situation and somebody asked for it, let's go. It's the same on the streets: I'm not the dude who's just in it for a fight, like "What're you lookin' at?" I'm not a hostile person. Some people are hostile as fuck. I'm like, "Bruh, I've seen it. I know where this goes. I know where this leads to. Why don't we both just leave? Let's just keep moving."

NIGEL Have we ever been in a situation outside that you assessed as dangerous and you didn't tell me?

EARLONNE I'm not sure. I may have seen things you missed but there was no need to even bring it up. You know what I'm saying?

NIGEL Do you think it makes you a better interviewer because you can see these little psychological tics and giveaways?

EARLONNE Interviewing somebody is totally different. But actually, as the interview goes on, I can see in someone's face if they want to tell you something but are holding it back.

NIGEL Recently we were interviewing someone who had just gotten out of San Quentin who had had COVID inside and was pretty sick. You asked such a great question: Had he written his own obituary. How did you know to ask him that?

EARLONNE Well, as we know, Carlos is one of them . . . Renaissance men. He's always doing plays; always wants to have a voice in the discussion. And I just can't see him allowing someone else to tell his story. I cannot see him just laying in that casket while somebody's reading what they think about him. He'd be there thinking, *Oh no, that's all wrong, what did you just say?* But I think everyone should write their own eulogy! You know, write it and update it every year.

   I used to tell people that when I die there's going to be a video of me clowning, 'cause they all thinking they heard the last from me but, nope, they're going to hear and see something new; something to acknowledge things and make them feel better, so they can walk away from the funeral happy and shit. They got that one last shot with you. Brighten up the eulogy and make it creative and fun. I don't want everybody crying. I'm gone. What the fuck y'all crying for over a stiff-ass, cold body down there? I ain't into that shit.

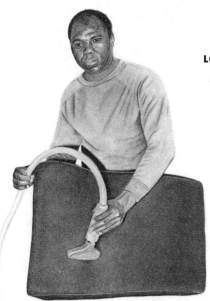

LONDON My name is London Crowdy. At the age of twenty-three I was sentenced to thirteen years and nine months in federal [women's] prison.

NIGEL Can you describe the photograph that you're holding?

LONDON Yes. First off, I see a middle-aged Black man who looks like he's in some type of warehouse, holding what looks to be a steamer or maybe a vacuum cleaner. He's using the device to clean a chair. And it looks like someone has asked him to be in the picture, 'cause he's almost looking at the camera.

NIGEL Anything interesting about his facial expression or his body language?

LONDON His facial expression is what made me choose this picture. His facial expression makes me think . . . well, let me say this: I can identify with it. I've seen this expression before. It's the face of loss of hope. He doesn't look angry, he doesn't look sad, his eyes are empty. He's a man who's just living, just surviving.

NIGEL I've looked at this picture a lot and always tried to figure out what his expression was about. I feel like you're describing somebody who's just resigned to what's happening. What does that picture remind you of?

LONDON It reminds me of when I was in prison. How can I explain this? I don't know . . . I love that word that you used, "resigned." It's like you're just doing your day-to-day routine; just trying to survive. The man in the photograph probably doesn't have the best prison job, but he doesn't have the worst one either. You just perform your duties and try to get by. You're part of the system.

NIGEL What were some of the jobs you had in prison?

LONDON I started off rocky, in the kitchen, but I was only there two weeks 'cause I couldn't handle it, the kitchen was just intense. I started off as a washer, washing dishes four to six hours a day. And I felt cut off. The kitchen is like a prison within a prison, because they lock you inside there. There were no windows, it was dark, and it smelled. But probably the funnest job I ever had was when I worked in recreation. I taught women how to jog . . . You know, recreational stuff.

NIGEL Like a personal trainer?

LONDON Yes, that was my side hustle in prison: personal training. I had gone through a depression right before prison, and went from maybe 125 pounds to almost 200 pounds. I'm height-challenged—five-foot-three—so yeah, I was very round. I was so out of shape I couldn't even run around a corner of the track, let alone run the entire thing.

I started to ask the women who worked out, "How long will it take me to lose thirty pounds?" They'd say, "It depends, but you can lose it in a month if you work hard." They'd have me out there, all two hundred pounds of me, never been athletic, never worked out, and they'd say, "Do a hundred burpees, run the track." I tried . . . and it was awful. They'd come and get me in the morning to work out and all of a sudden I'd have a head-ache or my stomach would hurt. That's when I realized I had to follow my own way. The trick was to fall in love with exercise and fall in love with my body. So I taught myself how to work out, and figured out what worked for my body, and that created a new lifestyle for me.

NIGEL How long did it take to lose the weight?

LONDON About seven months. I was in Alabama at this new federal prison that had a track, and I started running. The prison was in the middle of nowhere, nothing but cotton fields all around. As I was learning to jog, the only way I could keep going was to allow my mind to go places. Before I knew it, I was jogging nine miles a day and I lost seventy-five pounds. So other women were like, "Hey, you know the process . . . can you teach me?" So yeah, that's what I did. I taught group classes and did personal training.

I dealt with a lot of older women and I told them, "Okay, I love to eat right, so my whole thing was if you work out with London, I'm going to figure out what works for you. I'm gonna help you, my goal is to help you fall in love with working out. And I'm gonna help you find ways to eat what you like and is healthy. It's not a diet, it's a lifestyle." That was my approach.

NIGEL How did you get healthy food in prison?

LONDON One of my favorite dishes was also one a lot of the women I worked with loved. We called it sushi, but it's basically just tuna wrapped in a shell you make for it, with brown rice and oatmeal.

NIGEL As you started getting in better shape and helping other women do the same, did that change how you felt about yourself and your place in the world?

LONDON It made me feel good, 'cause when I started working out, I still had a lot of time ahead of me, and I couldn't see past that. For me, it was a great coping skill. Even though I didn't know when I was going to get out, I still felt like I was preparing myself for the next part of my life. I also felt like I was fighting against the system because I was focusing on the future. If I missed a day of working out, I felt guilty because I wasn't investing in my future. That was my whole mental game. And that was the attitude I tried to instill in the women I worked with: Invest in your future, that's what it's all about.

NIGEL If I came to you inside and said I want to work out with you, what would you do?

LONDON I'd talk about the lifestyle change and how we were going to work together in a healthy way. In the morning I worked with my older women, and it was all about keeping them active, walking around the track and teaching them techniques on how to enjoy their workout.

The way I enjoyed it was by visualization. I always told them, "This is what I want you to do: Think about the thing you're excited about, like attending your daughter's wedding. While you're walking, play that through, imagine all the details: What you're going to wear. What's she going to wear? Who will be there? What's the food? Think about the music. And pretty soon you forget about the track, you are just doing it." And that's how you fall in love with it.

NIGEL That's also a way of showing respect to them and helping them see that they should respect themselves and look to the future. It's a way of instilling love.

LONDON What I realized in there was that most of the women just lost hope. They needed to feel like somebody cared. A lot of them didn't know what love was. For some, no one ever told them that they could do anything better than what they were doing. It's a vicious cycle. They had never experienced what it meant to love themselves. They had to see themselves in a new way, and that brings me back to the photograph.

I'm glad we went other places with it. At first all I could see was his facial expression because it was so familiar. In prison everybody is in survival mode and you don't even know it; you're just pushing, day in and day out, you're just existing. That's what I see in his face, he's just there. But talking about that expression took us someplace else.

NIGEL Yeah, just like you did for those women on the track. Instead of an endless track and cotton fields, you helped them get their mind someplace else.

One of the things I love about photographs is, just like you said, you look and see one thing and then you start talking and it leads you into all these other conversations. The photograph is the jumping-off point.

LONDON That's a powerful thing.

NIGEL Earlonne, did you ever use exercise as a way to get your mind in other places?

EARLONNE I use exercise as a way to try to stay in shape and keep the gut down, because it always finds a way to expand. Nothing else expands; just the gut.

NIGEL I always wonder how people can gain weight in prison—there's just not that much food, is there?

EARLONNE It depends on your job. If you work in the kitchen . . . Imagine that, you know what I'm saying? I used to work in the kitchen and I caught myself caking it up, cookie-ing it up. If they come through with the sweets, I'm in.

NIGEL What do other people do inside to occupy themselves or to find value?

EARLONNE Some do drugs, or smoke cigarettes. Others try different types of shit—it all depends on the prison you're in. But sometimes you're in a prison where there's nothing to do but walk the yard.

NIGEL Seems like at San Quentin there's so much to do.

EARLONNE San Quentin's different. It has all kinds of stuff to do. You got classes, various groups, you can work in the hospital, you can be a gardener . . . But there are other prisons where there is just nothing. You walk the yard or you're in your cell.

NIGEL How much of your time in prison did you spend at a place like that?

EARLONNE Most of it. I did twenty-seven years, and I'd say twenty of them were in a prison where I had nothing to do.

NIGEL How did you keep from going crazy?

EARLONNE You just adjust to the circumstances and the situation around you. People look at a person going to the hole [solitary confinement] and being there for two years and are like, "Man, I don't know how you can do that." Or be in there for thirty years! But when it's all you have, then that's what you adjust to.

When I was in the hole, I just looked at it as another part of prison. I just didn't have any privileges. After the first couple of days, you adjust to it. And when you're in a prison with no programs, you adjust to that as well. What else are you gonna do? If there's nothing to do, you just roll with it, you know? It's sad being in those prisons, because there's nothing to do but fight, gamble, smoke, do drugs, drink. It's warehousing.

NIGEL Did spending so much time in prisons like that change you?

EARLONNE When I got to prison I already knew what I would do and what I wouldn't. At the end of the day, you adapt. We're adaptable creatures, even in the most confining spaces.

NORM My name is Norman. I arrived at San Quentin May 1981.

NIGEL How many years ago is that?

NORM I don't know, I guess thirty-eight years ago? Ronald Reagan was president in '81, but Jimmy Carter was president when I was arrested.

NIGEL How many presidents have there been since you've been in prison?

NORM Well, let's see: there was Jimmy Carter, Ronald Reagan, the first Bush, then Bill Clinton (aka Slick Willy), then there was the C student, and then Barack Obama.

NIGEL Six presidents.

NORM I was nineteen when I got here.

NIGEL Can you describe this picture?

NORM It looks like a training photo for people to learn about escapes. It shows the back of a pickup truck and there's a bunch of boxes with cans, like big tomato cans. But inside one of the boxes is an empty space, like it has been cleared out, and there is an inmate sitting in there, well, kind of curled up in there. Looks like he's planning to escape. I've known a few people who escaped from here.

NIGEL Really?

NORM Yes.

NIGEL Can you tell us about it?

NORM There was one dude, named Red. He escaped in a truck just like this one. I think it was '82. Once he got out the gate (inside that truck), he hung out and waited for it to get dark, then he hit the Bay, thinking he could swim away. Well, this is Alaskan Gulf water, this ain't the Caribbean—so pretty quick he started freezing and he had to get out. He got out of the water near the tower that's out back of the prison, and the cop who was on guard was asleep. Red was leaning up against the fence and hypothermia was setting in. He started shaking so badly that he rattled the fence, enough to where it woke the cop up. That's how he got caught.

Yup, there's been a lot of escapes from here, but most people don't get away. A lot of people get beyond the wall, but then they don't get away.

I had a neighbor who was one of the Rub-a-Dub-Dub guys—probably the most famous San Quentin escape period, in the seventies. Yup, that's what it was called. They took a bunch of raincoats and used them to craft a boat; then they made pontoons. They planned for their escape on the day the Marin County Yacht Club was having their regalia.

Somehow, they got outside the wall with their little makeshift boat and started floating away as part of the regalia. They had made a little sail and everything. The boat started to sink as they were going past the guard tower, so they began trying to get to shore real quick, but before they could, one of the cops pulled the window back and said, "Hey, you guys all right?" They yelled back, "Yeah, we're fine!" He goes, "Man, you look like you're sinking. You need any help?"

"No, we're almost to the shore, we got it!" They hit land and just took off. They had a car waiting for them and they jumped in and got away. Well, they all got caught eventually, but yeah, one of them was my cell neighbor and he used to tell me all the time how the gunner had offered them help.

I had another homeboy named Disney, who got into the pipe chases. They run behind all the cells; it's where the plumbing is. There's a walkway and he got to thinking that he could get down in there and go out through a drainage opening. Well, he got in there, so when they did count he was gone. They locked down the institution and started looking for him, but couldn't find him.

He wandered all through there for a few days looking for an exit . . . but the only thing he could find was a twelve-inch pipe drain. Well, that wasn't going to work. He kept looking for a way out and was crawling all around behind the walls. He didn't have any food or water, so eventually he started banging on the pipe chase gate so the cops would find him and he could turn himself in.

NIGEL Did it make you want to try to escape?

NORM No—'cause at that time they had *America's Most Wanted* and it would be worthless for me to be out, because I'd have to cut loose with my family. I'm a family-oriented person.

NIGEL Do you think anyone's ever had a realistic escape plan? Seems like eventually you're always gonna get caught.

NORM Oh yeah. With the surveillance that they have in every major American city, and with *America's Most Wanted* and TV and the Internet and cell phones . . . you're going to get caught.

NIGEL Did you ever make an escape plan?

EARLONNE Yeah, I made a couple of them, Nyge. I thought about it many times, especially when I was in Centinela State Prison. But Centinela is in the middle of a desert, so any plan has to be completely scripted, because if you get out you're in the middle of the desert . . . so how are you going to get away? But I had a few different ways that I was looking at.

NIGEL Can you share?

EARLONNE Inside the prison they had this thing called "hot trash," meaning dangerous stuff that can be used in ways the prison wouldn't want— contraband, like needles. When officers find such materials, they throw it away in a place that's always under lock and key. When bins of hot trash were full, other prisoners would take them outside the walls to be picked up. I used to try to figure out how to get inside one of those bins.

NIGEL But, like you said, it's not just getting outside the prison, it's getting away and staying out.

EARLONNE Yeah. Naturally, a lot of dudes dream about getting out, but to do so, you have people on the outside who are willing to participate and help you break out of prison. So, I've heard plenty of stories about plans, but very, very few people actually escape.

I did meet this OG dude (and it's a trip, because our lives had crossed paths years before, after he had escaped). For the background . . . In 1988, before I went to jail, my brother crashed my BMW. I went to pick him up and we arranged to have this guy come and tow my car to a repair place in our neighborhood. Unbeknownst to me, the guy who drove the tow truck had escaped from prison in 1982.

NIGEL 1988 . . . So you were heading to prison yourself pretty soon.

EARLONNE That's right, and I never saw that car again. Fast-forward to 1999 or 2000, when I was at Centinela State Prison. I met this guy who was from the same neighborhood as I was. We got to talking and he told me about this body shop he had worked at around there. I was like, "The one on so-and-so street?" He said, "Yeah." And I was like, "Damn! I had a little black BMW that got towed there." In the end, it turned out he was the guy who had towed it there.

NIGEL Come on . . . How could he possibly remember that?

EARLONNE He remembered because the car never got picked up! Every day he was at the shop, he would sit in the car and smoke pot because it was so clean and the seats were plush. Meanwhile, I was off in prison. So, of course, that connection bonded us and we used to hang out and talk. Once we got close enough, he told me that he had escaped from California Medical Facility, in Vacaville.

NIGEL How?

EARLONNE Well, remember this is 1982, so a long time ago. Things were real different. Security was different. Protocols were different. Anyway, he had a woman friend who used to visit him, right? Slowly, piece by piece, she was smuggling in clothes for him—women's clothes.

Eventually he got an entire outfit together, including a wig. Then one day, during a visiting session, he went behind a vending machine, put on the clothes and the wig, and even touched himself up with a little makeup. Once he was done, he just walked out like a visitor would. And he managed to stay out for fourteen years!

NIGEL How'd he get caught?

EARLONNE The only reason he got caught was because he worked at Jiffy Lube and was servicing cars for, among others, the FBI. But it wasn't even the FBI that caught him. Guys from the FBI who got their cars done at his shop liked him so much that they recommended him to people who were starting at the academy. One of those academy students recognized him from a wanted poster, because he had committed murder and had escaped from prison in 1982. Fourteen years later, in 1996, he was arrested and sent back.

NIGEL I can't believe that you put that all together; that seems so far-fetched!

EARLONNE Thing is, in some ways, prison is like a small community. When you meet people from your neighborhood, you start chopping it up and are bound to find connections.

NIGEL I don't know much about escaping from prison, but I do know one thing: The best plans are ones you never tell anyone about.

EARLONNE Exactly. You can't tell anybody, because people are so quick to tell your secrets to somebody. That somebody's gonna tell it to somebody else, who will tell it to somebody else. Somewhere down the line will be a person who will turn out to be a snitch.

NIGEL What is your first memory of stepping inside San Quentin in 1977?

JOHN I'm at the end of the world, life as I knew it is over. I'm going to die here.

NIGEL And what was San Quentin like?

JOHN It was very violent, very violent. I mean in one year there would be easy over a hundred guys murdered in this prison.

NIGEL What was a typical day like for you in 1977 here?

JOHN I was locked in a cell with a slab for a bunk. That's about it.

NIGEL Were you in the mainline?

JOHN I was on the row. I was sentenced to death originally. I went back to court in the last part of '81 or beginning of '82 and got a life sentence. I was one of the first twenty-five lifers, and I got sent back here.

NIGEL How many years were you on death row?

JOHN I'm pretty sure about close to five.

NIGEL Now I understand why you say you expected to die here.

JOHN Well, that's how you were treated. I remember having to go to South Block hospital and there's like eight guards that take you down to the elevator. I'd be shackled, with my leg chain, waist chains, and stuff, and I'm going to the hospital, they would yell out "Dead man walking!" And I'd slow-walk down the hall 'cause I could see guys on that upper yard that knew me and they'd slow walk too and try to talk with me at a distance.

NIGEL Who would yell that, "Dead man walking"?

JOHN The officer, whatever one that was ahead, to let other people know that there was a dead man walking, stay out of the way.

NIGEL I didn't know that was real. I thought that was just a movie.

JOHN Oh, that was very real. I still hear it in my head. And that's how you were treated: like you're dead.

NIGEL Who were you, if we met you back then?

JOHN A thug.

NIGEL What does that mean?

JOHN I was violent, I hung out with violent people, and I did violent stuff.

NIGEL Could I have sat down and had a casual conversation with you?

JOHN No, not really. I wouldn't have really cared about talking to anybody.

NIGEL John, how old are you now?

JOHN I'll be sixty-five in a couple of weeks.

NIGEL And out of your sixty-five years, how many years have you spent in prison?

JOHN Forty-two years.

JOHN These are old photographs. I'm looking at a medical staff, probably a doctor. And there's an inmate that's holding a black cat in his jacket and

there's a doctor there with a
stethoscope. It's listening to
the cat's heart, and the cat's
all wide-eyed and everything.
And I'm sure that would have
been in the South Block, in
the first tier, where they had
a medical lab. That's a strong
memory for me right there,
because that's how I used to
hold Bozo. I raised a cat in
West Block.

NIGEL How did you get a cat?

JOHN I worked maintenance, and down there was a pit we were exercising
in during our lunchtime. And one day I kept hearing this screaming, like a
little tiny cat or something. So I got into this hole and I reached in there
and there was a bunch of fur all torn up. And it's this little teeny baby cat
that didn't even have its eyes open. And I stuck him in my pocket and I took
him home. I attached a little barrel to a binky so I could feed it. I cleaned it
up and fed it powdered egg mix. Oh, he was hooked on that. I had to get up
every couple of hours, going, "Dude, what are you screaming for? You're
waking up everybody." And then I would feed him. It just got to be a regular
habit. 'Cause he was my buddy, I had something to go back to my cell for.
He also kept me mellow—that's pretty much why they let me keep him.

NIGEL Yeah, you had something to take care of.

JOHN Oh yeah. I had my little buddy, for eighteen months. And I had a little ID card for him on the wall. One time he scratched a guard who was
wanting to pet him—but they still let me raise him.

NIGEL What was the cat's name again?

JOHN Bozo, because he was always clowning me when I came back to the
cell. He just wanted to play and stuff. I never was a cat person until him.

NIGEL What happened to Bozo?

JOHN A friend of mine in the visiting room had a wife and she was a cat
girl. She wanted a cat and I said, "Well, I got one for you." He was getting
too big for me. I told him, "One of us has to parole and it ain't going to be

me." So I was out, waiting where all you guys come in, and one lieutenant came up on me and he says, "Hey, what are you doing here?" I says, "Well, I need to get my little buddy out," and I pulled Bozo from my jacket. You know, he got scared when he was outside of the cell; little cell soldier. I gave him to the lieutenant and he said, "Yeah, I'll take it, no problem. I'll take it right to her."

NIGEL Didn't you miss him?

JOHN Sure I did, but I had to think of his benefit, not mine, you know. He was a big cat—he'd been wanting to move on. So I was like, "You're grown up; time to go, kid."

NIGEL E., what does that story make you think about?

EARLONNE Nurturing. Looking out.

NIGEL Yeah, wasn't it kind of a surprise that John was such a big gruff guy and was so sweet about a little cat?

EARLONNE Oh yeah. You know, people get attached to things . . . like some people get attached to birds. Some people get attached to spiders and stuff like that. But John found that little cat was able to calm him down, you know, give him something to look forward to. He had his little friend.

NIGEL Did you ever have a critter?

EARLONNE In prison? I never did none of that shit . . . I can't do no lizards, can't do no spiders. Can't do none of that shit. That's, um, too much.

NIGEL Why? Why is it too much?

EARLONNE I mean, what am I going to do with it outside of just looking at it? And you know me, I'd think, *Why am I going to confine this thing?* You know what I'm saying? This thing is free to roam around in his habitat and I'm gonna put it in a box in my cell? Come on; that's pretty bad, a cell in a cell.

But people find all kinds of animals—and not just for pets. I was at one prison with this dude who was Native American and he got this idea that he could, you know, live off the land. So he would try to catch animals to eat. One time he caught this gopher and he boiled it to eat. Got sick as a motherfucker.

Another guy damn near died because he saw a baby rattlesnake on the yard and he thought it was so cute that he picked it up. The snake was like, BAM! He bit him good. And instead of dropping him, this dude changed it to his other hand and BAM! Bit him again. Finally the dude let it go, but then was so sick they had to helicopter him out. And, oh man. There were also the dudes on the yard who used to catch scorpions—if they weren't those black ones.

NIGEL What the hell did they do with them?

EARLONNE Just kept them in boxes. Wait a minute . . . Okay, I did have a pet in prison, way back in youth authority. I had a praying mantis. At that time I was still in a gang, so I had an East Coast praying mantis ('cause that was the name of my gang). The key to praying mantises is figuring out whether they're female—because those ones are the fighters.

NIGEL Did you set up little fights?

EARLONNE Yeah, we used to put them together and they'd go at it. It was some version of entertainment. What can I say? I was young. The crazy thing about them was that even if she was with a male, she would be ready to become a widow. The dude ain't never gonna win because she's gonna beat him up, you know, eat off his head and then have sex with him.

NIGEL I think it's the other way around: she beats him up, has sex with him, then bites his head off . . . Actually, I think she eats the entire body, no?

EARLONNE No, Nyge, biting the head off came first.

NIGEL I could fact-check that, my friend . . . but why don't we just live with the mystery on this one.

CHAPTER EIGHT

FAMILY

EARLONNE A couple years back, me and Nyge took a road trip to LA to meet Karen McDaniel. She had a whole lot to say about what it's like for the women who are—what we call in prison—"ride-or-die chicks." Women who stand by their men and basically do the time with them, no matter what they do or where they are.

NIGEL *Chicks?* Are there "ride-or-die dudes"?

EARLONNE Nyge, that's a completely different story. Anyhow, Karen met and fell in love with John, who was serving a thirty-five–year sentence.

NIGEL At the time, she was a professor. She was no stranger to complex human interactions, as her area of expertise was early childhood development, with a focus on traumatic experience.

EARLONNE She was smart, capable, and a real problem-solver.

NIGEL She was also in love, but about to find out what it meant to make a long-term commitment to an incarcerated man.

EARLONNE You want to tell them why we drove all the way to LA to get her story?

NIGEL We often talk about how important it is for guys inside to know people are thinking about them. But there's part of that equation that we never really covered, and it bothered me.

EARLONNE The perspective of women?

NIGEL Though we don't get too much hate mail, I did get an email from a woman who was upset with us . . . or with me. She wanted to know why our prison stories were so exclusively male.

EARLONNE She just wants to be heard. I appreciate her perspective.

NIGEL I ultimately had a good email correspondence with her, and told her we wanted to do a story about women's experiences. After some back-and-forth, she agreed to talk with us. But . . . our editor felt we should include her husband in the story. In my heart I didn't want to ask her for that, but I did. Guess what happened?

EARLONNE She was opposed.

NIGEL So for this chapter we did what I said we were going to do: get the female perspective from both sides on this topic—no dudes, no male voice.

SOUTHERN CALIFORNIA
December 2016

NIGEL Do you recognize these?

KAREN Oh my God. Of course. Those are underwires to a bra. They're considered weapons inside an institution. Women are told we can't have those in our bras when visiting our loved ones inside. I had researched everything, so I knew what I couldn't wear, for example.

I'm shocked that you found them in the parking lot. Do you know what can happen to women if they're caught taking those out? A woman who takes those out of her bra and discards those can be arrested. She can lose her visits with her loved one for a *minimum* of one year. That's like leaving contraband on prison grounds. We're threatened . . . Well, we learn quickly that that is not okay. Usually we have to go and change our clothes in a trailer or our cars.

The first time you visit prison, wearing a fancy Victoria's Secret bra, and you get told to go take the wire out, your whole wardrobe becomes a prison wardrobe. Suddenly every purchase that you make for yourself and your children becomes defined by *Can this get in the prison?* If it can't, should you really buy it? If your kids need sweaters and warm clothes, they need sweaters and warm clothes . . . that can also get in the prison. If you're buying a bra, it has to be a bra . . . that can get in the prison. Everything changes.

Women regularly drive ten, fifteen hours to see their loved ones. Their kids could have been crying the whole way. They could've spent God knows how much money to get there. After all that, we're told, "You can't see your loved one unless you can clear the metal detector." There's not usually a Walmart around the corner, and you can't go in without a bra.

I've heard many women, especially elderly women, say, "I'll just take my bra off." They respond, "Oh, no, you can't do that." Then they demand to see the straps of the bra again. I consider it sexual assault: I've been asked so many times to lift up my shirt and shake out my bra, then to take my hand and run my fingers around my belt. I've literally been asked if I'm wearing panties. A male officer has asked if my eight-year-old daughter had panties on. In front of all these people. What rulebook is that in? If a guard is physically touching my body, that's molestation. You're violating me.

NIGEL They don't try to make sure there's a woman who can do those kinds of searches?

KAREN That's what protocol *should* be. If there's reasonable cause to search a woman, a female officer is supposed to take her into a private area to do it. Instead, women are consistently violated by male officers, publicly. It's not reasonable—they do it to everyone, in front of children, even. It's never private.

EARLONNE Do you mind us asking how you and your guy met?

KAREN Letters. His family members were illiterate. I would read his letters to his family members, and then transcribe what his family members wanted to say back. This was all through my professional life and the work I was doing at the time.

I remember being shocked. I was so white and so naive. Just clueless about mass criminalization and what was going on around me. I learned that this man had been convicted to a thirty-five-year sentence as a nineteen-year-old, for robbing a McDonald's. No one was physically injured—his stupid ass walked into McDonald's at eight-thirty on a Saturday morning and said, "Give me all the money."

For that, he got thirty-five years in prison. I couldn't wrap my brain around it! I could see so clearly that he was a highly intelligent, deeply insightful man. Over time, we literally fell in love through those letters.

When I started loving someone in prison, I didn't understand what that would mean. My mom was fourteen years old when she had me, in 1968. She had a seventh-grade education. I worked really, really hard for many years to get to where I was—eventually a master's degree and a job as a professor. So, the first time I ever walked into a prison and was treated that way by officers, I looked at them like, "Are you kidding me? You went to the academy for sixteen fucking weeks! Who the fuck are you? I didn't commit a crime. Let's get that straight!"

But that's exactly how women like us are treated: not only like we committed a crime, but like we committed a crime *against* that officer . . . and his family! Many officers seem to take it personally that we're there to see someone who we love very much.

On my first visit, I was scared to death. I had researched everything, so I knew that I couldn't wear an underwire bra, for example. The prison's in Calipatria, which is in the middle of nowhere, just north of the Mexican border west of Arizona. When I first started going, there was no visiting system in place—so you had to line up your car the night before.

So, I drove to Calipatria and pulled up at the prison, looking for this car line—but didn't see any cars. I pulled onto the prison grounds, just looking for the line. It was ten o'clock at night and I was driving around the parking lot of the prison. Suddenly I got lit up by probably five different CDCR [California Department of Corrections and Rehabilitation] vehicles that swarmed my car and pulled me out to ask me what I was doing. "I'm going to visit tomorrow, so I was just looking for the car line," I said.

"It's back on the road. You are on prison grounds."

They put me back in my car and followed me out. That's when I saw the opposite direction from where I had come. Car after car after car, all lined up in a row in the middle of the desert. It was about 108 degrees out there. I drove to the end of the row, shocked both by the length and the orderliness.

Clearly, the people in those cars knew what was going on. I didn't. But I took my place, and waited. Just spent the night in that car, waiting. Visiting time only lasted for six hours. So to get the proper amount of time with your loved one, you wanted to get in as early as possible, because it took hours to even get processed into the prison. If you weren't there first, you might not get through until as late as twelve, and visits ended at two.

When it came time for the gates to open, everybody was ready. I'd brushed my teeth and used the outhouse they provide, out in the dirt and dust of the desert. Of course, we didn't have kids at that point, when I first started going. But I saw other women with children, making sure they'd all brushed their teeth and looked their best . . . I found the whole scene outrageous.

After a night of sleeping in your car, in over one-hundred-degree weather, it's *real* hard to look fresh in the morning. That first time, my plan was to go in looking completely fly. Unfortunately, that didn't work out. I didn't understand what was going to happen when I got processed. I had no idea (despite how much I had read about the rules) of the extent of what I could or couldn't wear. I didn't expect to be marginalized and degraded. It's already such an intense experience, and I wasn't ready to take it. Eventually, they broke me. But that took a while.

Calipatria had one motel: the Calipatria Inn. Women would bunk, say, six to a room. But you still had to have your car in line. After I became a regular, we developed a system.

By that time, I had moved out there, to Calipatria. So, on Friday nights I would get the car there early. As soon as my kids went to school, I'd drive there, leave my car, and have a friend from town pick me up and take me back to my apartment. The next morning, when all the other women arrived from LA and all over Southern California, they'd come to my place in a van, get me, and we'd go to my car, which would have been there overnight. We'd hop out and everybody would load into my car.

There were always the types of girls who would arrive at 6:30 a.m., directly from LA, and cut the line. If any of them pulled directly to the front, we'd end up fighting. They had no respect! If we were all in my car and saw someone cut, we'd pick who's gonna confront them. It usually ended up being me. So I'd bang on some woman's window and ask, "How are you gonna cut the line? You can't. My man's gonna talk to your man . . ."

EARLONNE When that happens, dudes will say something to each other; maybe in the visiting room, but more likely on the yard. "Look, man, we have this issue—we need to work this out."

NIGEL So there's a sense of cooperation between inside and outside to figure it out. But wasn't it scary to go up to someone's car and be like, "Get the fuck in line"?

KAREN It was very scary, especially for me. But I learned that I had to hold my own. In those conditions, you get gangster *real* quick. People absolutely respected it. They learned. Most would be like, "Really? Oh, okay, we won't cut the line." Or at least they'd be damn sure not to cut in front of *me*.

People otherwise never bothered us in line, though we would have been easy pickings for strangers. Church folks might come and offer a little Dixie cup with lemonade. Local businesses in any little prison town thrive off of the prisons. Everyone either works there or knows someone who works there or is there to visit. That's a captive audience. A typical visiting weekend for a family—let's say a woman traveling with two children— would cost about five hundred dollars, just to sit there. You buy food to feed your man and food for the kids. Plenty of times, when money was low, I wouldn't eat. Other times, I'd have to tell the kids, "We can only have water and chips at this visit." They'd know ahead of time. You do what you gotta do.

On my first day, I tried to wear my dream outfit. Which included cleavage. A hell of a lot of cleavage. I don't know how, but I got in. By the time I reached the yard, however, a female officer pulled me aside and told me, "Oh no, we're not doing this. Those are going back in your shirt, or you're leaving."

I was also wearing some cute capri pants. And high heels, of course, because those are just required. You've got to have high heels. Your man deserves to see you in those. Open-toed, and your toes need to be bangin'. We're really conscious about what we're wearing for the men and how we look. Legs are shaved; hair and makeup did; jewelry; everything. You used to be able to wear as much jewelry as you wanted. Now, many institutions limit it to one ring, one bracelet, and no facial piercings. Visitors get stopped for the facial piercings a lot.

Anyway, I looked totally hot on that first visit. I'd heard women say, "I'll just wear black. It's safe." *No! No!* was my first thought. *We need purple. We need pink. This man needs to see some flowers! He spends the rest of his time around all blue and all men.* After you become a sort of veteran, though, you get your visiting dresses. You can only go in so many times wearing something only to be told you have to go back to the car and change. So you stop trying to test the regulations. You settle. Fine. All black. Forget the purple; forget the flowers. You can still tell who's new by what they're wearing. If you're standing in line, talking with other women who have been there as much, we'll see some girl and say, "Ohhh . . . she's not getting in." But none of us would be foolish enough to say, "You cannot wear that; you should go back and change." We just say, "Good luck." You don't know who her man is. You don't know who *she* is! It's none of your business. Mind your motherfucking business with visitors you don't know. If you notice that some man is visiting multiple females? That's their business. That is *none* of yours.

I learned that one the hard way. There used to be an online prison group called PTO (Prison Talk Online). Us women used to go on it after visiting day. After one trip, someone asked, "Did anybody see that dude on A Yard who gets visits from two women?" I fell for it.

"Yes," I wrote, "I saw him today with the second female."

"Well I'm the first female. You just told on his ass," she wrote.

By doing that, I got my man in trouble, I got myself in trouble, and I almost lost my visiting privileges, because she pushed up on me the very next time she saw me. She was pissed. "What goes on between us is between us! That's *our* business. You had no right even answering." And she was right.

My husband used to take my glasses off at the beginning of my visit . . . He didn't even want me looking around the visiting room. I couldn't help it! I wanted to know what everyone was doing and how they were interacting. As a veteran female, you learn to tune in; you notice body language. All kinds of things. And there's so much waiting. It's hard to mind your own business. But again, you get schooled—and your loved one inside lets you know: *Don't do this. Don't do that. Mind your business. Don't go knocking on those females' cars again.*

It was also made very clear to me that I also shouldn't talk to certain females because their men were on the SNY (Sensitive Needs Yard, which means they're in for questionable crimes or they're gang dropouts). Just as there is a clear division inside—between the general population and SNY—there is that division outside, among families. It used to be much more so. But our movement is growing: family members are gaining more power and, in the process, realizing there's no benefit to treating anyone as "other." We *all* need our people to come home.

NIGEL How did you explain to your children, the first time, what was gonna happen on a visit?

KAREN Well . . . my children literally grew up going on prison visits. I didn't need to explain why we were suddenly going to see their dad there. They've never seen him anywhere else. They've spent their lives visiting prison; they were made there. Which is not something that I'm willing to get into. But they were both born into it. So, there were no questions. It was their normal.

We've always answered questions as they come. My background is in child development; I was a professor in the field. Often, with women and men inside, people lie to their kids and say, "This is where your dad works" or "Dad's away at college" or "He's in the military." We agreed early on that we would be honest with our kids whenever questions arose. As they grew up, they learned what prison was. Once they could read, they saw "Prisoner" written on their dad's [pant] leg.

It's not easy, but you learn. You cannot protect your kids from the trauma that they're going to experience there. You can minimize it as best you can. But I would advise any woman going to visit to learn the rules in advance, come prepared, and really talk with her kids about what they're going to experience. Tell them what it's going to look like, why they're going through a metal detector, and answer any questions they have honestly.

As a family, we developed hello and goodbye rituals. That becomes really, really hard. I would especially recommend a goodbye ritual, because taking your kids away from their father, [as you go] out of prison, is one of the most traumatic experiences—especially for little children. To have them crying and screaming for their father as you're walking away, with them trying to get back to him is . . . very, very difficult. If you can develop a ritual that will ease that for your children—whether it's putting your hands up against the glass with Dad, or blowing a certain special kiss or signal or a wave that they can do with him . . . that helps ease a deeply painful experience.

Every time you go, you're waiting so anxiously because every time a door opens, you're like, *Is that him? Is* that *him?* Once you see him, you do whatever you can to make it work within the parameters. It always fascinates me how the men inside learn to create what they need. They'll make incense out of toilet paper . . . I'm amazed at the ingenuity. And when *you* visit, you too learn to work with what you've got. I've figured out how to basically prepare a four-course meal in the waiting room. I can make some badass guacamole; then on to hamburger prep, with the tomato and onion already cut and ready.

That extends beyond food. Early on, before our kids, women taught me how to block for one another. One couple blocks for the next. You block the officers' line of vision, so that you can get your feel on right quick. Get you a good feel. Quick, get your grind on. Get it, girl.

EARLONNE We always said that when you go to a visit, you leave with wet pants and a dry mouth.

NIGEL But for men and women, traditionally, it takes women longer to reach some sort of satisfaction. But if this is too crude, we can skip it.

EARLONNE What do you mean, "too crude"? This is *Ear Hustle*!

KAREN I remember women on visiting days would be like, "Okay, I'm bringing in a burrito and she's bringing in K-Y gel—you want some?" The point is that, in prison, you come up with workarounds. And to your point, Nigel, in visiting rooms, the man's getting off. Not the woman. Let's be honest. You're there to please him. You're not getting yours.

And I'm just gonna call this out. Women over the years have claimed stuff like, "Oh, I haven't had sex in ten years. I have cobwebs." No, you don't. Just stop it. This is the one place where we need to stop judging, and just be fucking honest. Some of our men are in for decades. That takes everything from you. You are there to please him. Your desire is on the back burner.

NIGEL I wonder about the sexual dysfunction that women end up suffering, along with the other things they're suffering because the person they love is in prison.

KAREN That's so interesting, and not talked about. It's only acknowledged in the way that women often talk to women who have an incarcerated loved one. It's totally acceptable to talk about sex toys. "Girl, you need a vibrator," or this or that. But it's *never* okay, in my experience, to be real about the fact that a vibrator is not warm. It does not hold or cuddle you. That's not what women are about. For the most part, a man wants to get off. Women want to be touched, held, caressed. To go without that for years and years and years is not only devastating, it's traumatic.

That gets coupled with the other kind of minimizing—emotional. Which looks like this: Your husband calls at the end of the day and you tell him everything that happened with the kids. Then you tell him about how the car broke down, and how you're not going to make rent this month, and how you're at your wits' end. At the end of all that he says, "Yeah, but I'm in prison." That's very real. I get it. When there's *always* a "Yeah, but . . ." Your pain will never equal his. He's in prison! So your emotions and experiences are constantly minimized as lesser concerns.

EARLONNE We used to have these conversations in prison. Some of us had girlfriends. Some of us didn't. But we'd all talk about "What if your spouse, or your woman on the street, steps out and has a side relationship? Do you want to know, or do you not want to know?" Personally, I don't want to know. Because damn, they need it! Women need it just like men need it. People are human. And it might not just be decades in prison. It might be a *lockdown* for twelve months!

KAREN Yeah. Or he might go to the hole. Or lose visiting rights for three years. Or there's no contact allowed. I know people who agreed about how it was going to be, and the couple knew the score. For others, it was unspoken. And some men didn't know, or didn't want to know.

Of course, it's been much more complicated because of our children. But my kids got a very good model of a relationship. We created beautiful children that we are very proud of. And I'll say this: Marriages end, but family is forever. I'm proud of him and the man that he has become. I'm proud of myself. And I'm proud of what we built. We were able to model communication and love—even though our kids weren't able to see regular affection between us.

We agreed that if we ever had to do visits behind glass, I wouldn't bring the kids. Not that we were anticipating getting in trouble. But the sex stuff easily turns excessive. When you're trying to get your feel on in the visiting room—if you get caught, that's excessive contact. You can lose your visits for that. Same thing if you bring in contraband. People end up lying to their kids about what happened: "Oh, well, Daddy's working really hard on his college degree right now, so we can't visit for six months." In my opinion, the truth is the only way to go. Your kids will resent that lie. They'll eventually find out, and they'll resent you so badly. So we told them the truth about everything. The first questions are always: "Where are we?" "Is this really a prison?" "What did Dad do?" And then: "How long is Dad going to be here? When will he get out?" Time after time, people's answer is just: "Soon."

I can't tell you how many kids are told that. "Soon." Over and over again. And when he does not come back soon? Who do they hate? They hate their father, but their mother even more, for lying to them. You *have* to tell them the truth. Children can deal with the truth. Even when the truth is painful, it's manageable. What's not manageable is what they imagine.

Thirty years is manageable. They might say, "Wow. I'll probably be married with kids by then." But if you tell them "soon" and their tenth birthday passes, they graduate high school, they go off to college, and "soon" never comes? Nah. You have to go with the truth.

Kids need a marker in time, especially young ones. If it's a short sentence, you might say, "You know, Daddy will be closer to home when you're in fifth grade. That'll be about when he'll come home." If it's not a short sentence? You must speak that truth. For the child.

Though I believe that we've given our children a good model of a relationship, I wouldn't want my daughter to marry someone inside. Not because he wouldn't be a good man. I don't doubt that. The greatest people I know are sitting in cells. But I know what she would go through if she made that commitment. She'd have fifteen minutes for that phone call. She'd be reminded of the things that her man needs her to do. She'd be asked why they're not done yet. She doesn't need any of that. She needs to be heard. She deserves as much as she's giving. She needs a man who won't minimize her pain, her trauma, her sacrifices—because of his trauma. There's desperation inside when you have that much time. That's real. But there's desperation on our side, as well.

We only have fifteen minutes, too, and we have to share that with our kids. I understand you can't send red roses from inside prison, but you can find ways to let her know she's appreciated. Other than through cards and letters. Just listen to her. That's really, really important, because a lot of men don't do that. They take it for granted that their woman's always going to be there.

NIGEL Who do you end up taking care of—yourself or this other person? How do you possibly do both and maintain a healthy relationship?

KAREN It can be done. Unfortunately, I wasn't able to maintain it. In my case, I knew that I was compromising my own mental health and well-being. For me to leave like I did . . . it's not what women do. My loved one went inside at nineteen years old, for thirty-five years. We're near the end of that long haul. During that time, I helped him get an early release. I was with him for almost fifteen years. I'd be the first one visiting. There was pride in being the first woman in that room; your man could take pride in that too. I was that woman for all those years. Every weekend, every holiday, being that woman. But, though we're near the end, we didn't make it.

People look at me like, "What, you left him *now*?" Well, yeah, I did. I haven't abandoned him. He still gets his store money every month, and his package. I still answer every call and bring his kids to see him. But I left him, and that's made it hard to face other people. Everyone is judgmental about it. Everyone. It is a hard thing to hold my ground and say, "Yes, I left."

There are so many women that have stood by their men; some of those men are home. And that was their choice. I love and respect them. My choice is mine. Let's stop judging.

When the roles are reversed, men do not stay with their women, by and large. When you go into a women's prison—and I know this, because I now work in several of them—the visiting rooms are still filled with women. It's on our backs. We carry it.

When women go to prison, their mothers or their sisters take care of their children. My daughter came to me about her best friend at school, and said, "Mom, he has to move because his mom's going to prison."

"What do you mean he has to move because his mom's going to prison?"

"His dad's not gonna take care of the kids. They have to go live with the grandparents."

That is so typical: the grandmother or some other woman in the family takes care of the kids. It's very rare to see couples, men and women, in the visiting room at a women's prison.

One reason that I work primarily with men inside is because it's really obvious, when a woman goes to prison, that she needs access to her kids and her family. It's not as obvious that men still need access to their children, or that children absolutely need access to their fathers. Oftentimes the argument goes something like, "Oh, well, if you bring kids to see their daddy at prison, you're just making a new prisoner. That's going to be the next gang member." Not true. Our kids don't need random mentors. They need access to their fathers. I don't need some white man from the church coming and raising my child.

NIGEL I'm one hundred percent with you. I'm not trying to rail on men, but when we get into this topic, I just get frustrated.

EARLONNE You're not trying to rail on men?!

NIGEL I do actually like men! I love the men we work with at San Quentin.

EARLONNE Well, well, well. You have changed! When Nigel got into San Quentin, she didn't like to be around men.

NIGEL It's true. Going to prison is where I really learned to respect men.

KAREN Really? I'm scared of the women. The first time I ever got a contract to go into a women's prison, I was scared as hell. I had never been afraid like that. When I work with men, I'm never disrespected (by the incarcerated men, that is). Never, ever. But when I go to the women's prison, they look at me mean and curse me out and say all kinds of things.

With our literacy program, when I bring books to the men, they're like, "Oh my God, you have *Cat in the Hat*! Amazing. And *Clifford the Big Red Dog*?!" They don't care what books you have. They're just happy you're there and that they're going to get to read to their kid. But when I go into the women's prison, they'll say, "You don't have *Green Eggs and Ham*. The indignity." Even when I've just brought in two hundred books! So yeah, it's a very different energy.

EARLONNE How did you get involved with that program?

KAREN After enough visits, I got on the family reunification kick. With my background being what it is, I could not continue to go visit every weekend and not fight for systemic change. I'm not that passive woman.

Families need to recognize that we have power in numbers. As I mentioned, we need liberation for all of our people. But you're not allowed to cross-talk with other visitors, as a prison rule. Well, on Level IV yards, at least. I don't know what happens on lower-level yards.

There are all kinds of rules. It's all about "You will do what we say, when we say it. You are not going to question us." I went in having read everything available, probably knowing the rules better than the guards did. But I quickly learned how they hold all the control. Their power isn't only that they might retaliate against me. They would retaliate against *him*. They could take him to contraband watch after every family visit, and shackle him at his waist and feet and put him in a cell until he makes a bowel movement. They could potentially hurt our kids. Literally.

When I figured that out, I went through an arc of feeling broken. But once I got through it, I came back up and said, "Hell no. I'm not going to take this anymore." I was mobilized by seeing other women and their kids. It wasn't *my* pain—that wouldn't have been enough to rally me into taking back my power, which they had taken from me. But watching other kids and mothers made me say, "No. We can't do this anymore."

Camp Grace is a program that brings children to be with their dads for a full week. The families spend the week building life-sized murals based on "what a perfect day would look like if my dad wasn't in prison." They do things like dancing a *Soul Train* line with drums and shakers they make together, playing baseball in the grass (which is unheard of), and celebrating all the birthdays that they've missed. It is one hundred percent just the kids and their fathers. Mothers always ask, "Can I come?" Absolutely not. There's a different dynamic when children visit their father without other family members. I put children together directly with their dads, so they can ask what they want to ask, and say exactly what they want to say. They don't have to share him. They don't have to reserve one kiss for the beginning and one kiss for the end, like regular visits. They can lay on their dad, hug him, and wear his T-shirt.

It's about building a legacy bigger than prison. Love and pain is what our life has been in prison. Love and pain. If we don't talk about the pain, it just grows. We can't pretend that it's all good. It's not. There's *so* much pain. For our kids, our men, the mothers. It destroys entire families, entire generations. It creates generational trauma. And that's purposeful. When I say our people were stolen from us, I mean exactly that. I want them back. Every single one.

NIGEL Fifteen years being with this person. What have you given up for this?

EARLONNE Your retirement . . .

KAREN Well yeah, tangibly, I gave up my retirement and my financial security. I was a full-time professor of child development, and a known trauma expert. I was mobilized after disasters like the Northridge earthquakes, the LA riots, Hurricane Katrina. I went to South Houston to work with families.

But I never talked about my own trauma, because it seemed . . . unspeakable. I couldn't admit it. As a professor? That I fell in love with a man in prison, and married him? It diminished my credibility. So I lost a sense of my importance, my self-esteem. I'm not speaking for other women. I don't judge other women in this life. And I don't want to be judged. That's my call to action: Stop judging other women for our lives, our choices, and our stories.

Those are some of the losses. But I've gained *so* much more. I gained my whole life, my whole purpose . . . everything. I'm now the executive director of Place4Grace. I run programs in sixteen prisons across the state and help people come home to their loved ones in a way that's real, so they can reintegrate. You can't just come home after you've been gone for fifteen years if you haven't had any real time with your kids. You have to build that relationship. All that loss gave me my life's work, mobilizing children to help bring their parents home. Those years of pain empowered me to start the agency. Our pain can absolutely become our power.

It is scary as hell to love someone in prison. That's not why my relationship with my husband had to end. He questioned every parenting move I ever made. We'd negotiate, but I ultimately had to be the disciplinarian at home, of course. He'd argue with me about how I delivered it and I'd tell him, "The kids want to live with you when you get out. You'll take them for a while. Let's see how that goes."

We went through all those petty back-and-forths, ups and downs. He said, "You were never really a ride-or-die."

"I wasn't a ride-or-die for *fifteen years*?!" I said. I was furious. It took him about a week to take that one back.

"We need to work on this," I told him. "I'm dying over here. I'm dying over here. I am not just a mother. I am not just a prison wife." I begged, I pleaded to be heard: "I am a woman and I need you to respond to me as a woman, not as your secretary."

His position was always: "I'm doing what I have to do to get home to you. I'm doing everything I'm supposed to be doing."

"You're doing everything to come home to whom? Our relationship is *now*. It doesn't start when you come home. You are not going to have me to come home to." I said those words. But, bless his heart, even then, he still couldn't hear me.

CDCR played their role in breaking us too. Every time he would go down a level for good behavior, they would move him farther away. He's on a Level II yard now, six and a half hours away, in the prison where the officer asked our daughter if she had panties on. When I left that visit, I walked to the parking lot saying, "I'm never fucking coming back here." I knew that day that I was never going back. I was not going to take all my love and cram it into that life anymore. I deserve a full life, a full love, whatever that looks like. But I literally don't even know what that means.

I told him all this, but he wasn't hearing me. Finally, I wrote the "Dear John" letter. It was absolutely devastating. He hears me now, and has accepted his responsibility—but there is such a thing as too late. Still, it breaks my heart. I question my decision daily.

EARLONNE So when you're standing in a living room and your kids' father comes to the door, what's your response going to be?

KAREN When he comes to the door? What do you mean? We'll be picking him up. Like I said, family's forever. For his almost twenty years in prison, he has never had another visitor besides me and our children. And we'll be right there when he's released, to receive him and welcome him home. I don't know what that's gonna look like. It's scary. I'm worried about his transition. That will be a really difficult time, trying to figure out how to navigate that.

But I keep telling him, "There is a whole community here for you," and that he should just be fine. The fact that we've moved through this time and are now where we are? It's okay. No matter what, we'll receive him as well as if we were still together. We're a family. Forever.

EARLONNE In September 2020, we rented an SUV and headed to Central California and eventually to Ventura in Southern California, with interviews scheduled along the way. It was a tough time to travel: COVID and fires were raging throughout California. As we left the Bay Area, the skies were orange-brown and breathing wasn't pleasant.

NIGEL Driving south, we passed by prisons where E. served time. Each looked more grim than the next, and they were in the middle of nowhere. If you hadn't been traveling with your own personal prison tour guide, you easily could have missed those structures.

EARLONNE When we passed by Soledad, I couldn't help but recall when I was there in 2011, standing on Soledad's recreational yard, listening to the traffic going north and south on Highway 101. If you look in the distance and squint, you can see a clear hole to cars darting by. The other side of the gate was the freeway, with everything that goes along with its name . . . Something about that highway to me, well, that's true freedom. So, it felt pretty profound, having been out for two years, to be driving along freedom-way myself.

NIGEL We had three interviews planned, with the final one in Ventura, with Michelle Garcia. For years we've been saying, "We need more women in our stories," with listeners like Karen pointing out the obvious absence of female voices on the podcast. Michelle had been sentenced to ten years, and we planned to talk with her about what it was like to try to keep her family together from inside a women's prison.

VENTURA, CALIFORNIA
September 2020

MICHELLE We're at the Ventura training center for firefighting; it's a huge field. I work here as a program coordinator, and like to call it Fireman's Disneyland. There's gym equipment and shipping containers with extra equipment and safety gear. Some of them have these crazy training mazes inside—these blacked-out rooms with wiring where you have to maneuver your way through, with all your gear and tanks on your back.

It's quite an experience to see some of these men, who are definitely afraid. It's claustrophobic, it's dark, and you're carrying heavy equipment. The oxygen tanks beep to let you know you're running low, so you have to keep your breathing calm and steady. It's mind over matter, that's the key component. All about survival skills.

NIGEL Have you ever gone through one of those mazes?

MICHELLE Never. After I left fire camp, I never wanted to touch the tools again. Oh my gosh. Never, never, never. I wanted to go back to being a princess. But I've lived in this area my entire life. I was also previously incarcerated, and I believe in the benefits that fire camp brought to me—so this is now where I work.

EARLONNE How long have you been home?

MICHELLE Nine years. I'm very open about my incarceration, but one subject still stings: how it affected my family and kids. So don't let my tears freak you out.

NIGEL It still comes back?

MICHELLE There's a Band-Aid on it and soothing oil, but it never completely heals.

NIGEL We know there are a lot of incarcerated parents who do a good job and stay involved in their kids' lives as best as they can. We've also been talking with kids who have very difficult relationships with their parents, whose parents haven't made much of an effort. It's tough.

MICHELLE My first job when I came home was with a company called Get on the Bus. I'd been out for two years and was pro-incarcerated, meaning I wanted to defend my sisters and brothers inside to the families. I wanted to share our side of the story. After a few seasons of Get on the Bus, I realized not every parent is working hard to come home.

To see or hear a child tell you how their parent is letting them down is devastating. One girl told me, "I wish my mom would want to change, like you do." The first time I heard that was just like, *Wow*. What are you gonna say to that? How do you defend that? I get it: not every parent inside is a good parent. But we have to talk about that more; both sides need to be transparent and honest.

EARLONNE How old were your kids when you were arrested?

MICHELLE Six, eight, seventeen, and twenty.

NIGEL Can you describe the day that you had to leave your family?

MICHELLE It was March 6, 2006. I knew for about a week what the day would be, because I turned myself in. My younger ones—six and eight—how could I explain it to them? I basically told them, "Mom did something wrong, and needs to go see a judge." I think about that now and I'm like, *God, you couldn't think of anything better?* But I had never been through this before. It was my first rodeo. I didn't know how to explain it. And my oldest was in DC at college, so I had to call and tell her on the phone.

Years later, at the first Chowchilla [Central California Women's Facility] visit, I remember my daughter saying, "I thought you were going to jail. The sign out there says 'prison.'"

I had no idea that was going to happen. I had never imagined that I would get a ten-year sentence. If I had known what was going to happen to me on March 6, I probably would have gone to Mexico. I'm not lying. I would have just ran really, really fast . . . and never would have come back.

NIGEL You would have left your family?

MICHELLE Yes, I would have. Just to save them from all of this. It really got ugly. We had no idea what was ahead of us. No idea. When I surrendered that day, I didn't know my sentence, and I turned myself into county jail, too. Which was a mistake. I hadn't seen a judge, but I still had to spend eighteen months in county jail—which meant behind-glass for visits with my children, for a year and a half.

EARLONNE How long did you actually serve?

MICHELLE Six years.

NIGEL And what did you do the night before you turned yourself in?

MICHELLE We had pizza. I hadn't been able to eat for days and had already lost a lot of weight. The next morning I took my kids to school, then went home and had about two hours alone before I met up with my husband. We're Catholic and my mother-in-law had just died. So we had a gold rosary out. I took off my wedding ring, placed it on one of the arms of the crucifix, and left it on the table.

NIGEL Before you left the house did you look around and think, *This is the last time I'm going to sleep in this bed, the last time I'm going to take a shower here?*

MICHELLE No . . . I was holding on to this hope I was going to come home, that I was going to be okay. Like I said, we didn't know how bad it was going to be—which was a blessing in disguise. I left the house and met my husband and my brother-in-law at Starbucks across the street from the station. I had a chai latte and an old-fashioned donut. When I said goodbye to my husband, he started crying. In all the time we had been together, I'd only seen him cry twice. I just thought, *You really did it this time, Michelle.* Then I walked across the street and turned myself in.

I never did go back to that home. We lost our house through my incarceration. I can't even drive by the street, and it's literally minutes away from where we are now. When it comes to my home, my kids, my family—as I said—it never completely heals. I really fucked up. It's not a mistake where you can just do your time, then pick back up where you left off. It has a ripple effect. No matter how well we're doing, no matter how much I succeed in reentering society, it just lingers. It never goes away.

EARLONNE What got you to prison?

MICHELLE White-collar crime.

EARLONNE Can you tell us about those first eighteen months in the county jail?

MICHELLE Well, just about the only good thing was that my visits were regular. For anybody who is not familiar, that's not common in women's prison or jail. But every Tuesday, Thursday, and Saturday, I knew I would get to see my husband and one of my children (it was limited to two people). Like clockwork, my family would be there. That was the good part.

One of the really hard parts was slowly hearing and realizing what I was headed for, and learning what the system was going to be like in prison. Learning what I would have to endure, being bullied, being a person who looks like me—who doesn't look like she belongs in there—well, I learned what kinds of problems that would create for me. I didn't know anything about that world, and was tormented quite a bit at my own expense. At times, it was probably my own stupidity. I just didn't understand the system.

NIGEL You said you didn't look like the other people there. What do you mean?

MICHELLE I'm a princess. I don't like to be dirty. I like to have my nails done and my hair done. I like nice things . . . which is probably why I ended up there. So I stood out. That was hard, but not as hard as what it did to my family. The glass between us for those early visits did a number on my family. Being able to see your kids but not touch them when they're so close and are hurting and don't really understand . . . it's unbearable. Even if it was some six-year-old stuff, like, "He took my toy," I still couldn't comfort my kids. As a compassionate human being, there's nothing worse than seeing somebody in pain, and not being able to fix it or make it better. Being a mother and knowing that I was actually the root of their pain made it especially tough.

One time, I really saw the impact on my kids. We met in the corner, which is usually reserved for attorney visits, because it has a slot for paper to be passed through. My son saw that slot and his eyes lit up like silver dollars. He ran over and tried to put his little fingers through the slot so he could touch me.

Another time, the same son was pressing so hard against the glass that his fingertips went white. I realized then that as desperately as we long for our children, they long for us.

NIGEL I've heard from people that sometimes county is actually worse than prison.

EARLONNE If you can survive in county, you can survive in prison.

NIGEL When you got to prison, what was your first day like?

MICHELLE It was July 30. It was Chowchilla prison, so desert-hot. When I rolled out of county to become state property, they gave me the clothes that I had gone to jail in. For almost two years they had just been sitting in some dirty laundry room. It was crazy to see them again, plus I was like forty pounds heavier. I put them on for the trip from jail to prison.

As soon as you get to prison, you take all your clothes off, put them in a box, and they give you your state-issued stuff. Then they performed a strip search that found parts of my body I didn't even know I had. After all that, the CO asked me, "If you die, who do we contact?" I wanted to cry, but it's actually funny: I said, "My ex-husband. He can deal with it."

NIGEL By mistake?

MICHELLE Hell no! Why would I make my kids and my *current* husband go through that? I was like, let somebody I don't like deal with my dead body.

NIGEL What were some of the things you had to get used to that you thought, *I can't fucking do this*?

MICHELLE Honestly? Everything. I didn't think I could do any of it. It was hell. Prison is hell.

NIGEL Did you have any experiences of kindness in there?

MICHELLE Occasionally. I used to give my Reese's to everybody. One day I finally realized I was getting taken advantage of, all the time. I'd do things like give my phone time away . . . I just had no boundaries. And the first time I said no, it was to Big Mary. She got right up in my face. Mary Tucker, I can say her name. Rest in peace.

She was not happy I wasn't giving her my Reese's, and shit was about to go down. Out of nowhere, this young lady who was eight months pregnant came hauling around the corner and said, "Hell no," and pushed all three hundred pounds of Mary aside. "This is my girl; leave her alone," she said. We're still friends today.

NIGEL Why did she want to help you?

MICHELLE I don't know. I think she saw I was a newbie, a fresh fish, a poor thing. Maybe she saw my privilege and pitied me.

EARLONNE What was it like when your kids came to visit? What was the anticipation leading up to it, during the visit, and after they left?

MICHELLE They would visit prison every three to seven weeks. It was a seven-hour drive for them, plus hotel, gas . . . you know the whole story.

I couldn't wait to see them. I wouldn't be able to sleep the night before. I always laid my clothes under the mattress the night before, to get all the wrinkles out. You asked me about kindness inside . . . There was another woman who gave me the OG visiting clothes, so I'd look good at my first visit. The Nikes, the good jeans with pockets, the button-down shirt. Oh, and she gave me colored pencils for my eyeliner, and calamine lotion mixed with coffee grounds for foundation. I know it sounds silly, but learning how to be a person without makeup and hair . . . that can be a real issue for women. When your makeup's good and your hair's on point, you feel and act differently; you come to the table stronger because you have your groove on, you're feeling it. It builds up your confidence.

NIGEL It's also creating a sense of normality for yourself, right? Those are things you are accustomed to doing, so when you can find a workaround to take care of yourself, you're saying, "I'm in control." It also reflects, in some way, back to the life that was normal for you. I don't think it's silly at all. I think it's a very powerful gesture.

MICHELLE Yeah. It's also hard to feel attractive with your husband when you've got them granny panties on that go up to your fucking neck. Seriously, you can't feel it in those.

So the anticipation was always really good. Of course the departure of the visit was always . . . I mean, how do you even describe it? Their necks turned around . . . just staring at you, while they're walking in the opposite direction? Both of you looking backwards, with me just standing in line, crying, getting ready to be strip-searched? It's so emotionally upsetting. Then there's always that one CO who says, "What the fuck you crying about?" And it's like, "You know, I just had to say goodbye to my kids. I miss my kids, and—"

"Well, you should've thought about that shit when you did your crime."

Yeah, that was always just so demoralizing. And so common. That was much harder to deal with than being strip-searched. You get used to that. You learn to just kind of disconnect yourself from your body. Spread your cheeks, bend over. It's a freakin' process; you're a machine and you just deal with it. Male guards or female guards. If you have to take a tampon out, you do. You stop thinking. It loses its impact, but that process, and that numbness, has such a huge impact once you're out. How can I bend over for something or be put in that position and not feel shame and embarrassment anymore? I can't. That's trauma in itself.

But no, the hardest part was going from being a nurturing mom and getting a moment of feeling normal, to just BAM! Back to strip search, back to prison. To being a prisoner. It's just not normal. And I swear, certain COs love to play on that. The more upset you are, the more uncomfortable they would make it; they'd force you to go from A to Z just to prove a point that they had that power to humiliate you. That was the worst.

NIGEL I'd also think you had just been in a place where you had the touch of your family and children, the body of your husband, the smells, the textures. To then go through the complete opposite with the strip search. I wonder what that does to you, to have to switch like that.

MICHELLE It's caused lasting trauma that I am still trying to heal from. I don't know what that feeling is, but it's something that has to be respected and honored. Maybe one day I'll be able to put exact words to it. Right now, I just can't.

EARLONNE Can you describe the other people inside of a visiting room at a women's prison? Who occupied those tables?

MICHELLE Children, grandmas, sisters, maybe one or two men; maybe a dad.

EARLONNE Were people envious of you because you were married to one of the rare men who actually showed up to visiting?

MICHELLE Very much so. And people who are hurting hurt people. I know that now. Instead of just being envious and acting jealous, it would come out in evil ways. The more you have, the more you're taken care of, the more of a target you are back inside. I went through a lot of abuse.

NIGEL Is it too hard to talk about that?

MICHELLE It's not too hard to talk about, and it's not wrong to ask. But I work in this field now, and some of those women have changed their lives and are out. Others haven't changed their lives and are out. I wouldn't name them, but they would know.

Also, whereas I'm an open book, I don't want to revive anybody else's trauma. I was recently at Chowchilla for an event, and I was talking to the warden. I ran into a woman who, one time, had hit me upside the head with the clipboard that she was using for laundry sign-up. She had tormented me when we were both inside. When I saw her I was like, "Is that . . . you?" She didn't remember who I was, so I told her a version of the story and she was like, "Oh, yeah." But her face had changed; her spirit, her soul, had changed. I could see that. That gave me hope.

But yes. I definitely went through some torture in there.

NIGEL Did you ever tell your husband about what was happening? Or did you ever think it wasn't worth him coming, because of what would happen after?

MICHELLE Never. I enjoyed seeing my family too much, not to mention getting to have some decent food! But . . . I, well, yeah. I definitely kept my secrets when I was there. They all knew bad things were happening to Mom, we just didn't talk about it.

NIGEL Have your children reacted differently to your incarceration?

MICHELLE Yes. My husband worked really hard at keeping our family together; he was the glue. My youngest was a first grader and my oldest was in college. With three of the four, things went as well as they could have, because of my husband.

But my second child—my son, who was a senior in high school—was very angry. He didn't speak with me for years. I actually thought I might never see him again. I'd write him a letter every week, on Wednesday nights, week after week, year after year, with nothing in return. I would try to defer from the negativity of prison, you know, no "poor me." But I didn't make light of it either. My letters were probably nonsense. But I kept writing, week after week, and received nothing in return.

It wasn't until towards the end of my incarceration, when I was in fire camp, that he came to see me. We sat down and he let it all out; just let me have it. Didn't hold anything back. I took it, even when he was wrong or off base. I accepted it and just let go of the inaccuracies he had been holding on to.

My son deserves credit for sitting at a table, looking across at his mom, and telling her, "You fucked up my life." Oddly enough, today, that is the strongest relationship. He did what he had to do, and it's basically been smooth sailing ever since. I hear from him all the time. To the point where I always joke, "Watch what you pray for." For years, when I didn't hear from him, I would be crying, praying for him to reach out. Now, sometimes when the phone rings and I see his name I'm like, *Oh God, him again?*

In terms of the other two, the younger ones grew up with it. They knew family visiting better than the grown-ups; they had it down. They knew what they could bring, what they couldn't bring—they'd be in there telling me the rules. But they missed out on having a mom. My younger daughter, for example, started her period while I was gone. I talked to my husband about it on the phone. He told me they had gone to the store and he showed her the tampons and the pads. Thank God she chose the pads to start. Then they got home and went over how to use them.

A week later she was visiting me and said, "I started my period." Everything seemed fine and I thought, *Wow, he really did take care of this.* Then she said, "There is one thing I don't get . . . Why do the pads keep sliding up and down? They won't stay in place."

"Sweetie, did you take the tab of the sticky part off?" I asked her. She looked at me blankly. I explained that there's an adhesive on the bottom, and that you have to pull the cover off to make it stick to your underwear. She had no idea. So, even with my husband stepping up and taking care of the family as well as anybody possibly could, there are some things you just need your mom to tell you.

NIGEL What was Mother's Day like inside?

MICHELLE Bittersweet, always. It's so exciting to have your family and your kids with you. But you also know that they'll be going back to school Monday, and will be asked, "What'd you do for Mother's Day?" I'd spend a lot of time wondering what my kids would say.

I was in county jail for the first Mother's Day. When I was gone, my son entered a contest: Why You Have the Best Mom. His essay got selected as a finalist or maybe even the winner. My husband told me the teacher had called to ask if I would be able to be there to accept the award. When I heard that, I just felt like something you scrape off the bottom of your shoe. From that moment on out, I just wanted to erase Mother's Day off the calendar. I would start dreading it about three weeks beforehand, then it would take me about a month afterward just to shake it off.

NIGEL Do your children notice how you feel about it, still?

MICHELLE They do. I wish I could say it's all better and I'm completely healed, but this year—I think I'll take that tissue now. Yeah, Mother's Day was a doozy for me. I was deep in my self-pity. I had a breakdown. All of my insecurities came out. And even though it was just about me, when you're in the middle of that kind of a storm, you start blaming people, like, *If this damn family would understand how hard I've worked to make up for what I did*, and, you know, all of that.

After the Mother's Day breakdown, I came to this epiphany that if I didn't start forgiving myself, I'd be torturing my children all over again by not accepting their forgiveness. It took me nine years to figure that out. I don't know why. When my child is telling me, "Mom, we forgive you," and I still act out of unforgiveness, I'm basically saying, "F you, I don't believe you." And yet I want them to believe me when I tell them how sorry I am. I realized that I don't want to do that to them again. And I wish the power of that was enough to enable me to make that switch . . . but I'm just not there yet.

I've been so fortunate that my children have helped me realize that. That's the beauty of this amazing family: even through all this pain, we're teaching each other lessons and helping each other heal. None of us have all the answers. But together as a family, we fought and conquered this shit.

NIGEL Do you remember what your first night home was like, sleeping in a bed?

MICHELLE That's chapter two of life. But it's also the second sentence of incarceration. So, obviously, the first night is amazing. Curling up next to my husband, great sex, being able to just be held after the great sex, coffee in the morning in a ceramic mug, more great sex. Is that too much sex? Come on, that guy went a long time without it.

But then I got up to take a shower. Mind you, we're in a house that I hadn't lived in before. I was still excited about that ceramic cup of coffee and the sex and taking as long as I wanted in the shower. But then I got out . . . and I didn't know where the towels were kept in my house. And I know, I know, big deal; go look for one. But my first thought was *What kind of mother doesn't know where the towels are in her home?* That spiraled quickly into *What kind of mother goes to prison? What kind of mother doesn't think of her kids?* Then I was like, *Okay, come on, Michelle, dig deep, you got this. Just ask where the towels are.* I found out where they were, but that pattern kept going: Where's this, where's that?

School lunches

Jerelyn

Cakesters
uncrustables
Kiwi, strawberries
Pineapples, apples
Chips
- lunch meat
- granola bars
Yogurts

Zak

sandwich
- turkey, mayo, must
Peppers, lettuce
Chips
fruit
Cookies
yogurt

Eleven days after getting home was the first day of school. I couldn't wait. I was spinning. I had missed all these first days! I was going to make their lunches! And put a note in it with a smiley face! But I had no idea what my kids liked to eat. I had to go up to my kids' rooms, kids who are in junior high, and admit, "I'm sorry, kids, I don't know what you like to eat these days." What kind of mother is that? But I wanted to be a good mom. I stood there like a frickin' detective with my pen and paper, taking notes as they told me. I still have that piece of paper.

EARLONNE How did your relationship change with all of your children once you were out?

MICHELLE When I was gone, my husband was in charge, but my oldest daughter was the caretaker. She was also the one who would send me my pictures, my stationery kits, and supplies. She was the big sister and the mom—and was a big part of keeping our family together. She was in college in DC, but eventually had to leave because of financial reasons. I was deeply sorry about that.

When I first got home, she was there with pom-poms to greet me. But within like three, six months, you could see her resentment coming through. It's still a struggle today. She tries really hard and I try really hard, but there's damage there that hasn't been resolved yet, on both ends. It gets so difficult. I remember calling my friends after I'd been with my daughter. "Why is she being so mean to me?" I asked. It's not a hard question. Finally, somebody told me, "She's hurt. Maybe even she doesn't know how hurt she is."

NIGEL Obviously, roles really shifted with your daughter taking care of things that you probably would have been doing for her at some point. You describe her getting your schoolbooks, for example. That's a real shift in a parent-child relationship.

MICHELLE Yes. And I think me coming home and suddenly taking back my role as mother was also hard. Nine years later I have the clarity to see I probably took that role from her. Sometimes other family members will talk about Thanksgivings or Christmases that happened while I was gone, and will mention details about my kids. There's a part of me that's like, "What are you talking about, what do you know about that?" But the truth is, some of those people knew my kids better than I did, during those years. When I went in, we were a happy family. I lost my oldest son, then got him back; then when I came home I kind of lost my oldest daughter. That's been a huge part of my reentry struggle.

After I was out, I heard a woman named Karen McDaniel speak to men inside prison, telling the guys to stop writing eight-, ten-page letters— because they were causing too much pain. I got in the car and was like, *What the hell are you talking about, woman?* Then she educated me: she sent me the memo about what it does to the receiving end, the children, to read these long letters about how sad their parent is, about how hard things were, how much they are missed. It causes damage. Writing those letters is a kind of therapy inside, but not every letter has to be mailed. Unfortunately, I only learned that when I got home. I told my kids about it. "So this chick's telling me that my letters were bad, do you think that's true?" They answered honestly, and told me that they weren't bad, but that it was hard, heavy, and difficult to read them.

My reentry struggle extended beyond being a mom. Initially, I didn't know how to do anything for myself. I did not want to leave the house, because I was terrified of making an ass out of myself or doing something wrong. I didn't want to drive. I didn't know how to go to the grocery store alone. My husband had to stay home with me for a few days.

A hard six months later, I wanted to commit suicide. I didn't want to die, but I didn't know how to live my life, or what my life was. It was this battle of being this new person. Nothing made sense to me; I just felt defeated and beat-up.

Ventura County Jail called me and said, "We're doing an orientation for new volunteers. Could you come and speak to them?" I wasn't sure what they meant, but they said they just wanted me to share my perspective. I agreed, went, and got up—having never spoken publicly about my experience. I ended up breaking down into tears, admitting that I was still really struggling—to the point where I didn't even want to fucking live at that moment. Somehow, I got through the end of the talk. Afterward, this woman came up to me. She wasn't hysterically crying, but was just sort of silently breaking down.

She couldn't even get the words out, but her mouth was moving and I knew she was trying to say something. I signaled that I couldn't hear her, and she grabbed me, held my hands, and said, "Me too." I don't know what the words were before that, or what she said after. But I knew her pain, and she knew mine. Another woman was feeling the same way. It's so important for these stories to be shared. Today, we started this conversation by you saying that you wanted to bring more attention to the women. And, I want to say this without shaking or crying, but thank you. I understand we're a small population, but I say that with all love and respect.

Hearing that woman, her hearing me, knowing we shared that pain . . . for me that was like, *Holy crap.* I don't know who she was. I haven't seen her since. I don't even know if it was real. But that was a turning point for me. That's when the badass was born.

EARLONNE And your husband—is he a ride-or-die?

MICHELLE Oh my God. Yeah, he's my ride-or-die.

All those years he went through visiting me in prison . . . he was a pro. After I got out I was working for Defy Ventures, and there was a cool event inside Avenal State Prison that we went to. He had not been back to a prison in about five years. I was excited for him to be there to share my work with me and everything, but then all of a sudden, as we were going through security, I thought, *Oh, wow, I never thought about triggers for him.*

I just think he's Superman and can handle everything. But he had this really odd look on his face and I felt terrible, thinking he was being triggered. Well, he wasn't. He was fuming mad.

"God damn it," he said. "As a family member I had to go through this and that even though they saw me week after week. They knew me, and they treated me like shit, every time." As volunteers, we had just walked in. They didn't even ask for our names or IDs. Suddenly I could see all this pain he was holding for what he had gone through and what our kids had gone through. "Here we are at a Level IV prison and we just walk in? When we were visiting you at a Level II prison we had to go through hell! How does this make any sense?"

That's an incarcerated family. It sucks. We get so much shit thrown at us, but there's also this spirit. We're fighters and warriors. So when you meet that incarcerated family, don't be quick to judge. You just might be surprised at what the hell they're going through.

NIGEL So is that second term over?

MICHELLE No, but I'm learning. I finally started to come to grips with some of the forgiveness and with being friends with myself. When I'm beating myself up, just take a breath, sleep on it. (Isn't that the best advice ever? Sleep on it? See if you still feel the same way in the morning.) I also try to imagine I'm talking to someone in prison and they are telling me about these struggles. What advice would I give them? Then I try to treat myself the way I would treat them. The healing has started to come, but it's still a huge struggle.

It's been especially hard lately. Something triggers me and brings me back to the abuse and trauma that I endured inside. I'm trying to learn to separate those feelings and not revert back. It's not all rainbows and sprinkles. I don't know if I'll ever be able to forgive myself entirely for how much harm and pain I caused my family.

NIGEL We can't pretend like everybody finds their place in prison—or in families, for that matter.

EARLONNE And for some people, prison really is hell. Michelle will be all right, though.

NIGEL She's strong. But there have been times when I worry that because we concentrate on telling the everyday stories, the stories of persistence, the work-arounds that lead to some measure of satisfaction—that we might give people the impression that incarceration isn't so bad.

EARLONNE People know incarceration sucks. There are *way* more layers to the onion than what we show. We've never been about giving people a false reality.

NIGEL We've never sugarcoated anything—we are telling real stories about how you make a life inside and what happens when you get out.

EARLONNE A lot of people seem to think life stops when you're in prison. It doesn't. But nobody's tryin' to say it's easy.

NIGEL And I get that being incarcerated isn't a life anybody wants, but it is a life nonetheless: you work, you make friends, you deal with health, family, conflict, education; all the stuff that happens outside the walls happens inside.

EARLONNE But there are so many more emotions that the incarcerated person deals with on a minute-to-minute basis. Everything from being happy to losing someone close to you to just feeling helpless.

NIGEL I'm just really grateful to Michelle for telling us about what she went through so candidly. No bullshit. The good, the bad, and the troubling. She reminds us that the prison experience doesn't stop just because you walk out.

EARLONNE We're also grateful to Karen for being real with us about what it's like to love somebody who's incarcerated, and to try to create a family with that person. It's real easy to forget about all the people who suffer from the outside, and dedicate so much of their lives to waiting for their loved ones to come home.

CHAPTER NINE

THREE STRIKES

EARLONNE I got a call in the middle of our book meeting, right when we were talking about other voices we could bring into this chapter. Literally as we were discussing it, my phone rang. It was from an unknown number— the kind of calls that I rarely answer. But something compelled me to pick this one up, and I'm sure glad I did, because it was my homie Eric Post, aka E-Man. We had been at San Quentin together for seven years, and known each other for almost thirty.

"Hey, man, I'm out!" he blurted. "But peep what happened: *boom,* the dude that came and got me ended up getting pulled over. They took him to jail for warrants or something. So, I'm fresh out . . . but Wino and I are stuck on the side of the roads. Ain't nobody got a license."

I told him I'd be there right away. I needed somebody else to drive their car back, so I got on the phone with Yahya, my friend who was also formerly incarcerated. The two of us set off on a straight-up rescue mission. Imagine: E-Man ain't been out three hours, and we have to go rescue him in Dublin, California—about a half-hour drive from Oakland.

We rolled into the Honda dealership where they had been pulled over. E-Man was dressed all in black—LA hat, black long-sleeve T-shirt, black Levi's, and some black water-bead shoes. He was standing at the tailgate of the Dodge Ram 1500 truck they'd been in when they got pulled over. We got the truck they'd been left with, and Yahya and I took E-Man and his friend Wino to an IHOP across the street.

E-Man had been awake all night, waiting. His homies Boo Boo and Wino had picked him up, and he immediately started feeling carsick—like he was gonna throw up. He'd been out for two, maybe three hours (though he said it felt more like five minutes) and was feeling nauseous *and* cautious. Meanwhile, Boo Boo was driving a bit carelessly.

"I'm like, 'Fool, you bustin' U-turns and doing shit that I know you ain't supposed to be doing,'" he said, adding, "I was feeling more cautious, because I'm fresh out. And he was like, 'Man, the police ain't like that no more!' And then we got pulled over.

"I was scared. I ain't felt like that in a long time. It was like the feeling you get when you first go to jail, you know? You're in the car, heading to jail, and you're scared. It was close to that. I was trying to do everything right! But shit that's wrong was coming to me, and I ain't got no control. When I saw those lights behind us, I couldn't believe that shit. I was just like, 'Nah, hell no.' I mean, when my homies came and got me, I felt like I was back in 1982. They're there with their LA hats on, looking like hood motherfuck- ers. Those homies are not on parole or nothing. They're still wild. They don't get caught up in the shit that we used to when we was younger, but they still had a look. So *I'm* the one that was nervous.

"The policeman came to the car and said, 'Roll the window down.' All I could think was, *Ain't this a bitch*. You know, the last time I had been pulled over by the police, it was 'Step out of the car.' Then I was cuffed up, and see you later. That was the last time. So, you can imagine where my head was at. Fresh out after twenty-five years, and pulled over within min- utes. I was like, I ain't really out, all I got is one foot out.

"Also, I was picked up by Boo Boo, the same homeboy who I was with when I got taken to jail in the first place. The only difference was, last time they snatched *me*. Boo Boo went to jail this time, because he was the one driving . . . on a suspended license. But we were in the same situation: just driving along, then suddenly the police were behind us."

"E-Man," I say, "would there be a takeaway from all of this, like maybe . . . switch up homies?"

"You know what? I might have to catch the bus next time."

The basic sentence in California for your first DUI is a minimum of two days in jail, and a maximum of six months. That minimum can be avoided altogether if you agree to restrictions on your license, and if nobody was severely hurt.

E-Man had a history of DUIs and other warrants when he was last pulled over (meaning nobody was hurt, and he was not resisting the po- lice). I'm not here to judge or condone any of his behavior. Breaking the law should have consequences, and there are occasions when people need to get checked. But E-Man was in his twenties when he received his sentence. He's now in his mid-fifties, having spent about half of his life in prison for a reckless decision. *Twenty-five years.*

Of course, this is a personal issue for me. Due to this law, I was sentenced to 31 years to life for a crime that generally would have carried roughly three years or less. In my case, this brutal punishment was compounded by the devastating loss of my best friend, Furman Little.

I was convicted of attempted second-degree robbery. In the end, my crime was essentially tackling a person to the ground, then getting up, and leaving. The way it all shook out, when it came to my sentencing, instead of getting a handful of years, the Three Strikes Law was applied. As a result, I was given a potential life sentence in prison.

I didn't know it would be three strikes until I went to court and realized I had taken a plea bargain for *two* convictions in my first case—robbery and kidnapping—so my prior felonies were now considered strikes. I remember being sentenced and I was laughing because my co-defendant's paperwork said 2017, and I hadn't even thought about the 2000s. When they told me my first Board of Parole hearing date would be in 2028? In 1999, I just couldn't fathom that.

Back when I first started going to court, I saw a dude that I had been in juvenile hall with. He was sitting there eating a dry-ass baloney sandwich, and he was like, "Well, they just gave me 25 to life." I was looking at him like, you just got 25 to life and you have an appetite?! Seventeen months later, they give me 31 years to life plus 26 years to life. I was crushed. It was like . . . I'm a fucking lifer. For attempted second-degree robbery.

California's Proposition 184, the Three Strikes Law, was overwhelmingly passed by voters in 1994 after Richard Allen Davis was convicted of taking the life of a young girl named Polly Klaas. The law was touted as a means of incapacitating violent, depraved criminals like Davis. But that's not what it has done. Instead, it has given a life sentence to anyone who has two previous felony convictions if that individual is convicted of a third. So, a person who may have made a few bad decisions in his youth, then was hungry and stole a slice of pizza, or chose to drive home after just a little bit too much champagne, could be sentenced to a mandatory minimum of 25 years to life in prison. I ran across a whole lot of dudes in prison who were there on petty-ass cases, who had nonetheless been sentenced to a hundred or more years.

In my opinion, the Three Strikes Law is the most oppressive law since slavery was legal. The loophole can be found in the wording of the

Thirteenth Amendment to the United States Constitution: "Neither slavery nor involuntary servitude, except as a punishment for crime whereof the party shall have been duly convicted, shall exist within the United States." Hmm . . . How else could anybody possibly justify giving a life sentence to a human being for stealing a few VHS tapes, or some golf clubs, or a pack of cigarettes? These are punishable mistakes, of course. But a *life sentence*? Hell NO! Californians signed off on this either consciously or unconsciously. Maybe people wanted to see if it might lower rates of kidnapping or murder in the state. It didn't work. So how is it that, nearly three decades later, such an extreme system of penalization is still in effect?

Close to 100,000 lives have been affected by this law—and that's not including family members left behind. That's just the men and women who have been incarcerated. I couldn't accept the fact that I was going to serve out my life in prison. Not for what I'd done. And though I'm one of the fortunate ones who is sitting here writing about this as a free man, there are too many human beings serving out extreme sentences that they don't deserve. Something needs to change.

If we were to disqualify felonies committed prior to the enactment of Proposition 184 in 1994, that alone would clear *eight thousand people* out of prison.

Everyone who's on appeal begs the court to reverse their case. I've been that man. Every time, the court acts like their hands are tied . . . If they are, why not change the law? As a victim of the Three Strikes Law, one who was never willing to accept that fate, early on in my prison years I began my quest to understand that question. Why *not* change the law? And what would it take to do so?

EARLONNE I was in Centinela State Prison when I became determined to figure out this law and learn how to get rid of it. Prior to an extended lockdown in 2006, I started researching government codes (similar to penal codes) in the prison's law library. They were brand-new books, because nobody had ever checked them out. I had paid a library clerk to photocopy the areas of the books that interested me, so that I would have something to study in my cell during the lockdown.

I learned that, if I wanted to see a change in the Three Strikes Law, I would need to take matters into my own hands . . . or at least try. Back at the start of the 2000s, there weren't many organizations trying to help people get out of prison, or putting up any initiatives. Those that were trying to help were doing little more than holding banquets—nothing that moved us closer to abolishing this law. They were taking advantage of hope!

In 2004, that hope was reignited with the introduction of an initiative on the ballot called Proposition 66, which set out to demand that convictions be brought and tried separately. That would mean abolishing getting two strikes in one conviction. We were optimistic that it would pass, leading to our sentences being recalled. Under those standards, my sentence would have been three to six years.

For weeks, we were all excited, believing the life sentence enhancement would soon be gone, and that we would finally be able to get out of prison, go home, and catch up on lost time. Just prior to a consequential election, then governor of California Arnold Schwarzenegger weighed in, saturating every TV channel with commercials with the headline "26,000 murderers, rapists, and killers will be released if you vote 'yes' on Prop. 66."

We were all on the yard talking about how and why these commercials weren't being addressed with counterarguments to this classic "tough on crime" fear-mongering. What made it even worse was that our very own California Department of Corrections—which had put up money in 1993 to get the Three Strikes Law established—was campaigning to vote "no" on Prop. 66. This slap in our face—"NO ON PROP. 66"—was literally stamped on some of their paychecks. They even had posters up in the window facing the yard, promoting their position, for all of us to see.

The night of the election, most prisoners were still hopeful, talking about how this oppressive-ass law was finally going to be amended. For some of those guys throughout the California penal system, the presidential election was a sideshow. All they were thinking about was Prop. 66. And things were looking real good. When I went to sleep that night, I did so easily, feeling rather overjoyed. Drifting into dream world, all I could think was, *This struggle is over*. When I woke up the next morning, I immediately got word that about 5.6 million people had voted "yes" on Prop. 66—and 6.2 million had voted "no."

It absolutely broke my heart. It was like a bomb had gone off: everybody was walking around like zombies.

It was such a distinct moment in time; Nigel and I covered it while I was still inside. It was September 2017, and featured a fellow incarcerated individual named Curtis Roberts. The episode was called "Left Behind."

NIGEL Election night. Tuesday, November 2, 2004. George W. Bush was running for his second term; John Kerry was his opponent. But no matter who they wanted to win, prisoners could not vote.

EARLONNE Nope, but a lot of guys in prison had been following the campaign on TV. All we were thinking about was Prop. 66.

CURTIS Proposition 66. I remember watching the TV that night, and I was sitting in my prison cell, and I went to sleep knowing that we were way ahead, and I thought, *Tomorrow morning when I wake up, I'm gonna go home at some point.*

NIGEL The idea of Prop. 66 was to reform the California Three Strikes Law. One reform was that if your third conviction was not for a violent or serious crime, under Prop. 66, your sentence might be dramatically reduced.

EARLONNE Yeah. It was gonna be a huge change. Here's how Curtis got his third strike:

CURTIS The crime I committed was I walked into a liquor store and snatched two twenty-dollar bills out of the cash register; no weapon. After I got caught for stealing the forty dollars, I pled guilty to burglary and robbery. They gave me 50 years to life. Currently, I'm on my twenty-third year. The first time I'm eligible for parole is 2044.

EARLONNE But on Wednesday, November 3, 2004, Curtis and other Three Strikers woke up hopeful that Prop. 66 had passed and they just might be getting out sooner than expected.

CURTIS When I turned on the news and I saw that Prop. 66 had fallen, that it did not get passed, I along with a lot of other Three Strikers . . . It was . . . You could cut the tension with a knife. It was a really sad, sad moment. I mean it was. It was devastating, and a lot of Three Strikers were very at, um, at their wits' end, I would say.

EARLONNE This is life in prison. Things on the outside with the law, with our families, they happen beyond our control. Our hopes go up, our hopes go down, and when they're down, you gotta figure out how to carry on.

Some prisoners have every reason to hope because they may only have a few years left on their sentence, so they see light at the end of the tunnel, but for guys under the Three Strikes Law, hope is harder to come by.

EARLONNE We all felt lost. Our hope had been collectively inflated, only to be punctured and deflated. Witnessing those around me, seeing that everybody felt as crushed as I did, made me realize that action had to be taken. The courts weren't giving any love when it came to getting relief from the Three Strikes Law. Even the highest court in the land wasn't going to change it. It would have to be on the people. That's who we needed to get behind us. We needed to vote it out.

After looking into the election codes, I familiarized myself with the process. How do you file an initiative? What do you need? I spent a lot of time going through it, and after reading as much I could, and though I was well aware of the limitations that had been placed on me, I started telling cats, "Bruh, this shit ain't that hard." As far as I understood it, it was a money and numbers game.

In order to put up an initiative to change the Three Strikes Law, one needs the signatures of 5 percent of the total number of voters from the prior gubernatorial race. It's a tedious process, but not necessarily a difficult one. Once you have an initiative, it has to pass through the Attorney General's office, the Legislative Analyst's Office, a public review, then back to the Attorney General. From that point, you have six months to get the signatures. After that, you're on the ballot.

In theory, that didn't seem too bad: 650,000 signatures. How could I get it done? In California, *anybody* can put forth an initiative. I resolved to do just that. I educated myself, and tried to educate those around me. The hardest part about it was going to be getting it done from prison. But once I saw Prop. 66 fail, and saw the effect that loss had on those around me (not to mention myself), I was like, "Okay, we gotta re-run that."

NIGEL Do you remember what was going through your mind when you first heard your sentence?

EARLONNE *WHAT THE—?!* was going through my mind. You start to think the worst thoughts. You think, *Man, this system is racist. It's unjust . . .* I didn't even know I was a three-strike candidate. So, you start believing the system is against you. Like, *Oh, they fucking me.*

NIGEL E. and I went out to the yard to talk to some Three Strikers about their sentences:

> "They gave me biblical time. They thought people can live like Joseph and all them people lived in the Bible. What is it for a man? About seventy-five? seventy?"

> "My name is Stacy Bullock, and I have 150 years to life."

> "I have 425 to life, so I have to do at least 100 years before I'm eligible for parole."

> "I was sentenced to 1,010 years and 19 life terms for, uh, armed bank robbery."

> "I'm serving a sentence of 210 years to life. When I go to my first board appearance, I'll be approximately 250."

> "I won't go up for parole until . . . Jesus will come back first."

NIGEL Earlonne, Curtis said he'll be eligible for parole when he has served fifty years. So, compared to those guys in the Yard Talk segment, dare we say he actually got a light sentence?

EARLONNE Yeah, he got a light sentence—because if he gets out in 2044, he'll only be eighty-two. Meaning, he'll only be on crutches, using a walker or cane, or in a wheelchair. In comparison, they're going easy on him. As we know, Curtis don't feel that way.

> "I feel like somehow I have fallen into this type of loop, or hole, or whatever you want to call it," he told me, "that I have been labeled the worst criminal in the history of the United States of America. I've never shot a gun. I never molested no kids, never raped nobody, never put my hands on nobody. I mean, surely, they're going to see the error of their way of giving me 50 years to life. But you know, I just don't make no promises anymore. I'm here today. I'm making it today. You know? I'm making it through this hour, and that's kind of like where it's at for me. No promises. It's just a tough road, tough, tough road."

EARLONNE Back in Centinela, in 2005 and into 2006, I had come up with the idea for an organization called CHOOSE1: Could Hip-hop Overthrow Oppressive Sentence Enactments. The number "1" stood for the fact that all it takes is one person to spark a revolution.

My mission was to get individuals from the West Coast hip-hop industry involved, to help pull together the necessary funds to get my initiative on the ballot. From there, we could get this law changed and send home all these Black and brown faces. I wasn't under any illusions, and never lost sight of the fact that I was, in fact, in prison, but I also wasn't going to let that deter me. I've always prided myself on my ability to think outside the box and do what needs to be done to take care of business. I looked ahead toward steps I would have to take.

If I could somehow organize a few big-name artists to throw concerts, and maybe put out a compilation album, the proceeds could fund the initiative. Now, everybody loves to tell you that they know somebody in the hip-hop industry. But when you press them for details, they either don't really know the person or they'll say, "Ah, well, you know, I couldn't ask nothing from them." I know that every entertainer gets hit up for cash, all day every day. And it's hard to ask people for shit—but if you're able to present them with a cause they could get behind, I had to believe they'd at least look into it.

By the time the idea for my proposition was fully formed, I had arrived at San Quentin. That's where I found and recruited the type of people who would support my efforts. We launched a cool letter-writing campaign, and sought to get people involved on social media. I asked Arnulfo and Bonaru—the dudes who ran the *San Quentin News* (which goes to all the prisons in California)—to put the idea for CHOOSE1 in one of their issues. We were serious about it. Devoted to the cause. We developed a real live organization, and were all working hard to really push the line. San Quentin—with its stream of volunteers, Bay Area activists, and average people who are committed to progression—provided fertile grounds for growth and getting the project off the ground. Even beyond the immediate group of activists, we had a lot of people inside the prison system who were on board and supportive.

In 2015, we submitted an initiative that I drafted along with two of my boys from inside: Gino Atkins and James Benson. We sat down and hooked that shit up, which consisted of taking the existing penal code and revising it with additional language. Such details were a little complicated, but what we were requesting was simple. All we were asking for was that no felony prior to 1994 (when the law came out) could be used as a strike. That's all. If the law passed, it had the potential of saving into the high hundreds of millions of dollars just over the first couple of years. And then the low hundreds of millions for the few years after that.

Once we finished the initiative, I mailed it to my friend Julie Piccolotti, who had been working with us on the outside, and she drove it all the way to Sacramento and submitted it on my birthday, August 13, 2015. It was called the Three Strikes Rehabilitative Reform Act of 2016 [Initiative 15-0084]. United States vice president Kamala Harris (then the attorney general of California) gave us a good title and summary. It was cool—we were all happy with the way she articulated our mission. Now, all we needed was the funding and the signatures.

We turned our focus to acquiring the signatures, which is not as straightforward as one would hope. Lesson learned. As for the funding goals, we couldn't get the celebrity hip-hop motherfuckers to listen to us. They didn't want to be involved. They had no stakes in the Three Strikes Law. We had submitted our information and done everything we could within our power, from within the confines of prison. But one doesn't have representation behind those bars. There's no union. No advocates. No voting. Nothing. You're just an unrepresented class of people.

NIGEL Back out on the yard, we asked guys if they remembered what was going through their minds when they were first sentenced. We heard: "Life's over." "It don't matter no more." "I quit caring."

EARLONNE Life may be over, but here's what may be worse: you still have to keep on living it. And to live in this environment, you gotta have some hope that you're going to get through it. It's up to each prisoner to find their own reasons to keep going.

NIGEL When we interviewed Curtis, E., you had been in prison for twenty years. When we thought you had another eleven to go, I asked you, "How do you keep going? What keeps your hopes up?"

EARLONNE Well, I just kept getting up every morning. Thankful that I had another day. Thankful to be alive. In my mindset, regardless of where I'm at, I'm going to live to the best of my ability. Even in prison, I just tried to live to the best of my ability.

EARLONNE'S APARTMENT
December 2020

Though my own sentence has since been commuted, I have not let up on my Three Strikes fight. I never will. That has meant going out and spending a lot of time talking to invested individuals, whether they're from the DA's office or various philanthropy groups. But all the organizations we had been dealing with were like "We can't do it this year." No matter my vision, they were the ones who had the deep pockets. I didn't have shit. For them, everything hinged on whether or not they believed we could get the funding to make it onto the ballot.

I've often felt like I was just spinning my wheels, wasting my time—sharing my story and getting my hopes up, feeling like real progress was being made, only to have them just bag out and shut down the movement. Then again, I've gotten a first-class education on how this shit really plays out, which I know is invaluable.

We're still pushing in a big way for this. Hey, we might have something on the next ballot. And I won't be doing it on my own. As soon as they were released from prison, I hired two individuals (both Three Strikers) to join CHOOSE1: John "Yahya" Johnson and Fanon "Red" Figgers.

I recently sat down with Yahya and Fanon to discuss some of our residual feelings about the law, and posed the same questions to Curtis Roberts—who has since had his sentence commuted—and to E-Man, the unfortunate protagonist of the rescue mission in Dublin, California:

EARLONNE Do you guys feel you've reconciled with a sentence that never felt justified?

CURTIS No way. Even today, even though my sentence was commuted by Governor Jerry Brown, I still have times when I'm pissed off. I'm mad. Society has not understood the truth of what really happened to all of us.

FANON No, I could never accept nor justify it. I was sentenced to 210 years to life for what was actually a property crime. I felt a lot of despair. But I still had resilience. I don't know where it came from, but I never felt like giving up. Even when I felt hopeless, and just didn't know how to get out of the situation.

YAHYA Reconciled? No, I don't think that I've reconciled with receiving 30 years to life for a second-degree robbery. What I *have* reconciled with is my attitude and the mentality that put me in a position to receive a Three Strikes sentence in the first place. Reconciliation means that you come to some type of resolve, or some type of peace, with something that was done to you.

The Three Strikes Law is inherently racist and inherently unjust.

That, I can never reconcile. The only way that I can ultimately reconcile with the law is to repeal it. Get it off the books. Only then will I have peace of mind.

E-MAN Nah, man. To me, being sentenced as a Three Striker is a worse fate than being sentenced as a murderer. How could I justify getting more time than somebody who killed people? I don't think a worse law exists, other than the death penalty. And even with the death penalty, you know what crimes will get you a lifetime without parole. But when you go in for some bullshit that you could have got thirty days for, and then get hand-cuffed to a motherfucker who just killed two people, and *he* will go to the parole board and get out before you? While you're stuck because of a man-datory sentence for some shit that usually carries a month? That's deep.

For a cat to be able to stay sane and make it through that? There was a time where a lot of us thought, *Shit, what the fuck am I acting nice for, if I ain't never getting out of here? I'm going to make the life sentence worth me having. I may as well keep on fucking up.* But that's just giving in to what they wanted. That's the kind of behavior they were counting on, to prove that any of us deserved to be in there as long as we were. I really believe Three Strikes is the worst thing that they can give a dude.

EARLONNE Was it something that you dwelled on when you were in there?

CURTIS Well, yeah! I was sentenced to 50 years to life. So most certainly on the inside I felt hopelessness and tons of rage. But I couldn't do anything with all that rage. I still have the same rage, but now I have a voice and they can't shut me up.

YAHYA Yeah, absolutely. For the first ten years of my sentence, I was a rager. I had an attitude; I was angry. I had a "me against the world" mental-ity. But I think the most important thing for me to understand is that it was self-defeating to feel that way. I needed to shift my perspective and focus that anger in a more healthy way. What I did as a result was utilize that anger to study law, to join justice-reform groups and things of that nature, and to ultimately seek to affect the outcome of a law that I was unjustly in prison for.

But because I had such rage and anger, I realized that underneath those emotions were some unresolved conflicts with myself. I needed to cultivate that anger into something more productive. So I changed my life as a result of it. Now that anger is being utilized in a way that will ultimately repeal the Three Strikes, and ideally getting rid of enhancements. So, the unintended consequence of the law was that it has made me a crusader for justice reform, you know?

E-MAN For me, it actually brought a rage by itself, because I had allowed the system to catch me, because I didn't have my shit together. So, the rage and everything that I felt against the system, I just used it to make sure I never let them motherfuckers get me like that, ever again.

EARLONNE But your rage was more on yourself.

E-MAN Exactly. I'm the one who fell into the bigger trap, the one that I see now. Every time I went to jail, I was like, *Damn, you didn't see it back then.* As I got older, and was still sitting in this shit, it was like, *How did I fall into this trap?* The thing about getting caught up in the system is that you learn more about it, but by the time you do it's like, *Shit, now I'm all caught up in it.* And it's hard as hell to get out.

EARLONNE Once you're inside, you're inside. Does it matter what put you there?

CURTIS There was a clear line inside between lifers who were murderers and lifers who were Three Strikers. That was a very clear boundary, especially when many Three Strikers started getting vocal about the unjustness of our predicament. The guys convicted of murder didn't like it. They had the attitude that "This is our first time in prison, so we should get a chance to get out. Three Strikers?! You already had your chance. You blew it." That was their mindset.

I remember being interviewed by KQED and they asked me, "Hey, tell us about the worst day that you've had in prison." I said, "The worst day is when you let a murderer out before me." I received a ton of flak inside the prison for that. I mean, I was pointed at on the yard and people walking by would just spit hatred at me. They were all convicted murderers. I told them, "You go on the Board of Parole hearings and tell them that you're upset with me for making that statement."

EARLONNE I know they wanted to beat you up.

CURTIS They did. They hated me for that.

EARLONNE So, when another person arrived in jail under the Three Strikes Law, did that bond you to him?

FANON Yeah! We had something in common. Bonding with like-minded people—even through your anger—that can help us. We collaborated, for sure.

CURTIS Especially over the last ten years, when a lot of Three Strikers were coming together and fighting, there were a handful of us that were putting our faces and our cases out there to take on this law. That was a connection, at least at San Quentin.

YAHYA Being a Three Striker defined my prison experience and my identity. There wasn't a day that I didn't feel like I wore a scarlet letter. And by that I mean that having that weight on my shoulders and knowing that I walked the line with murderers and baby rapists and those kinds of people . . . I mean, I hate to put a status or a rank on felony conviction, but that's where my mind was.

I compared myself to different individuals in prison and so constantly felt wronged. Ultimately, I resolved that conflict in myself and stopped casting people in that way. But it took a while. I always gravitated toward Three Strikers because of the solidarity that we all had—that we were there for the wrong reasons, with these sentences that were . . . outrageous.

There was a connectedness among us, especially among those of us who formed groups, with a hope to end this. It really helped us to sit in that space and figure out creative ways to ultimately make it out of prison. I found more kindred spirits that way. Not that those were the only people I bonded with. But other Strikers could identify with issues a lot of people couldn't understand. We could empathize with each other. That's how our relationship kind of started, E. You was on a crusade to change the law. We formed a friendship beyond that, but initially it was all about being left behind on all of these initiatives that were passing us by.

We started communicating and you had this knowingness about who I was; I had this knowingness of who you were. We were both hiding behind masks, but at the same time, I'd see you on the yard and be like, "Okay, Dub'e Dub."

EARLONNE And I'd answer back with your nickname as well: "All right, Yahya."

E-MAN This is what I got a chance to see. A huddle of motherfuckers from all different flavors. When somebody was talking about some shit that came through about Three Strikes, it bonded a lot of motherfuckers, because we all wanted to find out what was going on—so we could get our ass out of prison. Yes, the sentence bonded a lot of motherfuckers that you probably wouldn't have never fucked with. We were all caught up under the same shit and were all just trying to find a way out.

EARLONNE Did you want to talk about it?

CURTIS It helped me have compassion for people if I knew they'd been sentenced due to the same law. That really opened the door for conversations with people from other races, who I may not have connected with otherwise. It kind of lowered the tension and gave us a reason to talk.

EARLONNE Did you always talk about your sentence?

YAHYA Every opportunity that I got, I'd talk about my sentence. I used to want to shame the system. I wanted to show how crazy it was that me and other Three Strikers were in there. Not for some bullshit, but for a crime that wasn't commensurate to the time that we got. Anybody who would listen, I would talk to them until I was blue in the face. Especially if I had an opportunity to talk to a politician, or some type of justice reformist. I'd talk about how inherently racist and biased the law is.

With other incarcerated individuals, we would sit in the yard and drink coffee and talk about our sentences. We would chop law—you know, interpret it and talk about what we thought it meant. We'd have these huge-ass debates about it. Sometimes that shit would go on for hours. Some people would leave angry or sad, but, nevertheless, we got some resolve out of it.

One time, this brother told me something that was so profound, but it had me depressed for a couple of years. He said, "Brother, the court system is not there to help you. The court system is there to make sure that district attorneys have done the right thing. If they violate your rights in the process of them 'doing the right thing,' the courts will give you relief. But by no means should you ever think that the judicial system is an advocate for you."

EARLONNE Do you all still resent the system?

CURTIS I do. This is a huge trigger for me. I am so angry at the system and at society that a man sentenced to first-degree murder gets 25 years to life. After twenty-one years, that killer is eligible to go to the board and potentially go home. A Three Striker has to do his entire base term. Mine was fifty years. I had to do all fifty before I was even eligible to go to the board. How is that just? So, yes, I resent that.

YAHYA I don't have resentment for the system. I used to. But resentment only runs counterproductive to my mental health. Now, I look at the system with the perspective that it's imperfect, and that we have to strive to make it as best we can under the circumstances. But abolition and a lot of criminal justice reform is necessary, because the system is so deeply racist.

I'm trying to utilize the energy I used to feel about the system being wrong to propel me to do the reform work that needs to be done. I try to turn it into a healthy type of anger, or else I'd just spiral down in rage. Instead, I look at the system as something that is a continual work-in-process. The way that its identity takes shape is how we can step up and respond to the need to change it.

Even though we were slaves, this government is for the people, by the people. When we realize that, we'll get our power. And when we say we need to speak truth to power, that's what we mean. Not that we speak to the government, because we've invested them with authority. But by remembering that as a society, we put those people in place. They're representatives of us. We have the power. The government's greatest trick has been to make us feel that we don't have that power of representation, and that our voice doesn't matter when it comes to steering who represents us. If we capitulate and let them do whatever they want to do to advance their own agenda? That's not democracy.

E-MAN Well, I definitely don't forgive the system. Hell no! No sir. Why would I forgive the system? And that extends to the people. Certain people really need to know that this shit is real. In the beginning, a lot of people thought, *Man, they ain't striking people out for little shit.* I'm like, *Well, I'm real.* I'm a motherfucking testimony that they are striking out human beings. Whoever would have thought that somebody would get struck out for what I did—getting pulled over, consenting, and getting busted with a DUI. I mean, it stopped a lot of motherfuckers from drinking and driving, after I got caught. So, I hope it saved some lives.

EARLONNE Do you feel that it sets up a different kind of resentment for the system to give an individual that much time?

E-MAN It's supposed to, but I understand. That shit was never meant to work for us Black men. I see it from that angle. This shit worked for them. It's not that the system is broken. It's that the system just works for them.

It's their shit. They wrote it. So I don't forgive it, but I'm not mad. At this point, I understand that this system works . . . it just don't work for us. They are eating off us. We are the new dope they're making money off of.

FANON To be real, I was pissed off then and I'm pissed off now. What really pissed me off the most is I still remember, when the judge gave me the 210 years to life, the sound of my mother screaming.

EARLONNE The scream of, like, "I'll never see my kid again"?

FANON Yeah. And the judge was, like, talking directly to her. So, when I think about the system, I get mad all over. Not mad in a violent way, but mad in a way that I want to do something productive to fight against this unjust law.

When Governor [Gavin] Newsom commuted my sentence in March 2020, my mother cried. She was proud of me.

EARLONNE I remember that. We were recording when we got the news, and I talked to you. Pretty sure you were crying, too!

FANON Yeah, I was, bruh.

EARLONNE So most of us had our sentences commuted, which means our sentences were reduced before we finished the intended time inside. With that in mind, do y'all feel a responsibility to abolish the law that kept you in prison for longer than you should have been there? Or any responsibility to the other Three Strikers who are still inside?

CURTIS I feel no obligation to abolish the law. I don't. I do feel an obligation for living up to who I became on the inside: a person who has grown up, been rehabilitated, and ready to be released amongst society. I want to live that out. As far as abolishing the law? No. I don't have the platform for that like you, Earlonne. In terms of fellow Three Strikers left behind, my heart goes out to them. And I'm very proactive about making sure that they have certain comforts.

FANON I do feel obligated to abolish the law, and obligated to live as a productive citizen. I want them to release other Three Strikers. People say "rehabilitated." I've just been *habilitated.* 'Cause I was always doing wrong, all my life—now I'm learning to do right, for the first time, after fifty years. So yes, to both questions.

E-MAN My way of giving back to those left behind is by hollering at the people that don't nobody come and holler at. Especially all those who we know should be out. Muthafuckas shouldn't have ever have done as much time as we did. We are all true peers.

YAHYA I feel a responsibility to abolish the law, largely because the vast majority of those affected by it are Black and brown people. One of the things that was mind-boggling to me is that when white people were struck out, they were already at retirement age. When Black and brown people were struck out, they were in their youth. I was struck out at twenty-three years old. Those I came across during my prison time . . . we were youth. And so, in my mind, I feel that they were trying to kill off a generation of people with a law. You know what I mean? So, yes, I have this undying loyalty to change the law, and an undying loyalty to those who were left behind.

I do feel very put off by having to go to the board and be treated the same way as somebody who, say, took a baby and threw it out the window, then killed five or six people. Why should I be held to those same standards when I'm in there for a completely nonviolent felony? Why do I have to go sit in front of a psychiatrist or a forensic psychologist and explain all my ills and how I've reconciled with them . . . Just to be found suitable for the board? It's bullshit.

It's way too much time, especially for a law that was initially conceived to curb violent crime from an old white guy who kidnapped and murdered a little white girl. They sold it to the people like that. And as a result, y'all brought a whole bunch of people under this law and gave them life sentences for petty crimes, you know? I feel an inherent duty to repeal that, and I feel beholden to other Three Strikers that have been left behind to help them get out.

NIGEL There's a lot of change happening, and much of it is positive.

EARLONNE Yup. And we have a strong coalition, one that's growing all the time. We are pushing forward to get it on the ballot. Ideally, with time we'll be able to hire a bigger crew as things get better and awareness continues to grow. Our goal is to have a major campaign that's backed by notable hip-hop individuals, like Ice Cube, Blacc Sam, Meek Mill, and Jay-Z—all artists who are already supporting opportunities to make real change in California.

NIGEL We concluded the "Left Behind" episode by hitting the yard in San Quentin to ask, "What gives you hope in prison?" People offered a bunch of different responses—their faith, the programs at San Quentin, working out.

EARLONNE But the most resounding source of hope was clear:

"Getting out. That's all I can hope for. Getting out."

PART III

INSIDE

OUT

CHAPTER TEN

COMMUTATION

EARLONNE From the very beginning of *Ear Hustle,* work-arounds were re-quired. Today, we just expect them. It's how we get shit done.

NIGEL Creating something in prison means working within an institution that has other priorities. Challenges, small and large, are built into *Ear Hustle*'s DNA. One could say the same of any production, but our chal-lenges have always been . . . a little more unusual. There's no manual on how to create a podcast inside a prison. During Season 1, I had to get a clearance level that would enable me to supervise the Media Lab, because the guy who was in charge of it would often decide to leave early, or just not come in at all. For years, it was the only place we could work, so it needed to stay open for as long as possible. On days when I couldn't come in, we had to find a legitimate phone for Earlonne to use so that we could catch up. This could take hours—because guys inside of course can't just pick up a phone whenever it's convenient or required, and calls made to certain people (especially volunteers) have to be made under supervision.

EARLONNE We did what we had to do. Which meant working around un-foreseen lockdowns, when we couldn't communicate, even if we had a strict deadline. We had to figure out what to do when our sound designer, Antwan Williams—who loves fashion and is a damn fine tailor—got in trou-ble for altering his clothes, and we had to work without him for about five months.

NIGEL No matter what the roadblock has been, we've responded with the same attitude: "Okay, let's figure this out." That attitude isn't rooted in ei-ther of us being blind optimists, as much as it's due to our shared determi-nation and tenacity. We believe strongly in the work we do, and even when it's hard—and it's never easy—*Ear Hustle* is bigger than any one person. That belief, along with our friendship, has kept us moving forward.

EARLONNE That's what's up.

NIGEL I think the most significant work-around, for me, was probably Earlonne's commutation. It was such a high point, such a relief, and yet I had no idea how the podcast was going to work or be received without him inside. We had spent three years working together, and had reached a level of synchronicity that we both felt, and that listeners seemed to appreciate.

EARLONNE Luckily, we figured it out real quick.

NIGEL We have different styles, but we understand innately how the other works and thinks. We know each other's strengths and weaknesses, and never need to discuss them in depth; we just adjust ourselves to balance out the other. When we interview somebody together—which is probably 90 percent of the time—we go into it with complete trust that we have each other's back.

I've always relied on that. Interviewing is a mind game. Not in the way something like chess is, where there are opposing sides and aggressive moves of attack. But you are leading the other person into areas of their experience that you want to explore, which requires being several steps ahead, guiding where the conversation is going, but always leaving room for unexpected detours.

EARLONNE We listen closely to where the other is going, and play off the direction either of us is taking the conversation. We just know, without needing to talk about it, who's a better fit to tackle a given area of our conversations. On the flip side, even when an interview is going south, we know how to change lanes, and can also both accept when it's time to call it a day.

We don't just have different styles, we're also very different people. But we delight in allowing the other to reveal their personality over the course of an interview. We don't censor the other's instincts—neither of us could work with a partner who did.

NIGEL I know when Earlonne is going to come in with humor or just the right amount of levity to ease a situation. And he knows I'm likely to push someone to go deeper or into uncharted territory whenever the answers feel canned. After five years, we can do this effortlessly, but when we started out there were times when we wobbled on the humor or the provocation, and we would call each other out. I've always welcomed criticism from Earlonne, because if he takes the time to call me out on something, I know he's right.

Finally, although so much of what we do is serious, the work is infused with joy. The humor and laughing heard throughout the narration are real; those parts aren't scripted. If ever I am scared or nervous, I'll tell Earlonne exactly what I'm feeling, and he never fails to get me past my anxiety.

But personally—and he knows how thrilled I am that he got out of there—I was nervous about going into San Quentin without him. I just couldn't imagine it. This was our creation. We'd been through a lot of hard stuff. I think we surprised ourselves with how hard we work and what we accomplished, and what a great professional relationship we've developed.

EARLONNE Yup. Both quiet, but we found our extroverted selves and did something amazing. We didn't set out to change shit. We just tried to tell stories, and that resonated with people. I knew it was going to be all good, even with my being absent inside.

NIGEL But when you find the person that is your best possible professional partner . . . Well, I hated saying any of this, because I didn't want to make it seem like I didn't want him out. Of course I did. I just didn't know how we'd continue to grow.

EARLONNE Come on, now. You know me, I'm not a worrier. And I definitely wasn't worried about what was going to happen to *Ear Hustle*. But it was indeed a hella looong process, which means we both had a lot of time to wonder about where we were headed.

I know you like to keep track of everything, Nyge. Let's dig into all that and see what we were going through.

———————— ⟨∿∿∿∿⟩ ————————

EARLONNE My commutation process began with filling out an application. It asked things like "What were your previous charges?" After naming the priors, you had to briefly describe the case and answer a question like "Why are you requesting this and therefore why do you deserve to be commuted?"

That alone was really interesting. You have to write down your negative behavior, then your good behavior, then what has rehabilitated you. It took some time to get all that down; it's almost like a résumé—except you're explaining everything about yourself in one document. It brought up a lot of questions that made me consider my youth and the causative factors of how and why I became the person that I did. Why did I start committing crimes? Why couldn't I just stay on the path of going to school and playing sports? A lot of that came up during the interview.

I submitted the application on December 28, 2017, and eventually received an interview with a parole agent named Chan. As soon as we sat down he was like, "I'm going to record this. And if you're lying, we'll disregard you."

It started off with a seemingly simple question: What is your name? "My name is Earlonne Woods," I said, and then, "Well, my name is Walter, legally, but when I was arrested I said my middle name." We went back and forth on this, and he kept pressing me for details. So I was there just thinking, *Wow, this is how it's going to be to start over*. We discussed everything about my history in prison: going to the SHU twice; my write-ups; my 128 Chrono (which is basically a verbal warning).

Then he pointed to my picture on my ID and said, "Man, you gotta start smiling for your pictures. It's important to understand. Presentation is everything. If a person only sees this picture, they'll assume you're standoffish, because you've got a mean mug on." The first thing that popped into my head was, *Twenty years ago, I had a smile on my ID, because I was sure my sentence was going to be reversed on appeal, and I wouldn't be going to prison for long.*

I think I got myself a new ID the next day. And when I left the interview, I initially felt confident that I might get out soon, maybe even within days or weeks or months. But the more I thought about the conversation, the more I felt like I hadn't said everything I wanted to . . . maybe because the stakes were so high. It was like an interview, and the job is whether or not you get the job of exiting this prison and going into society.

I started contemplating what I could have said differently. The dude had told me that if I had any questions or wanted to add anything to my file,

I should just get a letter to my counselor—which I eventually did. I wanted to add that I denounce gangs, because we had talked about my gang history in prison, but we never came back to the fact that I don't deal with gangs anymore, and that I had stopped doing that in like 1995 or 1996, when I got out of prison the first time.

My counselor assured me that she sent my letter to her partner. Hopefully he got it, as it clarified some things. Among them was that, in the crime that sent me to prison for 31 years to life, I had been accused of being the getaway driver—because the car (my Jeep Cherokee) was registered to me. When the victims came to the hospital, they said, "We've never seen him." Nobody identified me as the assailant. Which put me in the driver's seat. When I had the conversation with Chan, I told him, "I've been incarcerated for twenty years. I'm accountable for what I've done. My past life is my past life. I can't change things, but I *can* tell you exactly what actually happened on the night of December 27." I was the one who got out of the car and assaulted this guy. It only dawned on me after our conversation that what I had said is not what the record reflects.

They didn't have the right story in court, and we (myself, Chapple—the actual driver—and Deon Arnold, the passenger in the front) didn't take the stand in our own defense. (I later found out that was the dumbest shit one can do. I hid behind lawyers, because mine instructed me: "You've got a previous history and if you take the stand, they'll bring that up." Regardless of what your lawyers tell you, take the stand to represent yourself. If you don't, the jury assumes you're guilty.) I wrote all this in my letter, breaking it down and ending with "I told you what actually happened. It's not what the record states."

I also wrote about denouncing gangs. Growing up in gangs, we had this mentality where all these people you don't know are your enemies. There's no form of communication. And the cold part is, these are the same guys growing up just like you in poverty, just like you on welfare, probably with single moms. You grew up the same way, you know these dudes' struggles in life, and yet you're enemies, because someone said so and that's what you grew up into.

When I got to a Level IV prison, I remember looking around at these Crips sitting back smoking weed and drinking with their so-called enemies. Once you start talking to people, you get to understand each other, and you forge friendships. It takes people life sentences to finally talk. That changed my perspective.

I'd also been reading a lot of Black history books about the plight of

African Americans in the United States. With everything we were up against, why were we killing one another with this gang shit? All that was on my mind when I first got out of prison. And from the time I was sent back, I never associated with a gang. Dudes knew me, knew who I was and where I was from, but I told them I didn't fuck around with that shit no more. I wanted the commutation board to know that.

I knew I still wouldn't know anything until my board hearing. It could be anytime between then (October 2018) and November 2028 (my initial parole hearing) before anything was resolved. Getting my mindset together to be potentially released was crazy. I'd started to think of what it would mean to return to the real world and take care of shit, like finding a place to stay.

But it was a very profound thought to really consider that I could be free from San Quentin State Prison in 2018. Impossible to not start thinking, *After twenty years, what do I want to do? Who do I want to see?*

The first picture I wanted to take was a silhouette of me looking at a sunset on some beach. That's freedom to me. Walking down the beach and being able to absorb the moment. It's so different than being imprisoned. I wanted to go to the beach and watch as the waves come in. I wanted to jog down that beach if I chose to.

With my freedom, I wanted to reinvent myself as somebody totally different, independent from who I used to be. I wanted to move on with my life. Of course, I wanted to see my mom and my family and a couple of people down south. There were a few friends from inside that I'd keep— people whom I'd known for twenty or thirty years; people who have never wavered and always been there, always had my back. I'd continue those friendships. But if a person hasn't been in my life for the past ten, twenty years, I felt no need to rekindle that. It ain't their fault that I was in prison. But if I haven't been able to call on someone the whole time I've been inside, why should I reinvest in our relationship?

Anyone getting out of prison thinks it's going to be easy, or that he'll be able to acclimate easily or jump into something and get going. I know it's not like that at all. One, you have to find a job. Two, you gotta find some type of stable place to live. You need a wardrobe, furniture, hopefully a car. So you need a lot of stuff—you don't have to have it immediately, but if you want to save money you've got to get on that right away.

I didn't think that was going to be too hard for me. I have the drive and determination to do whatever is necessary. But I knew it would be a challenge to get out and try to establish myself in an area that I knew nothing about. See, I planned to parole in Northern California. At least for my first year. I'd observed that individuals from San Quentin transition into society better in the Bay Area, especially when it comes to jobs and outreach and support. I had friends here, but no family. I could have paroled down to Southern California with my family, but I wanted total change. I wanted to be able to create a new life. I wanted to remain a co-producer of *Ear Hustle*.

Of course, one day I hoped to find love, but I imagined that when I got out I'd just focus on the job. Two jobs. One, hopefully maintaining the podcast and taking it to the next level. But I also wanted to get, like, a construction job. I'm not trying to catch up for nothing.

Twenty years is a long time. When I came to jail, I still had a pager. There were no texts; we didn't have smartphones—none of that shit. The Internet was there but it wasn't cracking like it is today. There was no social media . . . The technology was completely different. I know enough to know the world is a totally different place, one in which people are tethered to their phones. I didn't think I'd be. Maybe, maybe not. Like most things in the future, I couldn't wait to find out.

I'd start in transitional housing, so I will tell stories about what it's like to get out of prison. What it's like to get a girlfriend. That'll be real interesting: Trying to date a girl for the first time. Trying to court a female. What it's like to get out of prison and have sex for the first time. To get out of prison and be rejected by a woman. What everyday life is like. That's the whole idea. Also, while I'm in transitional housing, I'd save as much money as I can, so that when I leave, I'll be okay.

I was a previous homeowner. Bought a home when I was twenty-four or twenty-five. I didn't have it long, of course, because I went to prison. At that time, the housing market would just sell you anything. It was 1997 and I bought the first house I saw. I think it cost me seven thousand dollars. I'd like to have a home again someday. No idea how I will be able to afford it, or where I want it to be. That will come.

To be financially literate and save for a comfortable life is something I've thought about a lot. By 2028, the year I was supposed to get out, I wanted to be hella successful. I thought about writing a book. I wanted to get my license. I had a license before, so hopefully I'll only have to answer a couple of questions or take a test. I wanted to ride a bike around and learn about new terrain. Explore my surroundings. Just learn the roads; how to get from point A to point B, whether I'm using public transportation or driving. What areas are good or bad. All that.

I thought about being able to say, "Hey I'm free. What do I feel like eating? I'm going to go get a nice double-bacon, eggs, and chili-cheese sandwich." Imagine having the freedom of not having to wait for prison food! I wanted to see if McDonald's still got them bomb-ass French fries. And I was looking forward to going grocery shopping. I wanted the freedom to take my time, thinking about what I needed. Like, maybe I'll want to get the ingredients for banana pudding, which ain't that many—just some bananas and some vanilla wafers. (I knew I was gonna make me a shot of banana pudding when I got out.)

I wanted to cook on the grill. Watch TV shows and cook . . . and have to go grab some ingredients and then rewind the show while I cook. I wanted to learn to make exciting stuff. But the first meal I cooked for myself would be something easy. Maybe a steak and mashed potatoes and corn. Yeah. Excited for cooking, going to the barber, putting gas in the car, shopping for clothes.

In terms of my first outfit . . . I got so clowned for mentioning that I wanted five sweat suits when I got out. I'm not too picky. I was just after something that I can go out in for at least the first couple of weeks. A sweat suit's easy, because I didn't really know my size. I'd gained weight in prison. So I would need to go shopping for myself. But I asked people looking out for me to get me five gray sweat suits. What was I gonna say? "Get me a Gucci sweat suit"? I'm low-maintenance; I just wanted to be comfortable.

I mean, if I had a choice and knew my size? In that case, I'd have requested a three-piece suit. With some nice shoes. But I won't be going as extravagant as I used to dress. I used to have what I considered unlimited funds, so would buy all kinds of fancy stuff. This time I knew I'd be going to thrift shops and stuff. Not for my whole wardrobe, but some items.

I was really looking forward to going to see Furman's kids. Over the years, I'd fathered his kids as much as I could, through letters and phone calls. I wanted to be able to hang out with them and answer any questions they may have, you know. My boy would have spent time with his kids.

And, of course, one of my primary goals when I got out was to put another initiative together against the Three Strikes Law. That's a big one, and something I'm very passionate about. A main mission will be to eradicate that. People should do the time they deserve.

I knew I would talk about life in prison—especially to the youth. Maybe go to juvenile halls and talk to them. Catch them in high school and junior high and on probation. Talk to the kids that have one foot in and one foot out. Those are the people that you can reach. I'd try to help by talking about my life inside, especially because my story includes this very powerful thing Nigel and myself created. Against all odds. And partly because we had people in prison that believed in us—one being Lieutenant Robinson. That's one of the nice stories.

I'm pretty comfortable being transparent, but the side I probably would not share as much about is being involved in riots and stuff like that. That might interest some people, because the average person only knows about the prison they see on TV—so if they really want to hear about it, I'll share it. Prisoners do divide themselves. They are segregated by race. If you weren't alive during segregation, you experience it in prison. It was definitely a rude awakening for me, in terms of race relations and the prevalence of intense racism. Every prisoner feels that their race is superior; it's their way or the highway.

I knew I wanted to be forthcoming about all I'd lost in prison. I'd lost a lot. My youth, my waistline . . . but I gained a lot as well. I mean, I'm still alive, still breathing. And I had plenty of things I wanted to do, if I got out.

SAN FRANCISCO BAY AREA / SACRAMENTO
May 2018

NIGEL It's Tuesday, May 15, 2018, at 6:39 a.m. If it were a normal day, I'd be going to the gym, then San Quentin to work with Earlonne. But today is no normal day.

Today I'm driving to Sacramento to go to Earlonne's en banc hearing, which is part of his commutation process. This has been going on for a really long time. Too long. Today we'll find out if his commutation will actually move forward. If it does, he'll be way, way closer to actually getting out of prison. It's amazing.

I hit the road first thing, 'cause I want to get there early and not be all nervous and sweaty. But it's frigging hot, compared to the Bay Area. I've been driving up here for fourteen or fifteen years, as a professor at Sacramento State, so I'm used to the drive. I haven't been going back for a year. I've been on sabbatical, and everything's been about *Ear Hustle*.

Today is about Earlonne and his future. By extension, it's about our future, and where *Ear Hustle* can go if he gets out. I'm going to be meeting up with Alex Mallick (the former associate director at Human Rights Watch in the Bay Area, and cofounder of Re:Store Justice). We'll be reading letters in support of E. and his future.

Obviously, I have a lot of emotions about today. It's, it's . . . a huge thing. Earlonne's a Three Striker with 31 years to life. Been inside for twenty years. I don't know if he ever thought he was going to get out. Actually, that's not true—he did. He's always had hope. That's the kind of person he is. I guess I didn't know if I really thought this could happen. I've certainly hoped this day would come. And once this process started, I had a lot of confidence just based on who Earlonne is. Thank God for Alex; she really pushed this and got him to submit and go through the commutation process.

At ten o'clock, there'll be a hearing in front of a board. It's a public hearing; anyone can go. I think three other incarcerated people are up for commutations before Earlonne. Then his name will come up and anyone there to speak on his behalf will get five minutes. Same goes for anybody who wants to speak against him . . . but I can't imagine that's going to happen. Then they'll make the decision this afternoon. By dinnertime tonight, we're going to know whether or not Earlonne's commutation was approved.

There's more to the process. If granted, it has to go to the governor, to the Supreme Court of California, then back to the governor. Not too sure about the timeline, but we figured it would be December, earliest. We're about to find out. I'm pretty nervous. Not because I don't think he'll get it . . . More because it's an official process with such high stakes. When official things happen, it puts me into a weird state. I don't have control—because it's about a process and not necessarily about individuals.

NIGEL It's 9:00 a.m. and I'm in the parking lot, getting ready to go into the hearing. I'm early; that's just how I fucking am. There's nothing worse than rushing around unprepared. I'm looking at my letter, reading it over. Hopefully when it's my turn, I can say this flawlessly:

Dear Committee,

Thank you for giving me the time to speak today on behalf of Earlonne Woods.

I understand that Earlonne is in prison for the crimes he committed some twenty years ago. And there is no doubt that there was reason for him to be incarcerated. But I want to speak about the man he is today. He is someone who could easily integrate back into society without causing a threat. In fact, he would come back as a contributing citizen . . .

When you first meet Earlonne, he's very quiet. He's a listener. Someone who carefully observes what's happening around him. He isn't the kind of person who tells you everything about himself the first time you meet him, he's what I call a slow reveal . . . He has no time for the drama or getting involved with the petty things that inevitably happen when you work in a situation where resources are scarce . . .

The creation of *Ear Hustle* is a perfect example of the man Earlonne is today. He is smart, dedicated, extraordinarily hardworking, trustworthy, and very creative. He possesses all of the assets that make him the person I want to work with, whether he's in prison or out. If and when Earlonne is released, I will be there to be part of his support system.

Our plan is to continue to work together on *Ear Hustle* and to figure out how to keep it about life inside—while also focusing on the very complex issue of re-entry, post-incarceration. I truly believe that Earlonne is ready for this next step, and that if given the chance he will leave the prison and enter a community of people who are ready to support him as he transitions back to being a free citizen.

Thank you,

Nigel Poor

I hope that's good enough. How could they say no, with all that he has done and is doing? It doesn't make sense. It's gotta be a yes.

NIGEL Now I'm in front of the Capitol Center, 1515 K Street. Waiting. Not sure what to expect. I imagine there's going to be a lot of hanging around before we get an opportunity to speak. It's interesting to be here—it's so much more beautiful than I remember. The trees are full and it smells so good. It feels like it's going to be a successful day. A day of possibilities. Good possibilities for Earlonne. Going up now. Getting into the elevator and heading to the fifth floor, where I'll be meeting Alex, as well as E.'s friend Joy.

ALEX Hey, Nigel! You're kind of dressed up.

NIGEL Yeah . . . I'm more nervous than I thought I was going to be.

ALEX I'm nervous, too. I am. I mean, just, this is a big day for Earlonne.

NIGEL I know. And it feels different. It's so official.

ALEX Did you see Earlonne yesterday? He knows this is happening, right? He got a letter.

NIGEL Yes, he was very cool.

ALEX He always is.

NIGEL At the very end, I was like, "You know, this is a big day," and he kind of underplayed it. But then he was like, "Yeah, it is. It's a big day. I'm gonna hate waiting."

ALEX They'll have the results later tonight. Then the governor decides to commute or not, and then it goes to the state supreme court. He needs a majority vote since he's a Third Striker. Struck out twice in one go, and for his last crime they used those juvenile offenses.

NIGEL Yeah, but if it gets passed here, it'd be hard for it to not go forward, right?

ALEX I think so.

NIGEL It's 11:30 a.m., and the commutation hearing is over. I don't know what to think. It seemed really great. Five of us spoke on Earlonne's behalf, saying wonderful things about him—about who he is, what he's doing. But then we were all shocked when the representative from the LA district attorney's office stood to speak against him. She said of course they were against the commutation, and that it should be immediately made void because Earlonne had perjured himself on the application. Then she said he has not been an exemplary inmate, and that he'd been involved in underground economy in prison, and has not been sober for as long as he says. It was a very odd process. With my bad memory, it was hard to take everything in, because of my shock. So, I don't know. I still feel really positive about it. He's going to get it. I just wasn't expecting to hear anybody speak against him.

Alex is going to San Quentin. I could go, but it's all so emotional. I need to take it in. It's great; Alex'll explain everything to Earlonne. She understands the process, and knows the ins and outs of the criminal justice system more comprehensively than I do.

I'm still worried about Earlonne. I know he's super strong; I know he'll act like, "Okay, it's the process." But I was hoping I'd be able to say, "It was a slam dunk," or that there wasn't anything that seemed like a potential hiccup or a bump in the road.

I'll check . . . in a few hours. I need to figure out how to get to the damn parole board hearing decisions. Finding stuff online is not my strong suit.

NIGEL I'm loading up the website. CDCR. Board of Parole hearing outcomes for everyone heard today, Tuesday, May 15, 2018. All right. "Belinda Anderson. Governor grants commutation of sentence." Deep breath. "Larry Martinez . . ."

"Earlonne Woods: Sentencing court, Los Angeles, governor referral, pursuant of Penal Code, section 4802. The application of Earlonne Woods for commutation of sentence, the Board with the majority of commissioners concurring, hereby makes the recommendation required by Penal Code 4813 for the governor to grant a commutation of sentence."

Makes the recommendation for the governor to grant it. Wow. That's the first step down a long road before Earlonne gets released. But it went through; this was the hard step. The board approved it. Now to the governor. I know how long this process will take. But it's happening. It's happening.

SAN QUENTIN
August 2018

NIGEL Hey, what's the date today?

EARLONNE Monday, August 13.

NIGEL What's special about it?

EARLONNE Aw, you made the effort to come in today. You're so sweet.

NIGEL I love Mondays—it's always a chance to start over again. Most people hate to go to work on Mondays. It depends on how much they partied or relaxed. When you're fortunate enough to love what you do, Mondays are special. But of course this one is particularly special, isn't it?

EARLONNE Yup! Today is special because it is the day that my mother went through a long labor with me. She always tells me that my birthday is not until 10:42 p.m. on August 13.

NIGEL How many birthdays have you spent in prison?

EARLONNE I have spent a total of twenty-seven or twenty-eight birthdays in prison. It's nice that this check-in just so happened to be on my forty-seventh birthday. Now I know what it feels like to be forty-seven. Just making it is good, you know? Life ain't promised, and prison is the worst spot to die, to me. It's like you've been stripped of everything. You don't get to get out and see your family or anything. It's just . . . over. I'm hoping I survive to get out and be free.

NIGEL What's going on with the commutation process?

EARLONNE Well, it's definitely a process. You know I sent in the application, had the interview, then you went to the en banc hearing and the Board of Prison Terms approved it back in May. After that, they sent the paperwork on to the Supreme Court of California. They sent the approval to the governor's office, and the governor's office wrote the report on what will be later the commutation certificate. That was sent on July 16, 2018. And now I'm on the docket list. The next thing I hear will be a date and time. That's where I'm at: waiting to get processed.

NIGEL Day to day, what's it been like to be in prison, knowing that it's most likely coming to an end? Has it changed the way you look at your life here?

EARLONNE Not at all. No, I haven't changed one bit. I mean, you know, we clown. But at the end of the day, I'm still here. It's not reality yet. But it's very uplifting to think that, very soon—after twenty-one years of prison—it could be over. I'm ready for it.

NIGEL What are you ready for?

EARLONNE All kinds of stuff. You know, love. I do want to be loved. I'm just going to be dating for a while, but I'm sure this new world of romance will be interesting. I'm more concerned with setting my path, though. You've heard me say that a person getting out of prison is $25,000 in the hole, because you have nothing—especially if you just get out with like $200, entering a world where that won't even get you across to the bridge. My main objective is to deal with *Ear Hustle* and jobs and get my 401(k) or 457 or one of them together and start building a future. Dating will come, but that's not my priority.

NIGEL We're about to return to work. We've had so many different struggles, trials, tribulations. We've had lockdowns. We've had construction. And now we're trying to get back into it. All kinds of things . . . It's going to be an interesting time.

SAN QUENTIN
September 2018

NIGEL Through all the relief and excitement about Earlonne's commutation, when it finally became real, we came together to figure out who was going to "take his place." I was never able to use the word "replace"; the very notion of doing so provoked anxiety.

But we both knew I needed a co-host inside. We set out to find him by presenting it as a professional job search. We were only going to hire one person, but figured it would be helpful to others to put in the time to present themselves for the position. We wanted it to be fair, and needed somebody who would be reliable and dedicated.

We wrote up a job description and explained the application process, then posted it around the prison. We asked for a résumé, a letter of interest explaining why they were right for the position, and requested applicants to tell us which was their favorite episode, and why they connected with it.

EARLONNE About thirty men applied. Most, if not all, stopped me—on the yard, in the housing unit, even naked in the shower—to ask about it. I didn't let on, but I had a couple of favorites, dudes who would do a good job and also protect the integrity of our program.

NIGEL We whittled it down to ten we wanted to interview. We brought each one to the Media Lab, and from those discussions selected three. The final stage required them to pitch us a story idea, get on the computer and try their hand at editing, and to study a script and record narration with me. Lieutenant Robinson suggested that we diversify the team, so we did our best to interview men from all races. In the end, however, our three strongest candidates were Black. Each was promising, and it seemed like it was going to be impossible to make a choice. They all fared well pitching a story and editing. The decision would be made based on how they worked with me on the mic doing narration.

Hopefully we make narrating a story sound easy, like two friends hanging out and talking about rather challenging subjects. That's how we engage, but striking that tone takes time and effort to achieve. Some of what you hear in an episode is scripted, keeping us on point, but a lot of it is improv. You have to be able to do several takes and keep it sounding spontaneous. A lot of people have the gift of gab and can be very funny and engaging—but you never know how they'll respond when the presence of a microphone is introduced. Many people either freeze up and sound stiff, or step into a larger-than-life persona that sounds phony—neither is the type of personality we wanted. You also have to prepare and actually read the script. It's impossible to just do it cold.

Before we did the final interviews, we ranked our remaining three candidates. They're all great human beings, and it's not in either of our natures to grade people, but we knew we needed to note any flaws or mistakes in their narration. Saying no to people you care about is hard. I hate to hurt people's feelings.

EARLONNE But, Nyge, I'm always telling you: this is business, we can't take it personally. So on the day of the narration tryouts, they did us a favor and made the decision easy. The first candidate hadn't looked at the script before he got on the mic, and really blew it. As good as he was at every other part, his lack of preparation took him out of the running.

NIGEL The second candidate was dedicated and prepared—but unfortunately there was an unforeseen issue with his ability to have banter. On mic, his mouth clicked and made distracting sounds. We hated to rule him out; everything else was ideal.

Our third candidate was a little performative, but we could both see that once he relaxed into the process he was going to be great—as a bonus, he had the best laugh around, and we knew he was a super-hard worker. So, after the long application process, we offered Rahsaan "New York" Thomas the job, making him our new inside co-host.

Turns out we liked the second candidate so much that we made a job for him as well, bringing on John "Yahya" Johnson as a producer.

EARLONNE See? It takes two guys to replace me.

NIGEL Sorry, my friend, it was never a replacement. New York and Yahya are *additions* to the *Ear Hustle* family.

EARLONNE Okay, okay. I know you have to say that. Either way, they were a crucial part of enabling us to work around my hopeful, forthcoming release from San Quentin.

SAN QUENTIN
September 2018

EARLONNE Today is September 17, 2018. The commutation process continues. A couple guys have left. My case is waiting to go to the supreme court. But I'm in line. My family members will be alerted when the case moves.

NIGEL I've noticed a change in you in the last month. You know what I'm talking about?

EARLONNE Nope.

NIGEL I feel like you are finally starting to talk about your life like you are actually getting out. Before, when I'd ask about the future, you never wanted to talk about it. It feels real now. I hear you talking about things outside, so I wonder if you actually feel differently.

EARLONNE The only thing I've been talking about is a black *Ear Hustle* T-shirt. Everybody has these maroon and gray ones, but I want a black one. Nah, I believe the time is coming to an end. I'm just sitting and waiting. Someone came through the other day and she was like, "Aren't you stressed out?" I'm like, "Not really." We got too much work to be doing for me to even consider being stressed out about the date. I'll be ready.

NIGEL I used to ask, "Are you excited?" You'd say, "Nigel, I've been in prison too long to count on anything or think it's going to happen." That doesn't seem to be your attitude now.

EARLONNE It's getting close. Even back then, I was prepared to be released. And it's not real yet—the final mechanisms haven't happened. Governor has to say, "I've commuted your sentence." At that point, I'll have seven days left. Until then, I'm still a lifer.

NIGEL I just wanted to put it out there that my sense is that you're more positive about it.

EARLONNE It wakes you up. When I was writing down my thoughts of my past time in prison, I remember talking about being on a slave ship. You're on this bus with shackles on your ankles, shackled to your waist, and everybody's shackled. You're looking out the window. Just looking in the cars that drive by, wishing you were in those cars. Wishing you could be free, driving a car, being the passenger, being in the back seat. Anywhere except for where you are. But you're not. You're stuck on this bus, going to some other prison. But in those moments you also get to be mentally free: you're out on the freeway with regular people. In prison, you don't see that. You just see the everyday monotony.

NIGEL I'll ask again. When I see you next time, in your fantasy, what happens? Who's out there; what do you do? You should think about it, because maybe you do want it to just be private with one special person. Maybe you want more. It's going to happen fast, and people are going to want to know. There could be press there. Who knows?

EARLONNE My only goal, or fantasy, is to look in the rearview mirror as San Quentin gets smaller and smaller. There's a lot of projects we can finish. I just want to continue onwards.

Who knows when it will be. You can come up with a good idea, but nobody will know when that day arrives. When it does, it can be small as an Uber driver. And as big as the few people who want to be there. Well, of course you're going to be out there.

NIGEL I plan to be, but I don't want to crowd you.

EARLONNE Come on, Nyge. You'd never be crowding me, plus you're going to have to record. It's going to be fun. If the press is there, we are not going to talk on San Quentin grounds. No conversations, no interviews. We can get in the car and go wherever, but we won't be in San Quentin during this interview.

My mom was like, "I want to come up, yeah, I want to be there." I'm like, "Hell, NO." I want to see her, but just a little later. You know what I'm saying? I want to see people much later, because this will be the day I'm out, and I want to get out. I've done enough time here.

NIGEL Sam will be there.

EARLONNE My whole incarceration at San Quentin, Lieutenant Robinson has been a stand-up dude. Just the same person that I met the first time. He's not a switch-wheel type. He's just . . . He's his way. He's always been straight with me, always calls it how he sees it. He's not here to press you. He's the person that gives everybody the opportunity. It's up to you to fuck that opportunity. And, of course, you know he's the person who gave us the go-ahead. Yeah, I will shake his hand, probably give him a cool hug, because he's been there.

SAN QUENTIN
November 2018

NIGEL So it was Election Day yesterday. November 6.

EARLONNE I know! Gavin Newsom for California, which was very interesting.

NIGEL What's your intuition telling you about any impending circumstances?

EARLONNE I have no intuition. I try my best not to occupy time and space for things that are not in my control. If it's not in my control, I try to say, "If it happens, it happens." But I do hope that it happens before Governor Brown leaves office. As long as it's before January 6, I'm good. It could happen this month.

NIGEL It could happen tomorrow. You don't have any feeling, one way or the other?

EARLONNE I'm not really trippin', but I am doing things to position me, *just in case.*

NIGEL Like what?

EARLONNE Like getting rid of excess stuff in my property. I shredded all of my transcripts.

NIGEL Was that a big deal? How many folders did you have?

EARLONNE It wasn't a big deal. You get tired of lugging that stuff around. Even though it's supposed to help you . . . it won't. I counted nine binders. Four from the preliminary hearing. Five from the trial. Probably about twenty pounds. It was hella heavy.

NIGEL By shredding, do you feel like you're saying, "I don't need this anymore and all my legal briefs, all my habeas corpus, is rid of search queries to the United States courts"?

EARLONNE It was more like, "This better work. If it don't . . . I'm really gonna need these back."

NIGEL Please tell me you recorded the sound of the shredder.

EARLONNE Of course! Shredding them was crazy. You start looking at shit that I might need in the future . . . whether to write a book and put a certain portion of it in there—like how in my case I knew the prosecutor kicked off all the Blacks on the jury. When we had the Batson-Wheeler motion, which is supposed to be on the record, the judge called everybody in chambers off-site. It was a trip. I sat in my cell for months with a graph outline of jurors. I had the numbers and was cataloging them by race. So, there was stuff like that.

NIGEL The fact that you shredded all that is such a big sign that you believe you're getting out. I mean . . . it was kind of reckless.

EARLONNE It was *very* reckless! But it was me saying, "I won't need this no more."

NIGEL How else are you preparing?

EARLONNE I'm having as many in-depth conversations as possible with Trevor, my brother. Ever since he got transferred to San Quentin a year and a half ago, and we celled up together, you know he's been talking a lot. But I don't really respond. Not for any reason, just that when I get back to the cell, it's my time to do me and think, listen to music, or just kick it and read. He gets the brunt of that, because I'm not talkative. But over the next month, I'm gonna engage him in conversation. I always tell him, "You dredge up old shit that should be dead and gone. It has no relevance." I'm not here to discuss some "Remember forty years ago, when you did this or you didn't do this?" I'm not into that. I'm about today. But there's a lot of things that, if he's granted the opportunity to be released, I want to do, family-wise.

NIGEL What are you hoping to resolve with him before you leave?

EARLONNE I won't be able to resolve shit, but I'm thinking of asking if there's anything he needs me specifically to do. He's very creative. He's a writer. Writes books and shit.

NIGEL I know I keep asking you this, but I haven't gotten an answer. Tell me what you want to have happen the day you get out.

EARLONNE What I *don't* want is for too much stuff to happen at the front gate. We can have a brief conversation, but the mission is to move it away from San Quentin. It's cool to be on that side of the gate but I want to get on the road. And we can continue recording.

This is going to be a moment that in my life will never happen again. So, it would be good for the story to own it. So, yes, I would like you to be out there.

I don't expect my family to be there. When I got out of prison before, my mother, my father, and my three sisters came to get me. Which was cool. But I've done that one.

I mean . . . I might have a limo come get me.

NIGEL Are you kidding?

EARLONNE I'm thinking about it. Bottom line, I just want to get away from here. I'm not trying to make it a shrine and shit, oh no. How long by the gate before we get the hell out?

NIGEL Where will we go?

EARLONNE Away from here. Let's say that when we get in the car we'll say what's next? You say what the destination is. I like the idea of a limo because nobody has to drive. We can just sit back and have an interview, just talk.

EARLONNE Today is November 20.

NIGEL You just made the funniest smile.

EARLONNE Well, I'm smiling because I have a notion in my head that the governor's possibly commuting my sentence tomorrow, on the eve of a religious situation. People show more mercy around religious holidays. More blessings.

The first thing I'm going to do, after going to the beach, is take a bath. Oh, hell yeah. And I'm talking about sitting in it long enough to let water out and pour more hot water in, for sure. I might try some oils or something. Just kick back. No phone, no nothing, just myself.

NIGEL What have you been doing?

EARLONNE I went to the prison canteen and spent $220, using the funds from my prison bank account—that's the max. In my mind, I was thinking I would just give it to my brother. I've been downsizing; throwing away all this stuff that I've been hoarding over twenty-one years. All the old paper-work, old cards that I usually keep.

I threw away my handcuff key along with those nine volumes of transcripts from the court. I've had them for probably like twelve years.

NIGEL You shredded them all. What does that represent to you?

EARLONNE That I hope that chapter of my life is over. That conviction is done. That I'm on my way home. If I'm not, I'll be paying a lot of money to reorder those damn transcripts.

NIGEL You know those little funny-looking pins that hold them together? I took them. I'll keep them safe. They're interesting . . . objects. When you leave, how many boxes will you have?

EARLONNE Well, speaking of boxes, I did another preemptive move. I packed up everything that's important to me. Mainly letters from my parents and my nephew Tyler, who was killed by the police. Most of the pictures I gave to my bro, but there were a few that I wanted. Two volumes, from beginning to end. Mailed them to the transition house that I'll be paroled into. The only thing I took out was my birth certificate.

NIGEL It feels very real. It's going to be a big adjustment. For you, of course, but also for the show. I wonder what listeners are going to think. They're going to be so glad you're out, but we hear a lot about how people like *Ear Hustle* because of our special, not overly familiar relationship. That's going to be different. I'm worried about who's going to control all the shit that happens here. You end all the bullshit, and that's so important.

EARLONNE That's just politics.

NIGEL You have very good politics. I don't know about prison politics. I'll learn.

EARLONNE I'll be able to interact with people and reassure them that everything's in good hands. That it's not over. People will understand quickly that it's just going to be different stories, not different personalities. And I'm certain that you, Nyge, will be just fine.

MEDIA LAB, SAN QUENTIN
Late November 2018

EARLONNE It's Wednesday, November 21, 1:45 p.m. Today, I got a call down here in the media center, from the warden's office. They told me to report to the captain, where I was then sent to the commutation place. I've never been to the captain's porch before—it's huge. They got a shoeshine spot in there!

A lady was waiting, and she took me to the associate warden's office. He called a lawyer from the governor's office. She said my name and I said, "Yes, that's me."

She said, "The governor feels that you've been running a great program and you're doing the work. So, he would like to commute your sentence immediately." Then she added, "And of course we love the podcast." All I could say was "Thank you." I mean, you have nothing left to say . . . The only thing I added was, "Please thank the governor, and tell him I won't let him down." Then she thanked me for calling in.

They took me to the lieutenant's office (which is just a few doors over from the associate warden's office), and when I got there they let me make a call. So I called my mom. When she picked up I was like, "Is this the mother of Earlonne Woods?" She said, "Well, it sounds like Earlonne Woods is . . . talking!?" Anyway, I laughed and told her, "Mama, it finally came. They commuted my sentence today." And she went through it. My mother is very religious, so she praised the Lord like a hundred times, which was cool. She was real happy. Then she said, "Oh my God, I'm so happy! My God, I get to have a man around the house!"

Walking back down here, the associate warden was like, "I feel happy for you." So that was cool. One of the officers knew, but he just sort of smiled and was like, "Let's go." It was interesting, a real special walk. Yeah. And there'll be more people called up today.

NIGEL You could be out Tuesday, Wednesday. There's so much to talk about. But let's take a moment, and consider who you were twenty-one years ago. Can you describe him to me?

EARLONNE I had given up on life, pretty much. I didn't have any real skills. I paroled from my first time in prison when I was about to turn twenty-four. I still hadn't completed my GED. I didn't have any certificates, no trades, none of that. So, I got back out into the world and took a few jobs, all under the table. I helped remodel a house and got paid a few dollars. I mean I was like, "Man, I just put in eight hours a day for two weeks and I got two hundred dollars?"

After a time, I pretty much gave up. When you give up, it becomes all about "I'm gonna get my money the best way I can." I knew what I knew best. Once you are successful, that's when it all goes bad. From then on you got to keep up a certain status, along with your bills. You start buying shit—houses, cars. You keep the hustle going.

In terms of what made me say, "I'm going to get my money off of other people"? I'd have to go back further, to when I was fourteen or fifteen and my mother was pretty much the only breadwinner in the house. We never had any extra money. Bills would be paid and we lived in a house, you know? So, we weren't poor. But if I wanted, say, a pair of Jordans, I couldn't get them. I was attracted to street life because we went out and made a lot of money, from a very young age. It was easy to get addicted to making fast money. I didn't work, and I had a father who was in the streets hustling, so I got into taking money. After my brother and I committed that first drug dealer robbery I was like, *I'm rich.* My mother was making like forty thousand dollars a year, and we made sixty grand in like ten minutes. You get engulfed in that lifestyle. You partying and you have no financial literacy, so you're fucking the money off as easy as it come. You feel like, I can go back out and get this.

On a personal level, I'd say I was always a cool dude. Just normal, humble—not a person that's around a lot of crowds or stuff like that. I was just a regular dude. And I tried my best to get jobs when I was out, but couldn't. Nobody would call me back. I played out living with people or begging for money—I didn't want that life.

NIGEL Once you made the decision you were going to go back to robbing people, how did you think your life was going to play out?

EARLONNE You always think, *I'm just gonna do it once, then make money to do something else.* Never works out that way. You get hooked. Crime is like drugs. You put in the time, just like people who work. Your work is crime sprees. It's a cold way of living; it's a cold way of life.

NIGEL What's changed? You're going to get out, but you're not going to go back to that.

EARLONNE When Furman was shot by the police and killed and I went to prison. That changed my perspective. He was the first person that I was around a lot—my road dog—and he was taken. He was really the first person I was close to who was killed in my presence.

We always had a philosophy of life or death, meaning we were going to run this and get ours—to the death, or whatever. When he died and I was in the hospital, the doctors and a detective brought me Polaroid pictures of him deceased, with tubes coming out and all that. I was looking at the picture and the reality of his death hurt so much. It was like, *For what? Why did he die? He didn't have a gun. Why did they shoot him?*

All of that was in my head, and I'm looking in and out, and finally was like, *You know what? I'm done with this life. Regardless of the situation, even if I get sentenced, I'm done.* On top of all that, for about fifteen months, I was charged for Furman's murder.

NIGEL That makes . . . no sense.

EARLONNE In their words, "Defendants, especially defendant Woods, performed provocative acts that proximately caused the officers to fear for their lives and shoot at all of the defendants, resulting in the death of Furman Little." Based on that language, Chapple Sims, Deon Arnold, and I were not just grieving—we were looking at a first-degree murder charge for my best friend's death. These officers lied about two things: one was me being the driver, when in fact I was sitting behind him (the video angle didn't reveal as much); and, two, they claimed that they saw a muzzle flash coming from my direction, which was what made them draw their guns. Imagine my relief that *that* angle *was* caught on video, and made plain that the officers opened fire without being provoked by any of the bullshit they had presented.

As I mentioned, a light switched on. I was done with gangs, done with that lifestyle. It never got me nothing but a long time in prison. I would have lived on the streets as an alternative to going back to prison. But I never went home and never got out.

Once I decided to refrain from the pretending—the preteen persona that I had picked up in the streets—and when I peeled all that shit off, I was back to a more authentic self.

NIGEL People always seem surprised when someone's been in prison for a long time and they change. But that's human nature. As you grow up and have more decades on this planet, you get more experience. It seems bizarre to me that people think someone wouldn't change.

EARLONNE Yeah, it's true. People change. Their ideologies become different. Especially if you *want* to. But some places don't allow you the space to do so. You may want to change your life in prison, but you could be in a war zone where people don't know you and are caught up in, let's say, race and politics. San Quentin's the flagship because you don't just have space to change, you have like seventy different programs to help you do it. In prison.

For me, my change always goes back to Furman. Knowing that he got killed based on some bullshit really affected me. No one needed to die that night. Knowing that if I had been running a hair faster the bullet would have penetrated my ribcage and heart . . . it's a lot. And I had a lot of time to think about it. It makes you say, "Enough. This shit ain't for me."

Then this crazy Three Strikes sentence. The sad part about having a lengthy sentence is that you just gotta do it. Because I don't believe in suicide. I don't have enough heart to kill myself. It was what it was. A no-hope situation. But I chose not to have that attitude. Instead, for a while I would smoke weed every day and try to train that shit away and just stay occupied and stay busy. At some point I stopped smoking, because I've always dreamed of getting out of prison and always figured that I'd get out somehow. I needed that clarity. That's when I started going to the law library and reading up on election codes to understand the initiative process.

NIGEL So getting involved politically is what kind of snapped you into being more awake?

EARLONNE Well, no, it was really the restorative justice group. I didn't even join the group, I'd just show up and sit in circles talking to victims of crime. Processing the impact that my life had on others solidified my decision to change my own life. That was very profound for me.

NIGEL So what do you think you've missed out on from being in prison for twenty years?

EARLONNE Time that I can't get back. I've lost twenty-one years of my life. I've missed out on family, friends, kids. It's so much; I can't put it into words. The main thing is family. Missing out on that has been hella stressful. My mother . . .

Plus, I missed out on just being able to get up and go to Magic Mountain, just because I had the free time to go. That freedom to get up and do what I want. I missed out on taking a shower by myself, on taking a dump by myself (otherwise known as taking the Browns to the Super Bowl).

I mean, of course prison hasn't been a total waste. I know that. I gained work. I completed five trades; really took them seriously. Took graphic arts. I'm proficient in computers. I completed an auto-body and auto-paint trade. And my work ethic is strong, as you know.

NIGEL Is there anything you're going to miss about prison?

EARLONNE Nothing. I'll say it like it is: prison sucks. I mean, there's a lot of things that you don't have to worry about, like paying rent and shit. And of course, most of all, I'll miss my brother. He's going to be stuck in here, but I'm going to do what I can do for him.

I'll miss doing the inside interviews for *Ear Hustle*. When we first sat down to talk about how we could share stories from inside prison, and worked on the idea for a podcast . . . that was dope. The details, doing the stories, bringing in Antwan for sound, all that. To see that idea go from nothing to us creating a podcast, to millions of people downloading it—that has been amazing. That's our history. And we're not stopping. I'll be a better spokesperson for guys in prison when I'm on the streets, doing this work.

But this will always be the place where we started that career. I didn't know anything about podcasts, then in you come, Nyge, this little white lady. And here we are. Our stories are being heard all around the world . . . It's crazy. Proof that no matter where you're at in life, you can effect change. That's been the highlight of my time inside. Sitting here creating stories and being supported and being co-hosts. Since we started, my life has been in this place.

And yes, I'll be leaving some good dudes behind, but it's my turn. Hopefully soon to be theirs. I'll miss Lieutenant Robinson.

But I'm not going to miss anything about being incarcerated. I'll never miss being strip-searched. No, I will not squat over and bend and cough and open up my ass cheeks. Never again.

And don't worry about us. We're going to do bigger and bigger things. We can keep it going. We'll figure it out . . . when I'm back from vacation.

NIGEL I know. Change is good. *This* change is great. But it's going to be a hard transition. How are we going to move this in a different direction once you're out? What are you thinking?

EARLONNE We've crafted a style or a technique where we're able to put windows in these walls, like we've been saying. Letting people from the outside see in. When I parole, we'll be able to do different types of stories. We'll go to different prisons, prisons in other states, prisons in other countries, you know. Just continue the work of telling stories.

NIGEL So, I don't need another co-host?

EARLONNE Yes, you do. San Quentin is our home. San Quentin is the birth of *Ear Hustle*. San Quentin is always going to be like that. The work that we'll do in the future is going to be different, but there will still be a place for it. *Ear Hustle* will always be our creed. That's never going to change, that's going to always be there. You know that's never going to change.

SAN QUENTIN
November 30, 2018

EARLONNE There I was, sitting in a holding cell, waiting to be released. I was also waiting to feel some kind of relief, because up to that point, the process of getting out had been weird as fuck. They were late coming to get me in the morning, which allowed me to get some much-needed sleep. I guess that was cool, but I kind of wanted the whole experience of waking up at like 2:00 a.m. and going through the process. At 4:20 a.m., the night officer came and woke me and told me to report to R&R after breakfast for release.

It was all sort of out-of-body. I got out of bed, washed up, and continued to clean up the mess I had made the night before. My bro had to get a new ID, which was his way of being able to walk me out. When we got to R&R, I gave Bro a kiss on the cheek and he did the same, saying, "Enjoy your freedom, man . . . Damn, I wish I could go with you."

After that, I had to just sit there, waiting on some parole officers somewhere in Fontana, California, to sign my paperwork. They were handling it all like this was some last-minute decision. I guess they were giving me my last opportunity to just sit in the tank—which was about the size of the cell I just vacated—waiting.

Just before the officer came to get me, Brown (the cellie of New York, my boy who we had chosen as the new inside co-host of *Ear Hustle*), who works in R&R, brought me my dress-out box. He came to the door with a tiny box with my last name on it. *Damn,* I thought, *that's a little-ass box. How could all my clothes fit in there?* I knew my mom, nephew, and Tyra (my nephew's mother) had sent me a couple of sweat suits, socks, underwear, and a pair of Nike Air Max 270 shoes to stride out in.

"Do you know what's in your box?" Brown asked. I got to naming stuff, and as I was doing so he held the box below the tray slot. I couldn't really see what was in there, only that there was something orange inside. I extended my arm through the slot and into the box, grabbed hold of some fabric, and pulled it into the holding cell. It was an orange prison jumpsuit that said "CDCR PRISONER" on it. Fuckin' New York. I laughed my ass off, thinking about the lengths he had gone to, to make sure he got to fool me on the way out.

After a while, which felt like a real long time, the officer had me sign for my real box. Inside was a black *Ear Hustle* T-shirt. It's a one-off; nobody else has this one. I immediately put on the street clothes. Pulling on that T-shirt felt amazing, with the soft fabric and all. I was so ready. But the crazy part is that I was still sitting in this empty cell, wondering how far behind I was from the other guys who were paroling that day. Would it be an hour? Two? All day? I had heard there was a whole camera crew outside waiting to pick me up and film me as I left San Quentin. Nigel, Julie Shapiro, our producer Pat, Emily Harris (who worked at the Ella Baker Center and used to call Sacramento and pester the powers that be on my behalf), and whomever else was supposed to be out there, waiting. The last time I spoke with Nyge, our plan was to go to breakfast.

It was probably around 9:00 a.m. by that point. Almost real. I got word that Tim Thompson, who was commuted the same day I was, and another guy had just left for release. I started getting nervous. Or just confused. This wasn't making any sense to me at all. How could there be one signature holding me up? What the fuck? Why wasn't I on the bridge by now, up out of this joint? That's what I would have loved. That's where I was supposed to be. Instead, I was stuck in a holding cage, with every minute dragging by like it was an hour. I started pacing back and forth, reading a California driver's handbook that got boring because my mind couldn't focus. *Did something get fucked up here? What if the Fontana parole office was closed and they don't sign off today?* All kinds of shit was racing through my mind. It was stressful as fuck. I kept getting distracted, wondering how Nigel and crew were doing with my delayed release. And then: *I WANT OUT!!!*

NIGEL I had been in that familiar parking lot for hours by that point. I had gotten up super early, because there was no way I wasn't going to be there waiting for E. when he stepped out of prison. I don't even know if I slept the night before. But I knew from being at the gate to meet other guys that no one ever comes out early. Just in case, however, I got there when it was still dark out.

I sat in my car and watched as the sky went from being dark to early dawn, to the sunrise lighting up the scene, to late morning. I knew he would be driven out in a van, so every time I saw a van my heart sped up and I got excited, thinking it would be him. After maybe four false starts, I accepted I was going to be waiting out there for a while.

EARLONNE My anxious mind got some relief when Officer Eagan came to the door, telling me that the counselor was on her way with my parole papers, which I clearly hadn't signed the day before. Finally, at 9:40 a.m., my counselor Ms. Howard arrived, had me sign papers, and hit me with a few words of encouragement: "I know I ain't gotta worry about seeing you again," she said. Then she took my parole papers and told me she had to run them upstairs to Records, and that I would be released within an hour. Sheesh. The paperwork I signed said, "Lifer's Special Conditions: five years parole." Hmm. I would argue that shit later. In that moment, I was signing under duress. I wanted out, and that's it. Finally, I had heard the words I'd been waiting for: "Woods, let's go . . ."

The holding tank opened and I grabbed my box of things. I walked out of R&R and stood next to a white prison van with two officers sitting in it. They'd be driving me off of the property. One of them asked me to state my name, CDCR prison number, and date of birth. "Earlonne Woods; P35554; August 13, 1971," I said. Before stepping into the van, I looked around at the yard. Someone yelled, "Stay up, E.! Don't forget about us!"

I got in, the van engine turned on, and we drove out of the gated area that R&R sits in. As we slowly curved around the yard, I looked at the people outside and at the tennis courts, at the geese on the baseball field, and the education building beyond it. Finally, I looked at the media center, where the trajectory of my life had been forever changed. I could only absorb it for the moment, while trying to ignore the officers up front talking shit about another officer's overtime or something.

We turned the corner and hit this long straightaway to the gate that would let us out of the back of the institution. We passed the back of the media center, the family-visiting duplex, then were at a gate where a guard looked under the van with a mirror on a stick and then looked under the hood. He opened the sliding door with some paperwork in his hand, and looked at my picture before studying my face carefully. He then asked the same questions: name, CDCR number, and date of birth.

OFFICER All good here. Enjoy your freedom, Mr. Woods.

EARLONNE We proceeded through a double gate. Once it closed behind us, the other gate in front of us opened. The sight was fucking amazing! All I saw as the van circled the outside of the institution was a huge body of water that you can't see when you're on the other side of that thirty-foot wall. The feeling of being on this side in that van was the moment I had longed for for so many years. Shit, it's what everyone dreams of, and there I was, taking it in. As we got to the front of the institution we passed a tower, where a sergeant approached the van, asked me to exit, had me repeat the answers to the same three questions, and sent us on our way.

Right as I was getting back in the van I saw two cool-ass officers: CO McGee and CO Smitty. They were like, "Bro! You looking good. Praise God!" I responded with a smile and a wave, and off we were to see everyone waiting on me.

NIGEL Finally, around 10:00 a.m., the white van carrying E. came out. People always talk about walking out the gate but that isn't what happens, at least not at San Quentin. Guys have to be driven off the prison property before they get out of the van. There is a yellow line about a hundred feet outside the prison gate, and once the van passes that line it pulls over and the guy can step out.

EARLONNE I saw Nyge, Pat Mesiti-Miller, our senior sound designer at the time, our producer Julie Shapiro, and a camera. The van pulled up and parked. As planned, we were recording the moment, as a means of claiming that once-in-a-lifetime look in the rearview mirror. In the end, I didn't

opt for a limo. The comfort of Nyge's car would do just fine. The officer opened the sliding door and gave me an envelope. Inside were my parole papers, a debit card with the standard two hundred dollars "gate money," and whatever money was left from my prison account. I stepped out of the van. And as soon as my feet hit the ground, I felt free. In a single moment, it was like twenty-one years of suspended animation had been wiped away.

NIGEL Hey!

EARLONNE How you doin'?

NIGEL I'm good . . . I'm good now. We're gonna get to sit next to each other in the car. Are you hungry?

EARLONNE Hold on, this is . . . This is what we don't get to see on the inside. All right, it's about time.

NIGEL You ready to see . . .

EARLONNE Yeah, I'm ready. That's a damn good view, though. This is interesting. I said I was gonna watch the place get little, but I ain't even turning around. My favorite word today? (I think it's always my favorite.) "Interesting."

NIGEL You know what's interesting? You look thinner already.

EARLONNE It's the prison clothes!

NIGEL The prison clothes are really unflattering. Anyway, you look great.

EARLONNE Well, I'm still about 230.

NIGEL A good 230!

EARLONNE Okay, first call, to Mom . . . Hey, what's up, Mama? It's your son.

ALYCE WOODS Are you out?

EARLONNE I am rolling across the bridge right now.

ALYCE *AAAHHHHHHHHHH!!!*

EARLONNE I think you just broke the phone, Mama.

PRX STUDIOS, EMERYVILLE, CALIFORNIA
December 2018

EARLONNE You're now tuned in to San Quentin's *Ear Hustle* from PRX's Radiotopia. I'm Earlonne Woods, a former resident at San Quentin State Prison in California.

NIGEL And I'm Nigel Poor, a visual artist, now podcaster. I've been working with the men at San Quentin for almost eight years now.

EARLONNE And together, we're gonna take you . . . Hmmm, where we gonna take 'em, Nyge?

NIGEL Outside, and then back in.

EARLONNE That's what's up.

NIGEL Earlonne, we are recording together for the first time outside the walls of San Quentin. After twenty-one years, you are no longer incarcerated.

EARLONNE Fuck no!

NIGEL As many listeners may already know, your sentence was commuted by the Honorable Governor Jerry Brown.

EARLONNE Good looking-out, Gub'na! Yeah, about a year ago I submitted for a commutation of my sentence, and it took a while, but the governor signed off on it a few weeks ago and I'm free as a bird . . . a bird who's got to check in with his parole officer from time to time. But hey, I'm cool with that. And I'm living in the Bay Area. Thanks to the good folks from Re:Store Justice, I'm in a nice transitional house.

NIGEL And what's that like for you?

EARLONNE It's love. It's peaceful. It's just sitting on the porch watching traffic go by.

NIGEL You know what's so cool? Driving up and parking in front of your house and walking up the stairs, and it's like *knock, knock, knock, knock, knock,* and you're like, "What's up, Nyge?!"

EARLONNE That's what's up.

NIGEL Oh, man, it's such a huge change. So, what are you thinking? What are you feeling? And most importantly, you know I have to know about what you're eating.

EARLONNE Well, hey, you was at my first meal.

NIGEL That's right. We stopped at a diner.

EARLONNE And I had to have what I've been thinking about for years: Steak and eggs. Breakfast of the champions. With toast, with a lemon or an orange. It tasted like someone sacrificed themselves for me. It was good, man.

NIGEL Earlonne, you were in prison for a long time. And now you have the chance to do and experience and eat many of the things you'd been missing out on.

EARLONNE Yeah, I gotta hella long list. Like, there's places I wanna go. Things I wanna see. Shit I wanna do. One of the things I missed out on the most was the freedom of choice.

NIGEL What do you mean?

EARLONNE Well, like today. I had the freedom to make the choice to take a bath this morning. Epsom salts and all. Bubble bath. Straight-up bubble bath.

NIGEL Oh wow! How long did you spend in there? Were you in there long enough that you had to add hot water?

EARLONNE I was in there long enough that I got out wrinkled. That's how long I was in there. Beautiful feeling.

NIGEL And you got to see your mom recently, in LA.

EARLONNE Yes, I did. I snuck up on her. Oh man, you know? It was good seeing her. It was, like, real profound. Like I can't even explain it. I can't express it. Just seeing her face.

NIGEL Aw. It was really sweet that you got to spend time with your family. But there was someone who was missing.

EARLONNE Yeah, my big brother, Trevor. I'm gonna miss him.

NIGEL I know you will. And he'll miss you.

Hey E., people are wondering what's gonna happen with *Ear Hustle*.

EARLONNE Well, I have to say, it's great getting out of prison with a job. It takes away so much stress about "How are you gonna make it on the outside?" That's like the biggest problem with reentry, and I'm delighted to say that I got a J-O-B.

NIGEL Yes, you are now a full-time PRX/Radiotopia employee, working as a producer for *Ear Hustle*.

EARLONNE Yep, but I'll still be co-hosting with you, Nyge. Just from the outside. Talking about stories of reentry from people like me, the formerly incarcerated.

NIGEL Thank God! And on the inside . . . We do have a very special new host who listeners will meet in Season 4.

EARLONNE Hoo boy! Y'all are in for a ride. And you're gonna love him.

NIGEL But you know what? You and me will always be partners. Partners from the start inside, and partners now outside.

EARLONNE Hell yeah! Professional partners on the outside now.

NIGEL *Ear Hustle* is produced by myself, Nigel Poor.

EARLONNE And me, the *free* Earlonne Woods.

CHAPTER ELEVEN

WITH AND WITHOUT

NIGEL E., after you took an intensely well-deserved vacation, we were right back to work. Actually, I'm not sure you ever took that vacation . . .

EARLONNE You kidding me, Nyge? *Every* day is a vacation out here on the bricks.

NIGEL We threw ourselves into the new circumstances, and it didn't take long to realize that it was true: we are partners, whether you were inside or—far better—when you were free.

EARLONNE Indubitably.

NIGEL But the first time I went in without you . . . that was a perplexing experience.

EARLONNE Was that, like, the week after I got out?

NIGEL I had grown accustomed to getting excited when I pulled into San Quentin, you know? Full of energy and ready to get to work. I had my routine: I'd see familiar faces, stop and chat with people along the way, you know. But I always knew that when I finally got to the Media Lab, you would be waiting for me. Everything would be organized, and we could just jump into work. I'd never have to worry, because you would have everything we had discussed set up and under control.

EARLONNE Well, I knew that you were taking time out of your life, away from your husband, Internet, and family, as well as paying tolls and all the administrative stuff that no one cares to see or acknowledge, so having everything on point waiting on your arrival was the least I could do to show my appreciation for your time.

NIGEL It's just that there was always a familiarity, a comfort—it was the way it was. The first day going in without you there, I felt out of my familiar zone. I didn't walk as fast, and even though I stopped to have my usual conversations, part of me just felt tired. I could go through the motions, but it was by rote. I wasn't exactly anxious; I was just off. Right before I reached the Media Lab, I realized I was sad, mourning what was gone. What we did together inside was so exciting, satisfying, and always surprising. Part of me felt like that was gone, and that all we had built together, all the struggles, all the intense good work we had done together might be coming to an end.

EARLONNE But you didn't have to worry.

NIGEL Nope. Not only did the work inside San Quentin move into an interesting new chapter, our collaboration evolved in fascinating new ways, which never would have been possible. In fact, though I missed seeing you at the end of that route, your freedom gave *Ear Hustle* much more flexibility to develop new stories.

EARLONNE Absolutely! And though we still do pretty much all of our interviews together, which is ultimately what we both prefer, there have been times when we knew it was necessary—and now possible—for one of us to handle it alone. Those times seem to be for sensitive, high-intensity interviews where we might not get a second chance. It's essential, in those scenarios, that one of us set out alone, and come back to the other with the interview we needed—or rather, with the most complete responses to our questions answered. After my sentence was commuted, we were able to pursue those complete responses by having one-on-one conversations, like the ones we both had with Ronnie Young, and you had with a victim's sister.

Back in July 2019, after I had been released, we did a story about what it's like *after* an incarcerated person gets out of prison. We called it "Kissing the Concrete." As we said in the episode description, serving a prison sentence is hard, but getting out isn't exactly a cakewalk either. We talked with several guys who were about to get out, then followed up with them once they had been released. One of those guys was Ronnie, who had struggled with drugs, homelessness, and being in and out of prison for most of his adult life. You interviewed him in San Quentin right before he was about to get out.

SAN QUENTIN
June 2019

NIGEL I gotta ask you a really hard question. I'm sorry. Are you better off staying in prison than getting out?

RONNIE No.

NIGEL Can you talk about that?

RONNIE Well . . . I don't even like that. Uh . . .

NIGEL I'm not judging you, and I'm not at all saying that you should stay in prison. But in prison, you have food, you have a place to sleep, you have the possibility of being in programs. So that's why I'm asking if you are better off in prison where you have all these things? Or is prison so horrible that it doesn't matter, and you just wanna be outside?

RONNIE Prison is horrible.

NIGEL There's no part of you that would stay here?

RONNIE No, absolutely not.

NIGEL All right.

RONNIE I hate it here.

EARLONNE I met Ronnie at the gate the day he got out, and helped him out a little in terms of settling into his new life outside. The idea for the next episode was that Nyge and I would catch up with him after a few weeks, to check in and see how things were going. Problem was, Ronnie stopped picking up his phone. Nigel has a bit of phone phobia, and would have stressed out trying to track him down. We agreed that this task would be on me.

I called him at least three times a week—but Ronnie never picked up. Finally, I got a text from him that he was in Stockton, which is about ninety minutes from the Bay Area. It would be a parole violation for me to go interview him without telling my parole agent; Ronnie was twenty or thirty miles beyond my allowed fifty-mile radius. The situation was a little challenging, as Ronnie obviously was not doing well, and was likely in street-survival mode, which was probably gonna be his ticket back to prison. After his response to Nigel asking whether he might be better off inside, she and I agreed that her presence at the follow-up interview might be misconstrued as a kind of "Fuck you, Ronnie. I was right." I had other concerns, about what might be a chaotic environment. We decided it would be better for me to go meet with him by myself. Given some of the similar life experiences I had shared, we knew he might just feel more comfortable speaking with me.

So I drove to Stockton to find him, and met him at the bus station. It was a windy day, so we sat in my car and talked, and the two of us got right into it.

EARLONNE So, since the time we left you, what have you been going through?

RONNIE Uh . . . Well, I've already been using. Look, I'm at the bus station and some dude comes up and he's going, "Hey Ronnie, hey Ronnie!" And I don't even know the dude, right?

EARLONNE And he knew your name and shit?

RONNIE Yeah. 'Cause I used to sell him shit, right?

EARLONNE Oh yeah, okay.

RONNIE And there it went. And . . . Yeah, I mean. Yeah. It was all bad.

EARLONNE Mmm. Does it make you feel better?

RONNIE No, absolutely not. It makes me feel worse. As soon as I got high, I don't wanna be around nobody, 'cause I certainly don't want people knowing. You know what I mean?

EARLONNE Right.

RONNIE Fuck, what's kept me in prison all my life, man, is drugs. I hate it, bro. I mean I'm sleeping on the streets. One night I slept . . . Ha, check this out: One night I went into the police department, to their lobby, curled my ass up on the floor, and went to sleep.

EARLONNE It was the safest spot, huh?

RONNIE Right? Nobody gave me a—nobody bothered me! But at Target in Manteca, they got them big huge-ass dumpsters, and that's where I slept the other night.

EARLONNE Was it cold or something? And that was the best spot?

RONNIE Well, I mean, there was a bunch of cardboard in there. You know what I mean? So it was the cleanest spot, probably. I don't know, man. I don't understand why they don't just put me in a program, man. Put me in a program.

EARLONNE What do you feel was one of the lowest points, being out here on the streets?

RONNIE Oh man, I don't know. Just walking and having no place to go. I mean nowhere to go. Unless I wanna get deep up in it again, you know? And I don't, bro.

[As we're driving, passing places he knows well] Right out here, French Camp Road, right? Homeboy, I was out here walking.

EARLONNE Yeah?

RONNIE Look, I was in this orchard right here, right? But then over here, you got the cemetery, right? That's where my kids were cremated. [Tragically, Ronnie's son and daughter died of a rare disease.] But man, I was just walking around out here, bro. Nothing to do. Nowhere to go . . .

Look at my feet, man. They're purple.

EARLONNE That's just from walking?

RONNIE Yeah.

EARLONNE It was a rough day. While all that was going on I had been recording, interviewing without a script.

Ronnie was in bad shape. After we spoke, I dropped him off at his friend's house, where Ronnie had stored a few boxes of his personal belongings prior to going to prison, as well as what he brought home. As I was pulling away, I noticed a heavily tatted-up white guy detailing a car in front of the house right next door to where I had just dropped Ronnie. Taking a moment to observe him, I recognized a familiar look in his eyes. I knew that look all too well; it was that "It's about to go down!" look.

I decided to wait a beat, and watched as the guy started walking towards Ronnie, yelling something and gesturing aggressively. To his credit, Ronnie started backpedaling, like he didn't want any problems. I stopped the car, quickly put it in reverse, and basically drove directly between the two of them. In my mind, I was thinking, *Okay, if this goes bad and the police come, they might run my name, and it could be a parole violation.* The tatted guy didn't know my disposition, and after pausing for a second he continued to spew insults. I knew I didn't want to get involved in whatever their situation was, so I yelled to Ronnie to get in the car, which he did. I sped away and took him to a park nearby, where I asked him what that had been all about. He told me, "We were in the same prison and I told him the next time we saw each other, he needed to have his paperwork [showing crimes committed] or who knows what time it is. Because some things were said about him . . . doing something to a younger girl." Prison drama on the streets. Anything could have happened. Clearly, this was an occasion when I was glad that Nyge wasn't around.

NIGEL I don't think I could have handled seeing Ronnie in such a bad situation, I might have wanted to give him money or figure out how to solve his problem, even though I know I couldn't have done anything. I heard the county actually offered him housing. So why didn't he take it? I mean, he had no place of his own.

EARLONNE At the time, he told me that he didn't want to live around other addicts. That's a trigger for him. Sometimes he stays in a hotel room with his friend Tammy, who pays, but he doesn't wanna break her bank, so he's been spending time on the streets. In any case, he wanted to go to Manteca, his hometown, about twenty minutes from Stockton. So I drove him as we talked.

NIGEL You understood how to be there for Ronnie while not stepping over the line. Ronnie felt at ease with you. He didn't feel paranoid about there being any judgment. He responded to the questions with honesty, and without any filter he might have put up had I been there.

As a team, we've also gone the other way—meaning there have been a few occasions when we decided that the person we wanted to interview would be more inclined to open up if I were to go alone. One unusual, indelible example of this came about in Season 6.

We did a very difficult story about a brutal sexual assault and its aftermath. The person who committed the rape is inside San Quentin—so I did that interview with New York and Yahya. As we were working on the story, COVID hit and we learned that we would not be getting back inside San Quentin anytime soon. While that in itself was a huge roadblock for *Ear Hustle,* it presented us with an interesting challenge when it came to this particular story. Originally, the story was being told only from the perspective of the man who had committed the crime. We still felt it was important to air it, but with the limitations imposed by the pandemic, we had to figure out a new direction for the episode.

After conversations with each other and the entire *Ear Hustle* crew, we decided it didn't feel right to put out a story about a sexual assault that only offered the perspective of the assailant. At a time when we knew we had to think beyond our typical structure in order to get the podcast fresh, we opted to try something very new and quite radical for us: we decided to track down the survivor and try to hear her side of the story.

It was a daunting option. I felt overwhelmed and even scared by the proposition, even though the attack had taken place almost thirty years ago. First of all, how would we find the victim? Then, if and when we did, how would we even begin that conversation—especially presuming she would not want to revisit the trauma? It definitely meant stepping outside the bounds of what had become familiar to us (speaking to incarcerated individuals).

Even before we got to that point, there were details we had to overcome. It took an incredible amount of research and we hit several roadblocks, which didn't deter either of us. If anything, it made us more determined to find her. We located several people who knew about the crime but either couldn't talk to us because of confidentiality issues, or simply didn't want to talk to us about it. Finally, our editor, Amy Standen, tracked down the sister of the woman who had been raped. That was when Earlonne and I made the final decision that, due to the subject matter and how sensitive the interview was going to be, it was best that I should talk to her by myself. To make things more complicated, the sister lives in another part of the country, so all of this was going to be done on the phone, no face-to-face contact. So, at the end of August 2020, I contacted Pat.

NIGEL I've heard your sister's name pronounced "Marah" and "Mira." I'm not sure what the correct pronunciation is.

PAT Well, her actual name is Mary. She assumed the name Marah later in life. She changed it after moving to Carmel, but her name is Mary. Mary Alice. That's how I think of her.

NIGEL Could you tell me a little about yourself?

PAT I live in Texas. I am post-retirement; back working full-time for a doctor and a doctor's office.

NIGEL Did you grow up in California?

PAT Oh, no, no, no. Our dad was in the military, so we moved around a lot. We lived in several different states, but my dad retired from the military when I was still in elementary school and we moved to Nashville, Tennessee. That's where Mary and I finished school.

NIGEL How much older is she?

PAT Mary's two and a half years older. She was always the older sister. She was the leader; I was the follower. She was very adventurous, fearless, outgoing; always had lots of friends. She was also a very talented musician and an artist. She was a busy person.

NIGEL Was she kind to you, did she tease you?

PAT Oh no, she was just a big sister. I remember one incident when we were spending the summer in Maine. My dad got us a little rowboat and, at such a young age, we would go out in this little rowboat, out into a very quiet inlet bay. I had just learned to swim and Mary said, "Jump in, Patty, you can swim now." I jumped into this water and it was ice cold and just took my breath away. I started floundering, and Mary jumped over and grabbed me and got me back in the boat. That was our

relationship. I would always follow her, but she was also the one there to pull me up by the collar.

NIGEL What was she like as an adult?

PAT The same: very adventurous. Very kind, spiritually sensitive, tender-hearted, artistic. She was a visual artist, so she really looked at things, and photographed all the time. She was outgoing—which is not to say she was outspoken, but she was profound. She read a lot and studied; constantly reading. And she kept a diary all the time.

NIGEL What did she look like?

PAT She was beautiful. Olive skin, blond hair, green eyes, very fit. She was an extraordinary person, inside and out.

NIGEL How did your relationship change or develop? Did you stay close?

PAT Well, she went off to college. Two years later I followed her (we both went to Brigham Young University in Utah). When she graduated from college she married a fellow that she met in college and they moved to Fresno, California. He was also an artist and a musician, and taught art. After I graduated, I also moved to Fresno and lived there for about three years, and then moved away. After that, we never lived geographically close, but we were always close.

NIGEL Were you raised Mormon?

PAT I was eight years old when I was baptized.

NIGEL Did your sister stay in the church?

PAT No, she didn't. After she left Utah and moved to Fresno, she and her husband kind of fell into the art culture and teaching, and grew away from the church. It didn't bother me at that time, because I really wasn't really active then. But I am very active in the church now.

NIGEL My understanding is that your sister was very spiritual. Did your different kinds of faith ever create a problem?

PAT No. Not at all, because the basic premise of being morally clean, of keeping your body healthy—those kinds of things are our core in the Mormon Church, and were core to her belief. She became a follower of Meher Baba. It's not exactly Buddhism, but it's similar. Their core belief is to be morally clean, take care of your body, and have reverence for nature.

NIGEL What was her life like in Carmel? Did you ever visit her?

PAT I would go out there on vacation and spend a week with her. It was always a wonderful time. We were sisters, you know. We would just enjoy being together. We didn't live close to each other, but we remained close and talked on the phone all the time.

NIGEL What did you think about her art?

PAT I'm not an artist. But her art was very, very beautiful. She did some kind of weird things in the later years, but it was still beautiful. I have many of her paintings hanging in my house. She loved this area—the Gulf, the water, seagulls, pelicans. A lot of her paintings reflected that.

NIGEL I'm going to move to a more difficult track. When did you first hear about the attack?

PAT I'm not sure how much later it was than the actual incident. I heard from my mother, who she had called. It wasn't something she wanted to talk about a lot, so she didn't. I knew about her injuries, which were quite extensive. But I never did actually question her about what happened. I felt like it was probably too painful, and it wasn't something that she wanted to dwell on.

NIGEL I hate to ask this, but do you know what her injuries were?

PAT I know he beat her up, because she fought him. She fought back. So her teeth were messed up, and her face was beaten pretty badly.

NIGEL When you hear news like that, when something happens to someone you really love, what is the reaction—the bodily, the emotional, the spiritual reaction to that kind of news?

PAT Well, you think nothing like that is going to happen to yourself or to somebody that you know. Those kinds of things happen to other people. So, when it happens to someone close to you or to yourself, it's just so hard to believe.

My sister was always fearless. She went on many, many trips just by herself. When the incident happened, she was by herself. She probably had her camera with her. She always did, because of being a visual artist. She was always taking photographs. She was walking in a beautiful place when this happened.

She passed this man on the path—he was going in the opposite direction and she didn't think anything of it. Obviously he turned around, attacked her, and dragged her off the path.

NIGEL You've mentioned that she was fearless many times. Do you think that experience changed her fearlessness and the way she operated in the world?

PAT Well, she didn't take extended trips by herself anymore. She became more self-aware and a little bit . . . not fearful, but just aware of not putting herself into those kinds of situations.

NIGEL Did you visit with her after?

PAT Yes. This happened in 1990 and I visited her in Carmel many times. I would go and spend a week or so. One of our favorite things to do was to go outside of Carmel, where there's a Zen Buddhist monastery. We would go there in the summertime. They open it to the public and we would spend probably three days there. It was just beautiful. A really wonderful experience.

NIGEL Did you notice a change in her then?

PAT She was still the same person that I remembered. She was an early riser and got up every morning to meditate. I think she actually became even more spiritual after the incident. She went on a trip to India to the headquarters of Meher Baba and spent a week there, I think largely to work through what had happened. There was part of her that was concerned about the role she played in the attack. The people who worked with her helped her see that of course that wasn't the case. Being violently raped and beaten cannot *not* affect someone's life forever. But she chose not to dwell on it and not to let it define her. She became celibate, but I'm not sure if that was before or after the attack. I think it may have been before.

NIGEL Do you think she stayed celibate?

PAT I do. She always had a lot of male friends, but they were platonic.

NIGEL You talked about her really honoring her body and also that she was very spiritual, as are you. Given that, how do you think about forgiveness, or about understanding this kind of incredibly vile act? In other words, how do you wrap your mind around having compassion for that person? How do you deal with your rage and your frustration over something like that?

PAT Personally, I choose not to judge, because I do not know what led him to a point where he would commit something like that. That is not for me to judge. I feel like men who are capable of committing violent sexual crimes on women or on children . . . I don't think they are ever able to completely rid themselves of that. Whether they'll commit that crime again, I don't know. I think it's something so deep that it will always be within him. But again, it's not for me to judge. He will receive his judgment when he stands before his savior, Jesus Christ. So, it's not for me to judge the man. I don't know what his story is. I don't know anything about him.

NIGEL I'm not going to say your sister forgave him, but when we were talking to the man who raped her, he said that even at the trial she talked about having compassion for him. I just didn't believe it. But we talked with other people who confirmed as much. What do you make of that?

PAT Hate is a very toxic emotion. For people to carry hate and those kinds of emotions within themselves, it doesn't do any harm to the other person. It harms yourself. And so you make a choice. You make a choice to *not* carry those things, and instead to have compassion. It's a conscious choice. My sister made a conscious choice that she was not going to let those emotions eat away at her. So for her to have some compassion for the guy . . . yes, I can see she would feel that way. She was not going to release those negative feelings and let them eat away at her.

NIGEL It's a very enlightened way to deal with that situation. I don't know many people who could. It's so healthy, but seems very difficult. I have heard people talk about that kind of forgiveness; how it ultimately allows you to move on with your life and not be mired in the darkness of what happened.

PAT As I said, she didn't want to dwell on it. It wasn't going to define her.

NIGEL Were you surprised when we reached out to you?

PAT Yes. It was like, *What? Marah?* She passed away in 2004, so kind of a long time ago. To get a call out of the blue . . . it was like, *Okay, well, that's interesting.* I thought it was something about her art and life in Carmel— until you explained to me what the topic was.

NIGEL Was that disappointing?

PAT No, not necessarily. Just surprising. I started looking at the *Ear Hustle* website. I really haven't given much thought to prison systems. Sometimes

I think that people in prison have it too good. They get three square meals, college education, free medical, they get this and that. I don't think very many people end up in hard prisons who do not deserve to be there. And I don't know if very many people are actually reformed by their prison experience. I'm sure some are. But I don't know. It's not something that I've really thought too much about.

And I don't have any feelings either way for the man who attacked her. He will face the consequences of his action, at some point in time. For sure. That's all I can say.

NIGEL Understood. I know your sister died of cancer, which can also be a very rigorous, difficult process. Did she face that experience in the same way she faced her life?

PAT Her story of cancer is one for the textbooks. She had no symptoms at all. And I work in the medical community. We were talking on the phone and she told me that she was getting her hair done and the hairdresser noticed a little lesion on the back of her head. She thought it was maybe an ingrown hair or something. She went back a couple months later and the hairdresser said, "This looks worse—you should get it checked out."

She was the poster child of a healthy person: she didn't drink, she was a vegetarian, she took care of her body, she felt good. But she decided to get it checked out and went to see her dermatologist and got a biopsy done. Then all of a sudden, she got deathly ill. I mean, she couldn't stand. Her equilibrium was off. Her roommate found her in the bathroom and couldn't get her up. She called a couple of friends and they got her to the hospital. She mentioned the biopsy, and when they got it back the doctor told her she had to see an oncologist right away.

Her friends talked her into checking herself into the hospital and they ran scans on her. She was covered with cancer; I mean she had cancer everywhere, and tumors in her brain.

I got a call the next day from her roommate, and she said, "Marah's not doing very well. You need to come right away." That was on a Saturday. I made arrangements, got on a plane Sunday. She never left the hospital, and twenty-six days later she was dead.

All through the time that she was in the hospital, she was very upbeat, very kind to the nurses. She had a wonderful doctor. Her friends came and took care of her; gave her massages.

I was there the whole time. She was certain she was going to get out. She was going to beat this. She stayed that way until the day before she died. Fortunately, she did not suffer through long bouts of treatment, but they started doing radiation immediately on the tumors in her head—to try and shrink them down and alleviate the symptoms.

My sister loved her hair. She had very fine baby hair. And she took good care of it. I came in one morning and they had given her a shower and had washed her hair and it was just a matted holy mess. She didn't want anybody to take care of it except for me. So, I got some spray that you put on babies' hair to get the tangles out. I combed her hair, just trying to take care of it; minute strands at a time. As I was combing it, her hair was just coming out in clumps in my hand. I didn't let her know what was happening. I put the hair in my pocket and did the very best that I could. I don't think she ever knew, but that was heartbreaking.

It was a very spiritual experience for me, because the morning that she passed, I came in and I just knew. It was the day. I kneeled down by the side of her bed and at that point she was in that in-between place. She was conscious, but she had her eyes closed. She was able to chew ice. And I just said, "Mary, it's time for you to go. Everything's taken care of. Mom and Dad are waiting for you. You need to go now, it's fine. We're good, you're all right." I just talked to her very quietly until she took her last breath.

She passed very peacefully. Two of her very best friends were in the room with me at the time, and we all just stayed very quiet. We didn't rush out and tell the nurses or the doctors. We just sat with her for a little while. Then finally I went out and let them know that she had passed.

I asked if it would be all right if we cleaned her up, and they said yes. They brought in warm, wet towels and we cleaned her and fixed her as best we could. It was very spiritual, and I was grateful. Grateful that it happened quickly and that she did not have to go through a bunch of suffering or chemotherapy. It happened very quickly. I've always been very, very grateful for that. She had completed what she needed to do here on earth, and it was time for her to go.

NIGEL You really shepherded her through that. The story about her hair is so poignant and beautiful and sad.

PAT I'm here in my bedroom right now and on my wall, I have a beautiful picture of her. It's a self-portrait that she did. If you would like, I could take a picture of it and send that to you.

NIGEL That would be wonderful.

PAT It would give you a kind of insight. It's a self-portrait, but not a typical self-portrait. You see a very spiritual side of her. That's how she chose to live and that's how she passed. She did not carry bad karma with her; she did not take the rape with her to the other side.

NIGEL I hope that I would have the strength to do what you did. You must be an extraordinary person. That's not an easy thing you did for your sister.

PAT I am sure that I was guided and directed by the Spirit to be able to accomplish what I needed to do. I will be united with her again. She's on the other side, she's happy, she's fulfilling whatever she needs to do. She's still the same beautiful person: she's artistic and musical and all of those things. She took all of that with her. That never changes. Your spirit does not change.

NIGEL Well, thank you for being so open to a stranger calling and asking you to talk about your sister. Not only did you bring her to life in such a beautiful way, but you gave me such a clear understanding of your relationship and who you are and how you both operated in the world. I love that strangers can connect like this and understand each other. It makes the world seem like a better place. So, I really deeply appreciate your time.

PAT Mary was a beautiful, beautiful, beautiful person. Just lovely. You know?

EARLONNE Afterward, when I heard the recording of Pat speaking about her sister's last days, it made me sad. Sometimes, in those kinds of situations, I have to have questions on paper in front of me. Otherwise, I find myself at a loss for words. I get like that whenever we've done interviews that are just so deeply emotional that I don't want to impose or ask the wrong question or unknowingly trigger someone. At the same time, I know that it can be helpful, and a real good feeling, to bring someone back to life via conversation and relive the past through stories. But when I heard Pat say she was combing Marah's hair and how easily it was falling out, I couldn't help but think of my cousin Arrika, who painfully passed away of cancer at the young age of thirty-four, while I was incarcerated. Pat was describing a situation that was real similar to everything I had been hearing about Arrika. That would have distracted me. Overall, we both understood that this was a conversation better handled one-on-one, just between Pat and Nyge.

NIGEL Finding the balance for a given episode isn't always as stark or as dramatic as it was with Ronnie and Earlonne, or with me and Pat. We've had guys whose stories were slanted or inauthentic because they were clearly trying to impress Earlonne. We've had others who refused to speak with us, but together we persisted until we found a way to get them to open up. When we were seeking a Latino voice or interviews with white guys inside, Earlonne would send me to the yard to approach them. Conversely, older Black men almost always needed a few extra words of encouragement or explanation from Earlonne before they'd agree to speak with us.

The balance we find once we're deep into the conversations is based on intuition—on the language between us that we are now fluent in. Over the years of working together, we have developed an intuitive style. Which isn't to suggest that we do our work off the cuff—just the opposite. We're always prepared, we do our research about the person or people with whom we are speaking, and we arrive with a thorough list of questions. When we started *Ear Hustle,* we hardly ever approached an interview with a set of questions. We came with curiosity and let the conversation unfold. That made for much longer interviews, which of course makes for a more exhausting editing process. Though it has its value, our list of questions can be bothersome, almost a burden, as if it were a heavy weight pulling our encounter away from the rhythm and improvisation of a natural conversation. Following the list, it's easy to forget to just listen and let the conversation go where it needs to go. Both of us are very cued into our surroundings. We have a mutual curiosity that steers conversations toward surprising places.

The other important ingredient is that we are comfortable with silence. Pauses in conversation are essential. They hold meaning, and it's important to allow them to happen. Even if it gets uncomfortable, that silence indicates the turning point where everyone has relaxed into the conversation and it's about to get real. There is a kind of silence that tells you the person you are speaking with is deciding if they trust you. If you allow them the space and patience to have that interior experience, all of a sudden the feeling in the room shifts. It is often like a big exhalation, everyone's bodies relax, and whatever is being revealed often becomes more profound.

CHAPTER TWELVE

LOCKED OUT

NIGEL We thought we had weathered it all, until we were faced with an incomprehensible threat to the continuation of *Ear Hustle*. In early March 2020, the reality of COVID-19 was finally sinking in and starting to be widely accepted as the lethal virus it is, though official regulations had not been put in place yet. I was worried about the danger of bringing COVID into the prison, so on March 11, 2020, I had to tell New York and the other guys I wouldn't be able to return to San Quentin until the situation was clearer. In my mind, that absence from the prison would maybe last a week or two. But the situation changed drastically on March 16, when the shelter-in-place order for six Bay Area counties was announced. We would be going on lockdown.

Earlonne, our producer Bruce Wallace, and I were at our office/recording studio in Emeryville. The space is usually filled with people but over the course of the month, fewer and fewer folks were coming in to work. We were part of the small contingent of people who were determined to keep moving forward and showing up to the office. In hindsight, that may have been ill-advised, but none of us were prepared to accept what was actually happening, and it's not in any of our natures to be idle. We had all heard that a possible shutdown of the state was going to happen, but I honestly just didn't believe it.

We were recording narration for Episode 3 of Season 5 in the sound-proof room, so we were pretty isolated. It was late in the afternoon and we stepped out to take a break. There were two or three other people still lingering around the office, and they told us Governor Gavin Newsom had just made it official, and that starting at 10:00 p.m., California would be sheltering in place for three weeks. I remember being scared and thinking, *Three weeks is an eternity*, and also, *Damn, we are not getting back into San Quentin anytime soon.*

EARLONNE I was like, *Cool—we get to work from home! This will be fun. I've always wanted to work from home.* My excitement was partially because I live like thirty-two minutes from the job, so, on a good day, an hour in traffic. Like Nyge, I never could have imagined how long this shit was going to last. So, I was just like, "Let's do this. We're about to have a cool, laid-back, pajama sort of vacation."

I remember thinking as I was driving home, listening to *Snap Judgment's* episode "This Is Not a Drill," about the time people in Hawaii were panicking when they thought a missile was heading their way, how crazy it was to contemplate a lockdown on the streets. I even thought, *Shit, did we low-key get hit with the fallout of a secret missile?* A happy thought overtook me: I had an ounce of a good grade of marijuana for the lockdown. That's like a self–Hail Mary pass, or a self-alley-oops! I'm not a drinker, so my bar of about eight bottles would hold me a couple of years if need be.

NIGEL When we were done, we shared a good, long, strong hug, then Earlonne got in his car and drove home, and Bruce and I got in my car to drive back to San Francisco. We talked about the coming situation, but I was still in denial about what it meant. I dropped Bruce off and decided it might be a good idea to go grocery shopping—I didn't completely understand what "shelter in place" meant, but it seemed like a good idea to stock up. I pulled into the parking lot of Trader Joe's and was startled to see that the line to even get into the store stretched straight across the parking lot. I waited in it for about thirty minutes and, when I finally entered the store, was stunned to see the shelves emptied out.

There wasn't any chaos—nobody was arguing over the last rolls of toilet paper (those had sold out days prior)—but it was unnerving to be in a grocery store utterly depleted of items. Being more sensitive to a visual display than to an overheard newsbit, it was the sight of those empty shelves that pushed me to accept the fact that this was very real. I would not be returning to San Quentin for a long time.

On March 17, 2020, the spread of COVID closed and barred shut the doors of San Quentin. None of us knew exactly what that would mean for our access to the prison, or for how long we would be denied the ability to speak with the men inside. We continued to hope that—at worst—we might not be able to venture in for several weeks. Weeks turned to months, and in

August it was announced publicly that San Quentin was experiencing the deadliest outbreak of the virus of any prison in the state. People were dying. While it was deeply upsetting for us to be so far away from our colleagues inside, we didn't allow ourselves to call a halt on the podcast, or to give up hope.

We had only aired one episode of Season 5 when that shelter-in-place mandate was issued. We gave ourselves a week or so to adjust to the shock and uncertainty—then did what we do best, and figured out how we were going to get back to work. We each set up makeshift recording "studios" in our closets. For almost five months, that's how we worked: Earlonne in his closet, me in mine, connecting via Zoom with our producer, Bruce Wallace, who coached us through recording narration.

EARLONNE A closet is generally the best place to record, when stuck inside one's home, because—unless you've got a big-ass linen closet large enough to sit in—it's the place most likely to be filled with soft materials that absorb sound. A bathroom might offer more space, but all the hard surfaces make the recording sound hollow and cold. Initially we were prepared to just sit on our closet floors holding a mic and recorder. But we ended up spending hours in there, recording narrations and also holding interviews over Zoom. Definitely called for an alternative workaround.

NIGEL For us, a closet studio requires: a chair, something to rest your computer on, a mic stand, a small portable recorder, a headset, Internet access, freedom from claustrophobic tendencies, and buckets of patience. We were used to recording in person, so had to learn to work off each other over the computer screen. Naturally, there were also a host of technical challenges: we needed very good Internet connections for all parties, and that often wasn't the case. Sometimes one of us would drop out or freeze up—causing the conversation to do the same. We had to explain to people how to record themselves and send us the audio. That was E.'s job. He can talk anyone through a setup, whereas I panic, until remembering that E. will always make it work.

In our own ways, both of us love clothes and shoes. Our tastes may not always align, and we don't exactly share outfits, but we both enjoy fashion to some extent. Once we both found ourselves jammed into our closets, we got a full-on peep at how the other deals with clothes. For both of us, it is all about being organized. But I also got to see just how many pairs of Vans Earlonne owns, and how he has various colors to coordinate with his outfits.

EARLONNE Nyge also has way more shoes than one person needs, but hers are all these Fluevog boots and crazy-colored high heels that would probably add about six inches to her height, and definitely wouldn't be allowed inside of a prison. I started to think Rick, her husband, definitely had to have his own closet, because all I could ever see was Nigel's shoes and clothes. We'd usually warm up by teasing each other about the contents of the other's closets.

NIGEL E., do you really need *that* many T-shirts?

EARLONNE Yeah, well, what about those zebra-striped pants?!

NIGEL Our mutual tendency toward close observation goes beyond listening. We are careful lookers—what we call "mapping" a photograph. We look at a situation and see what we can glean, even if all we see is an arrangement of clothing and footwear.

When we first started recording in our closets, Earlonne would say, "I'm mapping you, Nyge." "Don't worry; I'm mapping you too," I'd reply. Safe to say, we know each other's closets far better than we do the rest of the other's apartment.

To buy some time as we adjusted to our new work environments, we revisited a 2018 episode that held particular significance. It resonated with the social climate, and was applicable to the situation we and many of our listeners had suddenly found ourselves in. The decision to air it underscored one of the primary goals of our stories: to reveal the commonalities between life inside and out.

EARLONNE We had an episode all ready. But then the team got to talking about how a lot of folks are about to experience what many incarcerated people are familiar with: a lockdown.

NIGEL And at the beginning of Season 3, we did a whole episode about just that.

EARLONNE It was back when I was still a resident of San Quentin, and everyone had just come off of a lockdown.

NIGEL Lockdowns happen when the administration deems there's a credible threat to the safety and security of the institution, like when keys go missing.

EARLONNE Or they're looking for a weapon. Either way, a prison-wide search begins and we prisoners are stuck in our cells—can't go to class, can't go to the yard, can't go to our jobs. For three weeks, Nigel, *Ear Hustle* was on ice.

NIGEL As soon as that summer lockdown was over, we started recording.

MICHAEL I love graham crackers, banana, and peanut butter and jelly sandwiches.

NIGEL That's Michael Williams, and like a lot of other guys, man, they really talked about food during the lockdown. I mean . . . a lot.

MICHAEL Well, you know, one day you may get graham crackers, so you got to hold on to the graham crackers. Then the next day you'll get a banana. So you save that. And then when you get your peanut butter and jelly, you can make a graham cracker, peanut butter, and banana sandwich . . . jelly sandwich. And those are the best.

EARLONNE I think he might be right.

NIGEL Really? Is that your favorite sandwich?

EARLONNE Nah, that's like the easiest go-to sandwich. You know, my favorite sandwiches—when I got a chance to—put together bologna, lettuce, cheese, mayonnaise, mustard, pickle.

NIGEL Oh, pickles. Yeah.

EARLONNE We don't get all that shit at the same time. You gotta put that shit together. Food is what gets you through the day, and most guys are really careful about how and when they eat the meals that's brought to them during lockdown.

Lunch is delivered in the morning with breakfast, and I asked this one cat named Jay about his strategy of saving his lunch for later.

JAY I'm gonna mix the vegetables with the main course, and put half of it in the bowl to eat later with the lunch. You know, the stuff that you would never eat . . . like the soggy-ass salad. The salad is . . . just horrible. I mean, it's a lot of stuff that you wouldn't eat normally. You eating it and you try to convince yourself, *Man, this ain't that bad.* And it's horrible. I think that's when you . . . when you know you really about to lose it. This shit ain't never been good. You know what I mean? And all of a sudden it's like, *Damn, man. That was kinda good.*

NIGEL So, E., from what I've heard, on a lockdown, the prison gives you the daily recommended amount of calories, but nothing more.

EARLONNE Nothing more. Right.

NIGEL So here's my question. I didn't see you for about three weeks during the lockdown and I can't help but notice . . . that you don't really . . .

EARLONNE I know you not finna—

NIGEL . . . look any thinner.

EARLONNE Look like I put on a few pounds? Look healthy? Didn't miss a beat?

NIGEL Didn't miss a beat.

EARLONNE Well, you gotta understand, Nigel, I've been locked up twenty-one years, so the extra weight is because I'm a planner.

NIGEL Okay. I'm going to ask you about that in a minute, but here's another guy who told us about lockdown boxes. We caught up with Aaron Taylor by the basketball court and, man, he loves to play. But because of the lockdown, he hadn't been able to play in weeks.

AARON A lockdown box is . . . well, we call it an earthquake kit. It originates from being on the Level IV, where them lockdowns extend. They can go minimum three months all the way up to two years, if necessary. So, you want to have food in your lockdown box, because if you're getting served in the cell, they're going to bring you only so much food and it's not really enough to sustain a grown man, it'll just keep you alive. So, you want to have some food in there.

You want to have some cosmetics, because you won't be going to the store. So you want to keep at minimum two toothpastes and a minimum of two deodorants inside of a lockdown box. You want to have some soap up in there because you're going to be taking birdbaths. On a real lockdown you're only going to be in the shower area once every seventy-two hours. You want to have a couple of writing tablets and at least one book of stamps for your letters, because you will not be using the telephone.

NIGEL Aaron mentioned taking birdbaths. Can you explain how it's done?

EARLONNE Taking a birdbath . . . It works just like a bird in a puddle, just shaking around.

NIGEL Just dipping into the water?

EARLONNE But, instead of a puddle, I use my lockdown box.

NIGEL So that's one of those large plastic storage containers.

EARLONNE Exactly. And what I do is I just take it and I dump all that stuff on my bunk; I fill it up halfway with water, step into it, and get my lather on. And I take some regular water, clean water, and just pour it over me, and it's over. I'm clean and fresh, smelling good.

NIGEL Nice. Okay. Then when you're done you put everything back in your lockbox?

EARLONNE Then when I'm done, I've got to clean up, wash everything out, and I put all my food back in my lockbox neatly.

NIGEL Okay. So now I've got to know: What's in your lockbox?

EARLONNE All right. So usually I have potato chips, cheese popcorn, golden puffs. I have about twenty bags of rice, some sweet corn. I have cookies, three cases of twenty-four noodles, twenty-four clams in a box, sausages, gang of oatmeal, tin roast beef, chocolate peanut clusters. This is that fat boy shit. Famous Amos cookies, coffee. You've gotta have coffee. You need hot sauce. I have salt and pepper, cheese sticks, coffee creamer, sugar, loose mackerels, and tuna, salted peanuts. Peanuts, they used to cost a dollar. Now they went down to seventy cents. Brisk iced tea, Buddy Bars, which is another part of my fat boy diet. Hold on, hold on, hold on. I've got one more thing.

Let's see if these tater chips need to be freshened up a little bit. Maybe I need to— No. They're not stale. They're good. But I'm gonna have to go and eat them, since I opened the bag. They're good. They're salty as fuck, though.

NIGEL So I've also heard about guys getting written up for having too much state-issued food squirreled away. How come you're not written up?

EARLONNE State food is the food that the state provides for you. And like your lunch, you have to consume that within four hours, but canteen food and packaged food, that's your personal property.

NIGEL Oh, so you can have as much of that as you're able to buy?

EARLONNE As long as it fits within six cubic feet (the maximum allowed for personal property). But if the lockdown is really long, no matter how strict your routine is or how well stocked your lockbox is, you're going to run out of zoom-zooms and wham-whams.

NIGEL What can you do when you're on lockdown? You're stuck in that tiny cell, and it can be for weeks and sometimes months.

EARLONNE Ain't nothing to do, really. We're stuck there . . .

MICHAEL They give us fifteen minutes to shower, and once you get out you can run around on the tier and grab books and magazines. People would give me *Time, People,* and I would read every single page, every page, even the advertisement pages, where it talks about medicine and tells you what will happen if you take this medicine . . . If you read it too fast or if you just read the pages you like, you're going to be bored. You're not going to have nothing to read, so you have to read it page to page.

EARLONNE For some men, it was like a vacation. They watch all kinds of TV.

NIGEL So what about you, E.? Were you relieved to not have to go to work every day?

EARLONNE So the lockdown . . . Well, I did watch *The Young and the Restless* . . . That's something you watch when you come to prison. Probably 1988 was when I first got up on soap operas, because they just help pass the time.

NIGEL How many evil twins have they had in the plotlines?

EARLONNE You have a few. Right now, the plotlines ain't that—sorry—*Young and the Restless* . . . But I also got my sleep. I read a little bit. I responded to letters . . .

NIGEL Were you ever lying in your bunk and thought, *Man, this just sucks*?

EARLONNE Not one minute of it. Not one second of it. You got to think: prior to being locked down those eighteen days, we've probably been running raggedly since the first season!

NIGEL This is true. We were running raggedly. So were a lot of guys here at San Quentin.

EARLONNE We're working hard. We run a tight schedule over here, Nyge. San Quentin has a lot of programming, a lot of classes. Guys have jobs. A lot of us are busy trying to keep up with things.

NIGEL Yeah, just like people on the outside. Since I've been here, there's never been any super-long lockdowns. The longest was three, maybe four weeks. But maximum security prisons—they can go on for months, right? I can see how three weeks off might feel like a vacation.

EARLONNE True. I mean, we have it easier here in San Quentin than most prisons, but some things are the same no matter where you go. You have bad food, TV, books, and, shall we say, limited social opportunities. I mean, basically, it's just you and your cellie . . . in a five-foot-by-ten-foot concrete box.

NIGEL'S AND EARLONNE'S HOME CLOSET STUDIOS
April 2020

NIGEL Hey over there, Earlonne.

EARLONNE What's up, Nyge. How's it going all the way over there?

NIGEL Well, clearly, I've been better.

EARLONNE Yup. America has too. Right now, the world is grappling with this coronavirus.

NIGEL Yes, they are. So this morning I could have gone into San Quentin, but as a team we decided that it wasn't a good idea. As far as I know, I'm not sick.

EARLONNE Yeah, you didn't want to take the chance to bring any germs inside. Which is very smart.

NIGEL But a lot of our listeners have been asking us: What's going on inside with the virus?

EARLONNE So, we called the Media Lab and got our co-host, Rahsaan "New York" Thomas on the phone, and we asked him, "What's happening?"

NEW YORK Man, a lot's happening. There's a lot of fears, a lot of concerns. A lot of people are concerned for their loved ones that are over sixty-five that are in danger, both inside and outside of prison. They canceled family visiting. So I don't know where I'm gonna get a hug again. Your brother, he's tripping. He was scheduled for a family visit today. And he's not getting it, 'cause they stopped, as of today.

NIGEL And are guys inside nervous?

NEW YORK I don't know if "nervous" is the right word. I do have one major concern, and that is the elderly people here. I worry that we're gonna go on lockdown, and come up thirty to sixty days later, and some OGs that I love ain't going to be here no more.

But also people are wondering, are they ready for it? Can they sustain sixty days on lockdown? The state's not gonna give anything extra. You gonna get the same stuff. And we're wondering if they're going to make special provisions to get people to canteen or get people packages and bring them to our cells or whatever. So it doesn't feel like a punishment.

EARLONNE Having been through lockdowns, what's your advice for getting through?

NEW YORK I would say . . . use the time. It's a great time to catch up. We live in a rat race, right? We runnin' here, we runnin' there. We on social media. We doing this, we doing that. This is the time that you can finally write to your favorite incarcerated person, or write that book you always said you were gonna write. You can do all the little things that you been overlooking around the house, right? Use that time really productively and don't panic. You know, God is the greatest. It's gonna be aight.

EARLONNE Hey, you know the cold part? I'm free and they finna put me on lockdown out here.

NEW YORK I've been tripping on that.

NIGEL Hey, guess what Earlonne bought when he went to the store?

NEW YORK The same thing I bought, I'm guessing.

NIGEL What's that?

NEW YORK I got five cases of Top Ramen.

EARLONNE Hey, trust me, I got what I know is gonna work.

NIGEL As long as you can, you check in with me and Earlonne so we know what's going on?

NEW YORK Yup. The day I don't call is the day we've gone on lockdown.

NIGEL Soon after this phone call, the day came when we didn't receive a call from New York. The pandemic shut things down entirely. As of April 2020, we could no longer go in, and over a year later we still had no idea when we'd be able to enter and really engage with the men inside.

EARLONNE All the programs stopped running inside the prison.

NIGEL On two occasions we were allowed entry, with Lieutenant Robinson, but just to pick up equipment. We saw a few guys in the yard; everyone was excited and wanted to talk. It was the briefest flash of what our interaction had been. Then we went down to the Media Lab. To be in that space when it's quiet was . . . eerie, given how full of life and activity it always was. I was happy to see Lieutenant Robinson and some other COs, but the experience felt very sad—it drove home how far away from one another we are. I said to a few guys, "You know we haven't forgotten you, right?" They said they knew we hadn't, but we also acknowledged how much we missed the "before" times. We weren't able to see New York on either visit, which was hard.

EARLONNE We do know that New York's staying positive inside, and focusing on his writing. He writes articles for The Marshall Project and other news outlets.

NIGEL Hopefully we'll manage to get him a recorder, to interview people for the upcoming season—but things move very slowly inside, so we're not sure when that will happen. Apparently, vaccines are slowly rolling out for staff and tiers of incarcerated people, and things won't open up until people are vaccinated. Like the rest of the world, we just keep adapting to these very uncertain circumstances. Unpredictable situations are just about the only thing that's predictable about *Ear Hustle*.

Once we accepted the new reality, we decided to get back on the road—safely—and travel to various places to record interviews for upcoming stories we had been planning. We adapted, learning how best to record outside, got used to doing interviews while wearing masks and sitting far away from our interviewees, and found out you can get kicked out of public city parks if you are recording without a permit.

  Ear Hustle in the age of COVID is imperfect, frustrating, and, at times, devastating. But giving up isn't our style, nor is it our desire. At no point have either of us wavered on whether we would keep finding new ways to share stories about everyday prison life.

  We miss our colleagues inside and are trying our best to keep New York part of the episodes. That means getting on the phone and recording him in the fifteen-minute increments that the system allows, which means dealing with the nagging automated voice reminding us every few minutes that "this call and your telephone number will be monitored and recorded."

Despite those frustrations and limits, the current moment has pushed us to expand the variety of stories we tell. Without the ability to enter San Quentin, our lens was forced to widen, if we were going to keep *Ear Hustle* fresh. We set our minds to concentrating on stories about life post-incarceration, and discussions with those who have never been inside a prison cell but whose lives have nonetheless been defined by loved ones' incarcerations.

We talked with a group of men just out, who are training to help fight the fires ravaging California. We called kids with incarcerated parents, to hear about their experiences from this side of the glass, and spoke to formerly incarcerated moms like Michelle. We sought out people who have served their sentence, and asked them to replicate meals they used to make inside their cells, using only the tools and ingredients they would have had access to in prison. It allowed us (and hopefully our listeners) to gain a more profound appreciation for the ripple effect of incarceration: of the echoes—some traumatic, some familiar—heard and felt, long beyond a sentence has been served.

So, yes, being locked out of San Quentin changed the type of people we spend our days interviewing, but it didn't change our style, our connection, or our intention. Different stories, not different personalities. Our mission has never changed. We'll continue to bring everyday prison stories to life, as a means of revealing the commonalities we share as human beings. There are myriad stories waiting to be told, from San Quentin to prisons around the globe. Together, we're ready to seek them out.

We're confident that—as a show—we'll get through this crisis, just as we've found routes around or through prior uncontrollable obstacles. But we're not forecasters, nor have we ever aspired to be. Unpredictability is just one of the constants we've learned to expect. Of course, it is our sincere hope that by the time this is being read, it will be safe enough to visit our friends inside, and that our man New York will have received that big hug he was wondering when he'd get.

Ear Hustle is our creed. Our friendship and everything we've created since we first sat down in the Media Lab, while trapped birds in the rafters interrupted early attempts at recording. That world is branded onto the fabric of our beings. It branded us intellectually, emotionally, artistically, and—as of January 2021—physically.

INKED

SAN FRANCISCO BAY AREA
January 2021

NIGEL How many years ago did you and I start discussing making some permanent, visual statement about our commitment to *Ear Hustle* and each other?

EARLONNE You talking tats, Nyge?

NIGEL Yes.

EARLONNE I don't remember the exact date, but it's definitely been a few years, 'cause I was still inside when you brought it up. You said you wanted a prison tattoo!

NIGEL I kind of did . . .

EARLONNE And I was like, "Hold up, you cannot do that." Don't get me wrong . . . I admired your commitment and bravery, because it hurts bad, but you'd been going inside long enough to know that doing that was out of the question. It would have gotten you kicked out real quick.

NIGEL I know. It wasn't a great idea. I had just seen so much incredible tattoo art in prison and I thought it would be amazing if we got something like that done together—something special that documented our hard work and our dream.

EARLONNE A dream that is bigger than the reality, as you like to say?

NIGEL Exactly.

EARLONNE Well, you know I'm always up for adventure! Saying no just isn't part of my DNA, so . . .

NIGEL It needs to be the right person, though.

EARLONNE What about that lady who wrote to me, like, two years ago? She said if I ever wanted a tat, I should look her up. I could try to see if she's still around?

NIGEL Let's do this.

NIGEL Now that's it been a few days . . . what do you think?

EARLONNE What do I think? I think that shit was painful!

NIGEL It wasn't *that* bad—definitely not as bad as I thought. But I was nervous heading in.

EARLONNE Yeah, you were. How many times did you text her after the consultation? You were starting to make me anxious.

NIGEL Well, I had no idea what it would feel like, I was nervous about the design, and I didn't know whether I was going to be able to handle the pain. You seemed all casual and had that "whatever" attitude going. So I'm glad I went first. Once she started, I found the whole process pretty cool. I don't know if it was my expectations, but mine hardly hurt at all.

EARLONNE Mine was painful as fuck.

NIGEL You started yelling as soon as the needle hit your arm! I don't know if I've ever seen you that inconsolable . . . It was surprising. You're always the calm one. Not being able to help you was actually the most painful part of the whole experience. But then you kept making me laugh—like when you said that getting a tat was more painful than childbirth.

EARLONNE Okay, maybe that was out of my league. You kept asking me if I wanted to stop!

NIGEL Well, it was terrible to see you in such pain. I asked you if it hurt more than being shot.

EARLONNE Without question—it hurt way more than being shot! Some guys don't even feel getting shot. For real. And Nyge, mine was way more intense than yours. You got some lines and shit. Did you see how many needles she used for me!? Look, yours is already healed up all nicely and mine's still red; I'm gonna be wearing long sleeves for months.

NIGEL Yeah, all right, maybe yours was more painful. It's just wild, though. I never, never thought I would actually get a tattoo. But every time I see it, it makes me happy.

EARLONNE Why's that?

NIGEL Because it reminds me of what you and I have done together. It's beautiful—it makes me feel proud about the past, excited about the present, and optimistic about the future, all at once.

EARLONNE That's a whole lot of symbolism to get from a tattoo. You know I feel it too, though. Maybe not every time I look at my arm. But I'm definitely proud about what we've created. And the future's lookin' bright as well. Indubitably.

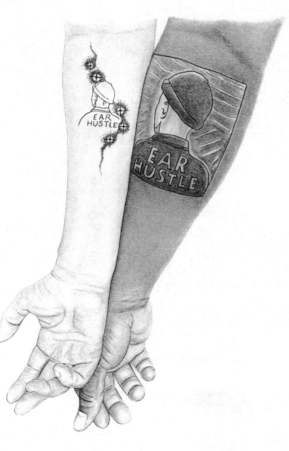

THIS GUY HERE

NIGEL Listeners over the years know that no episodes can be aired without the approval of Lieutenant Sam Robinson. He is the public information officer at San Quentin, which means that he oversees all of the media that's produced within the prison. He's also the point man for outside media that wants to come into the prison. San Quentin attracts a lot of attention from the public, keeping him very busy.

Our relationship with Lieutenant Robinson is a very special one. He championed and has been witness to our project from the very beginning. Maybe he was slightly dubious that we could actually win the PRX/Radiotopia Podquest, but he was still willing to let us try. Since then, he has been an essential, steadfast source of support to us, as a team and as individuals. There is no way to overstate the reality that—if not for his trust and respect—*Ear Hustle* would never have become what it is.

EARLONNE Indeed. We want to make sure he knows that we will never forget that *Ear Hustle* was made possible through him. Lieutenant Sam Robinson is a good brother. I remember him saying, when I was still incarcerated, "As long as what you are doing doesn't violate the safety of this institution or the safety of the general public population, I'm good." So, we have always tried to do our best to stay within that, and will always respect the boundaries that he upholds.

Though it is not in an official capacity, it didn't feel right for us to close out our storytelling without his sign-off. And so, as we've said many, many times, this episode of *Ear Hustle* has to be approved by this guy here:

I have thrived and enjoyed my career in Corrections from day one. But I believe that when I retire and look back on the span of my career, being a part of *Ear Hustle* will be up there as a crowning achievement.

When this journey began, my greatest vision for it was that it would play inside the prison and would be a creative, continuing project for the guys inside to immerse themselves in. When Nigel presented the idea of submitting an entry in the quest for the next great podcast, I thought it sounded like a cool exercise, but that the best we could hope for would be to receive feedback to help realize the dream of making that internal podcast.

I wondered, *How would this work?* Nigel is a visual artist, not a vocal artist. And Earlonne did not talk! I had known him for several years, and though he was a dedicated media center jack-of-all-tradesman, I had barely heard him speak. I didn't consider him to be a storyteller. There are hundreds of guys in prison who *are* storytellers, comedians, and just plain hustlers. Earlonne wasn't in any of those categories.

We submitted the application anyway, and when Nigel informed me that our San Quentin entry had advanced to the top fifty, I got butterflies. I don't think she could read it on my face, but I immediately thought, *We are going to do a podcast, for real!* I surmised that there could be nothing more intriguing than an authentic podcast coming out of one of the most infamous prisons in the world, San Quentin State Prison.

But then I went back to my same question: How can you do a podcast with a guy who doesn't talk? So after those initial butterflies, I returned to presuming that—despite the advanced placement in the contest—there was no way we were going to win.

As you all know, I was wrong. The partnership between Nigel and Earlonne has been groundbreaking and award-winning. Many people, whether employed at a correctional facility or incarcerated, struggle to relay what they see, feel, and experience every day in a prison environment, but *Ear Hustle* brings that reality to life in a very authentic way. The podcast has resonated with people inside and outside of the prison. I feel very blessed to have been on the ground floor, to watch this amazing adventure build, and to have had a small part in this creation. (And I have been honored to learn that some dedicated listeners even find my voice to be mellifluous.)

With that, I will sign off, but not before affirming:

I am Lieutenant Sam Robinson, the Public Information Officer at San Quentin State Prison. Just as I have approved every *Ear Hustle* podcast, I now have the pleasure and privilege of approving of this book.

LT. SAM ROBINSON

ACKNOWLEDGMENTS

This Is Ear Hustle has been a true collaboration, one that could never have come to be without the support, love, and care of many people. We would like to express our sincerest gratitude to all the individuals who agreed to contribute their voices and experiences to this book.

The *Ear Hustle* podcast team started small, and has grown over the years. It includes our co-creator and sound designer Antwan Williams, who shared the original dream; our intrepid senior producer Bruce Wallace, without whom we could not function; our man inside, co-host and producer Rahsaan "New York" Thomas; producer, book contributor, and dear friend John "Yahya" Johnson; editor Amy Standen; digital producer Shabnam Sigman; emeritus editor Curtis Fox; emeritus sound designer Pat Mesiti-Miller; and emeritus digital producer Erin Wade.

Thank you to all who have supplied beats and music, helping craft the *Ear Hustle* sound that has always been so crucial to our show: David Jassy, Eric "Maserati-E" Abercrombie, E. Phil Phillips, Rhashiyd Zinnamon, Lee Jaspar, Richie Morris, Dwight Krizman, Charlie Spencer of Quentin Blue, and Gregg Sayers.

Special love and respect to our executive producer, Julie Shapiro, who has been indispensable to our success from the start. Although you don't hear her voice on the show or see her contribution on these pages, she is part of the architecture of everything we create. Julie brings her knowledge, enthusiasm, and care to all things *Ear Hustle*.

Much gratitude to Kerri Hoffman, the CEO of PRX, and to Radiotopia for taking a chance on us, and for offering unwavering support over these years. It is an amazing affiliation and we appreciate all they do. Special shout-outs to Gina James, David Cotrone, Charlotte Cooper, and Donna Hardwick.

There would be no book or podcast if not for the community of San Quentin State Prison. Unending gratitude goes out to all those who have shared their stories with us, and to Acting Warden Ron Broomfield for supporting the project. Of course, we could never mention the community of San Quentin without giving love, tribute, and respect to Public Information Officer Lieutenant Sam Robinson. Our podcast could never have been made without his support and encouragement.

Writing this book has been an incredible process, another kind of collaboration, and we want to thank our literary agent Eve Attermann at William Morris Endeavor and our ever-supportive editor, Lorena Jones of Crown Publishing at Random House. Lorena offered enthusiasm from the start, and has been a steadfast source of insight, thoughtfulness, and constancy ever since. Lizzie Allen brought her incredible book-designing skills to the page, and (re)connected us with the amazingly talented Damien Linnane, whose gorgeous illustrations enhance our stories throughout the book. From Crown, we would also like to extend our sincere thanks to president David Drake, publisher Gillian Blake, deputy publisher Annsley Rosner, executive managing editor Sally Franklin, production director Linnea Knollmueller, production editor Mark Birkey, marketing director Julie Cepler, marketing manager Chantelle Walker, publicity director Dyana Messina, and publicist Stacey Stein. We will always be indebted to Cal Tabuena-Frolli for creating the original *Ear Hustle* logo, used for both our podcast and on the cover of this book. Our gratitude goes to Megan Wilson for the beautiful *Ear Hustle* tattoos she did for us.

Through engaging in this writing process, we were fortunate to be introduced to Domenica Alioto, who became our collaborator and writing partner. It is impossible to imagine this book coming together without her. In Domenica we found an extraordinary friend and tireless supporter who helped us every step of the way to bring the story of *Ear Hustle* to the page. Together, we formed a mighty trio we now call Team DEN.

We would also like to acknowledge two of our earliest and most ardent supporters, Patty Quillin of Meadow Fund and Aly Tamboura, a former San Quentin resident, now a manager in the Criminal Justice Reform program at the Chan Zuckerberg Initiative.

EARLONNE

I would like to thank my ride-or-die Momz—Alyce Faye Woods (even though she'll say she would only die for Jesus). I love you, Mother. You supported your baby boy through it all. Thanks to my sisters Cameia, La,

Sha, and Ty for always being there for me, 100 percent. Thanks to my brother Trevor for misguiding me into a life of crime, and for never giving me a moment's peace when we were cellies. Thanks to Jonathan, and to all my godkids. Thanks to my good friend Kenya Solomon, who never switched up on her boy. Much appreciation to everyone who visited, wrote, or looked out for me during that total of twenty-seven years in suspended animation.

Many thanks to Alex Mallick, Joy Alferness, Dr. Lesa R. Woodson, and Nigel Poor, who all spoke up for my release at the en banc hearing and who wrote letters of support. Thanks also to Emily Harris, and to Anne Irwin for being sooo cool and sponsoring CHOOSE1 with her SJC org.

Last but never least, endless thanks to my first white ride-or-die friend, Nigel Poor.

I dedicate this book, and all of my endeavors, to my best friend, Furman Little, and my nephew Tyler Woods. Both men were unarmed and were shot multiple times by the police.

NIGEL

I would like to thank my parents, Stephen and Phyllis, and my siblings, Aimee, Sarah, and Stephen, for being so present and for always asking what is next for *Ear Hustle*. Also, love to my son Robert, daughter-in-law Mira, and grandson C.J., who collectively remind me that having joy in one's life makes everything else work.

I would never have co-created *Ear Hustle* without the support and benefit of dear friends who were always ready to talk and give their encouragement. Thanks in particular to Jody Lewen, executive director of Mount Tamalpais College (formerly the Prison University Project), Frish Brandt, Lisa Sutcliffe, Valarie Wade, and Eliza Fischer. Thank you to Graham Green and Spencer Weisbroth for their advice. And thanks to California State University, Sacramento, and the Department of Design for supporting my work.

Thank you to my ever-loving Ricky P, whose kindness, support, and love make everything possible.

And finally, to my ride-or-die partner in all things *Ear Hustle*, Earlonne Woods. Here's to making the reality bigger than the dream . . . I love you in a non-overfamiliar way.

INDEX